# David Fraser

For twenty-six years David Fraser served in what is now the National Probation Service, both in the field and as a senior probation officer. He worked in several busy Inner London court areas, as well as in different prisons in the capital and the south-west. He also worked for almost a decade as a Criminal Intelligence Analyst with the National Criminal Intelligence Service, (which is now the National Crime Agency). He has been researching and writing about crime and sentencing policy in England and Wales since the 1980s. He has lectured to a wide variety of audiences in Britain and New Zealand and has had numerous articles published in a variety of justice journals. The first of his three published books, *A Land Fit for Criminals*, was recommended for the George Orwell Prize in Literature. It provoked wide interest in this country and abroad and was commended to the House of Commons during a speech by an MP. He has given evidence to three All Party Parliamentary Committees investigating sentencing and prisons. *Licence to Kill: Britain's Surrender to Violence* is the result of six years of considered research and involvement with the criminal justice system. David Fraser is married with two grown-up children and two grandchildren and lives with his wife in the south-west of England.

Other books by the author

*A Land Fit for Criminals*
*An Insider's View of Crime*
*Punishment and Justice in the UK*

Published by the Book Guild, 2006

# Licence to Kill

## Britain's Surrender to Violence

David Fraser

THE CHOIR PRESS

*In memory of*
*Florence Susan Fraser*

*Those who allow violent criminals the opportunity to kill, maim and rape, share the responsibility for it and the tragedy such crimes produce. More, they allow these monsters to create for all of us a world as dark and evil as their own.*

(unknown)

# Contents

# Foreword

by Leo McKinstry

David Fraser has long been a heroic voice against the moral cowardice and progressive ideology that grips our failing criminal justice system. The power of his analysis stems not just from his own experience of working with offenders for 25 years but also from the depth of his research and the strength of his logic.

Those qualities shine through his excellent new book, which I commend to anyone who cares about the fabric of our society. With lucid prose, a wealth of information and a clear sense of purpose, he presents a formidable challenge to the prevailing official orthodoxy that has so profoundly undermined the fight against criminality. His book is a magnificent trumpet blast against institutionalised leniency and soft justice. He brilliantly demolishes the myth that prison does not work, demonstrating that effective jail terms are the only way of keeping the public safe and that so-called 'community punishments' are nothing more than 'a licence to offend', to use a typically compelling phrase of his.

In contradiction of the government's manipulation of crime statistics, he provides irrefutable evidence of the dramatic rise in offending over recent decades. In one shocking figure, he reveals that there are now 15 times more 'acts of wounding and endangering life' than there were in 1950. He further points out that the rate of homicide has more than doubled since the abolition of the death penalty in 1965, a political move that had little support from the public. Indeed, one of the themes of the book is the chasm between the political establishment and the British citizenry over attitudes towards crime.

In his bracing catalogue of censure, David Fraser rightly targets the woeful Crown Prosecution Service, of which he rightly says: "No organisation could have done more to make the lives of criminals easier." But he is just as withering about the parole board, as well as "the enormous, self-serving, self-perpetuating medical-social bureaucracy" which has been created to treat drug addicts. A central part of the problem, as he argues, is the malignant influence since the 1960s of academic theories which absolve criminals of responsibility for their actions. In this handwringing narrative of exculpation, offenders' behaviour is driven, not by selfish or brutal impulses, but by poverty, or racism, or unemployment or inequality. According to this outlook, crime is a symptom of social malaise, while thugs and thieves are really victims who need support rather than punishment.

But as George Orwell put it: "some ideas are so foolish that only an intellectual would believe them." The public knows better than the lofty theorisers. Dangerous people belong behind bars, not on the street. There is nothing reactionary about wanting tougher, longer sentences. On the contrary, such an approach represents true compassion for the vulnerable and the victims of crimes. David Fraser makes this case superbly. Those in charge of the justice system would do well to heed his words.

# Acknowledgements

I am indebted to Theodore Dalrymple, whose support throughout the writing of this book, has been invaluable, and for the generous access to his written work.

I must also thank Gabrielle Brown for allowing me to use her diary notes and other written material, detailing her experience of the violent sex crime which so disrupted her life, and the response of criminal justice officials to her plight.

I must also express my thanks to Dan Collins for his suggestions concerning the structure of this book.

I am grateful to Adam Stevens and Linda Lee, for their timely and always effective IT support when this was needed.

I must thank Leo McKinstry for his support and for writing the foreword.

I must also express my thanks and appreciation to the following for their time and willing help in proofreading the manuscript: Julie Hatton, Patricia Alston, Rosemarie Fraser and Leslie Stickland.

Finally, I must thank my wife for putting up with what must have seemed endless readings of draft versions of the manuscript, over a period of more than five years.

# Author's Note

In 1967 I joined the probation service with the then commonly held expectation that offenders, given help and support, could be persuaded to lead the straight life. It soon became obvious that this was a forlorn hope. The vast majority of the criminals on our caseloads never gave up crime, and treated the courts' leniency with contempt. Thus the theories taught us on our training courses about how to deal with offenders were of no help. The evidence of the failure of probation supervision, and other forms of lenient sentencing, has been recorded and stored by the government in their archives, but assiduously ignored. In particular, from the early 1970s, the senior management of the probation service, and the majority of the rank and file officers adopted a mindset of denial over what we all knew to be the case, that the criminals on our books were treating their periods on probation as a licence to offend and committed violence and mayhem wherever and whenever they liked. But few dared speak up about this.

We can get a sense of the extraordinary nature of official attitude towards this failure by imagining what the effect would be if the government insisted on doctors using a form of medical provision known to be harmful. Yet, despite the obvious case to do so, nothing has changed and the denial continues, and for the last five decades our ruling elites have continued to promote lenient sentencing policies for criminals, even for those who commit violence. Large swathes of legislation have made life easier, safer and more rewarding for those who whether for gain, to impose their will, or just for the pleasure of it, attack us, burgle our houses, or rob us in the street. Victims frequently discover that the most severe and life-threatening crimes of violence are often treated lightly by the courts. Even killing has been made far less risky for the perpetrators.

Many academics, civil servants, Ministers of the Crown, MPs and lawyers, supported by the anti-prison and pro-criminal lobbies outside of government, have condescendingly told us that those who commit crime do so because of pressure from social, financial and personal problems, for which they need help and understanding.

They can display such compassion and virtuousness because generally, due to their wealthier life styles, gated communities and country seats, they enjoy a level of security not available to the general public. As a result they are not affected by the crimes committed by those they have campaigned to keep out of jail.

They have routinely and patronisingly belittled the everyday concerns about crime and violence of the general public and their wish for more protection. They have rubbished their calls for more severe sentencing, and imply that they do not understand the 'complexities' of crime. Prison, they say is repressive, authoritarian and itself a cause of crime. Their double standards were revealed when it was announced that there had been a 15-fold increase in the money spent on security for MPs following the killing of Labour MP Jo Cox in June 2016. No such increases are announced following the murders of ordinary members of the public. In July 2017, MPs enthusiastically supported a Bill to introduce more severe prison sentences for those who attack or threaten 'members of the security services'. The reason? In March 2017, parliament was attacked by a lone wolf jihadi criminal. He had tried to get into the House in order to kill as many MPs as he could. Although he was shot dead by a security guard before he could carry out this part of the attack, MPs had nevertheless felt the cold threat of homicidal violence directed at them by a criminal who was only yards away. While they are prepared for the public to be exposed to such risks, they are not.

This book sets out the evidence which shows that the campaign of increased leniency shown towards violent (and other criminals) since the 1960s, has both failed to reform them, and put the public in danger, and that our ruling elites have ignored this failure with cold indifference. It also demonstrates that longer prison sentences are the only effective deterrent to further crime by dangerous and violent criminals. A large part of this evidence is drawn from government records, and although supplemented with many case examples, those I collected and did not include would have been enough to fill at least another two manuscripts.

The book also includes a discussion about the death penalty, and its abolition despite strong public support for its retention – a subject tabooed by current orthodoxy. But I do not include it in order to argue for its reinstatement. I acknowledge that politics have hardened over this matter, and change is unlikely. Many remain uncomfortable with the idea that the State should have the right to take life; indeed this is close to my position, despite the evidence I put forward to show that it was an effective deterrent to homicide.

Reference to the abolition of the death penalty is included because it is an important part of the story of increased leniency, shown towards violent and other criminals. Abolition provided this campaign with a powerful boost, because once the sentence for killing had been reduced, it followed that the severity of punishment for all other violent crimes was reduced. As succinctly put by Peter Hitchins, "it is now harder to get into prison than into university." Yet, to repeat the point, a careful analysis of the evidence shows that the death penalty was an effective deterrent to homicide. No one has presented an alternative argument to explain why the homicide rate doubled, and why the rate of homicidal attacks also significantly increased, following its abolition in 1964. Thus by acknowledging how well it worked, we can more clearly understand what we have lost since it was abolished, namely that the sentencing system which replaced it, exercises far less restraint on would-be killers, than did the hangman's noose. Members of the public and police officers are now far more likely to be murdered by criminals than they were before 1964, and are generally far more exposed to their violence. These are facts beyond the reach of contrary opinion.

Despite this, the purpose of the book is *not* to set out to win converts for the return of capital punishment, but to point out the undeniable case for a sentencing system which is at least as effective as was the death penalty.

# Introduction

A young woman is beaten to death in her own home by a burglar. A teenage girl is machine-gunned to death while she is in a pizza shop. A home owner is kicked to death by thugs a few paces from his front door. A pensioner is bludgeoned to death as he enters his flat. A young girl is gang-raped and then doused with acid to remove any links to her attackers. This is Britain in the 21$^{st}$ century. While it is true that violent crimes have occurred throughout our history, they are now increasing, and these anecdotes are but a tiny sample of the thousands committed in Britain every year, most of them courtesy of the government's lenient sentencing policies which allow persistent, violent and dangerous criminals freedom to roam and so continue their killing, maiming and raping. Many of these assaults go undetected and therefore unpunished. Most criminals must commit many crimes before they face even the slightest risk of being caught. Likewise, most will be convicted several times before they face the possibility of a prison sentence. Yet police officers will privately confide that they are overwhelmed by the numbers of violent offences.

In addition, the police have been demoralised by the Crown Prosecution Service which closes thousands (and sometimes hundreds of thousands) of criminal files every year without prosecution; by lenient sentencing; by false accusations of institutionalised racism;

by political correctness, so-called diversity and bureaucracy. These pressures have undermined their ability to fight crime and protect the public, whose confidence in the police has fallen to levels not imagined 40 years ago.

This book argues that, whether crime is said to be rising or falling, we need a re-vamped sentencing system that would stop dangerous and violent offenders from harming anyone else again.

I have used, among other sources, the criminal justice statistics produced by the Home Office and more latterly, the Ministry of Justice, to track the course of violent crime in Britain over the last six decades. At one time these were produced in paper form; to have possession of these reports gave the researcher a sense of security. The information they contained could not be altered or removed.

For the last seven years, these government figures and other criminal justice information have only been available online. This has triggered a data explosion in the Ministry of Justice. Forests of information are now produced, and it is now difficult, if not impossible to work out what this ever-expanding mountain of data is telling us, without the commitment of considerable time and effort, normally beyond the reach of most busy members of the public (and I suspect, of many MPs and ministers). I believe this is deliberate. Nowhere is a clear overview provided which would enable the public to see, at a glance, the reality – that the criminal justice system's sentencing policies do not work. This in turn robs both public and politicians of the ability to demand they are changed.

Thus, claims that violent crime is falling and that generally crime is not the problem that it was 15–20 years ago, remain largely unchallenged. Such claims have become routine, part of an ingrained culture of deception. This, to quote from Peter Oborne's book, *The Rise of Political Lying*, "strips us of the ability to make soundly based judgements, and turns us into dupes".

I believe that the officials saw the arrival of the web as a gift – a bottomless pit into which they could pour endless information, and by so doing, create the means to hide the truth concerning the failure of their sentencing methods. The more information they provide, the less we are informed.

Based on more than five years of research, this book argues that violent crime has risen steeply over the last 60 years, in parallel with government attempts to hide this phenomenon, often successfully, by focusing on recent developments and ignoring the longer-term past.

It also sets out to familiarise the public with three important principles denied by current penal philosophy. First, that there is nothing intrinsically wrong or unjust with a severe sentence of imprisonment; to the contrary, provided that it follows conviction for a serious violent offence in a fair trial Secondly, that 'society' is not to blame for the criminal's wrong-doing – that is a matter of his own choosing – and therefore society is not responsible for his fate or his choice whether or not to reoffend. Thirdly, that the public's interests are paramount, not the offenders', and the public has an inalienable right to be protected from them, not just in the short term.

I feel this book is an important contribution to a debate that should be, but rarely is, held.

# 1

## The Story of Gabrielle Browne

This is the story of one of the hundreds of serious sex and violent crimes committed every year by offenders under supervision in the community. By passing community sentences, courts perpetuate the lie that the probation service can protect the public from dangerous, violent criminals. It can be told because of the persistence and bravery of the victim. Her preparedness to make her ordeal public means that an event that would otherwise have been recorded as no more than a criminal statistic, has been brought vividly to life. What it reveals about how the British justice system operates, is disturbing.

On the 6th March 2003, 38-year-old Gabrielle Browne set off for a training run in Burgess Park, Southwark, not far from her home in Camberwell, where she lived with her husband and two children. She was preparing for the London Marathon. Gabrielle worked in IT for a law firm. An intelligent, educated individual with lots of interests, she had been a keen runner for 12 years.

This training session started off like the many that had preceded it. She set out at approximately 8.30 in the morning and after dropping off both of her children at their school, and completing one or two other errands, she started her run and was soon in the park, which stretches from Camberwell and Walworth in the west, to Peckham and Old Kent Road in the East.

It was a crisp, sunny, dry morning, perfect conditions for running. There were five weeks to go before the big race and Gabrielle settled into her stride, pacing strongly along the canal pathway. Crouched behind a wall, watching her approach was 16-year-old Mohammed Kendeh, from Sierra Leone, whose immigrant status was shrouded in mystery. He had already established himself as a dangerous felon, with convictions for robbery, burglary and sex crimes and he had been out of prison for just seven days. As Gabrielle approached, he stepped out from his hiding place and barred her way. Just three days before he sprung this ambush, he had attended an appointment with his supervisor from the local Youth Offending Team, and signed an agreement to follow the conditions of a community supervision order, made in the summer of 2002 in relation to six sex offences he had committed in Burgess Park, some of them in front of the victim's children. The conditions with which he had agreed to comply included the requirement to be law abiding and keep in touch with his supervisor.

The harrowing story of what happened next is told using Gabrielle's own words.

"He crouched behind a blind corner on the canal path in Burgess Park so he could see me on approach but I had no view of him. He stepped out blocking my way, asking me the time. I was wary of him, but had a heart rate monitor on my wrist so couldn't say I didn't know the time. It was a pretext, I had barely told him when he spun on his heels, grinned at me and then his right arm whipped round my throat – still to this day not sure if I lost consciousness or if it is just too painful to remember – when I was next consciously aware of what was happening I was some 150 metres away against a wall, being pinned by his head in my chest, his body at right angles, his hands working to remove my running shorts.

Stupidly overwhelmed by what was happening to me, I was too afraid to scream not knowing if he had a knife and initially hit him with my left arm (deliberately as it was my weaker side!) – no response. I then punched him hard in the head with my right hand. His head smashed into my lip, instantly swelling and bleeding. He was becoming more violent and sexually aroused. His hands started to explore, by this stage I had been thrown onto the ground, knee bleeding. My shorts had been twisted into a tourniquet but that restricted his access to me, so he pulled my shorts and underwear off. Instantly this freed my legs, allowing me to kick him as hard and often as I possibly could. I realised the possibility that this was now a fight for my very survival. After a few minutes, it was becoming too difficult for him, so he ran off.

I took my phone out from my pocket to call the police, the thought in my head being, so that he could not do this to anyone else. How naïve was I to think that?"

As a result of this attack Kendeh was arrested and charged with attempted rape, an offence fully justified by Gabrielle's description of what he did to her. Had she not been strong enough to resist him, he would have raped her. He should also have been charged with violence for battering her face with his head. To begin with she had every expectation that the justice system would work on her behalf, that it would show it recognised the seriousness of what had happened by pulling out the stops to convict and punish Kendeh properly, and avoid unnecessary delays.

None of these expectations were met. For example, it took two years from the date of the offence for Kendeh to be sentenced. The incompetence and attitude of officials stunned her, and her experience of the justice system following the attack was almost as bruising and traumatic as the crime itself. Her struggle for justice, carried out over nine years, at the end of which period Kendeh was finally deported, provides a window through which the public is given a glimpse of how the justice system works – something which the majority know little or nothing about, until that is, they are targeted by a criminal.

What becomes clear from these events is that first, this was an avoidable crime. Kendeh had been apprehended several times for serious violent and sex crimes, before his attack on Gabrielle, but had been dealt with lightly on each occasion. A suitably long prison sentence would have saved Gabrielle and other victims from his further offending. Secondly, it soon became obvious that the justice system did not want to go ahead with this prosecution, despite the serious nature of the crime. Gabrielle was shocked when the police invited her to drop the charges. Likewise, the Crown Prosecution Service would have dropped this case, adding it to the thousands of others it discontinues every year, had it not been for Gabrielle's continued insistence that they prosecute her attacker. The CPS and the police were wrong footed by her tenacity; the confidence of most victims is so undermined by the violence and or sexual violation they have experienced, that they are left as putty when faced with similar obduracy from officials.

Not only did the justice system's response lack urgency, but the officials she encountered seemed unaware or unbothered by the fact that their lassitude poured salt into her wounds. Time and again, Gabrielle had to drag unwilling officials into action, by writing letters, sending e-mails, and making telephone calls to the CPS, parole board, probation officials, police, and MPs. She was made to fight every inch of the way to get the justice system to do its job, namely to put the defendant up for trial and if convicted, pass a sentence that reflected the seriousness of the crime. She achieved the first of these objectives, but not the second.

Yet throughout this ordeal she witnessed the system provide every possible benefit to the attacker. It tried not to prosecute him; it reduced the seriousness of the charge against him; it released him on bail while he was waiting to be tried, during which time he committed more offences; officials dragged their feet for two years before bringing him to court; he was given a discount against his sentence because of the long delay in process; he was given another discount for pleading guilty; he was given a light sentence; the Attorney General refused Gabrielle permission to appeal against the sentence; after Kendeh's release in March 2007 a judge supported his appeal against deportation and ruled he could stay in Britain.

Yet it is poignant to record that immediately following the attack, Gabrielle never expected the justice system would react this way. As a law-abiding person, she had unquestionable faith that it was there to work for her, not just for the criminal, and would respond with the urgency she naturally felt her situation merited. After all, attempted rape is a serious offence; it had been carried out by a dangerous predatory male, prepared to attack a stranger, who was therefore likely to strike again if given the chance. The ambush suggested he knew her running route and had planned the assault.

As a newcomer to the operations of the criminal justice system, she was surprised that it took three weeks to organise an ID parade, thinking that the system would see the necessity to act more quickly. Further, she was dismayed to learn that the new VIPER ID system, which the police used, was known to be far less effective at successfully identifying suspects than the traditional method. Instead of recruiting a group of volunteers who resembled the suspect, to be paraded in front of the victim, this system allowed the police to retrieve a selection of pre-recorded video images of people who resembled the suspect, but who were otherwise unconnected to him or the case in hand. These images, viewed by the victim on a monitor are of head and shoulders only, and provide front and profile views only. Researchers have found that the success rate for victims in picking out suspects was 54% using the traditional method and 34% when using the VIPER system.[1] Some researchers concluded that the VIPER system was therefore 'fairer'.[2]

Despite the physical proximity of Kendeh to her during the attack, Gabrielle failed to pick Kendeh out using the VIPER method. This is not surprising because of the effect of fear and heightened stress levels associated with the assault. Gabrielle believed she would have identified him if a traditional line-up had been organised; she could have then used height, weight, stance and gait, to make a judgement, all factors known to be important in identifying someone, but which were hidden by the VIPER system. Nevertheless, the results from the forensic analysis of Kendeh's clothing were still pending, and such evidence is known to be more reliable than witness or victim's memory.

Gabrielle's initial confidence in the justice system soon faded. In September 2003, forensic analysis established a fibre match on Kendeh's clothes, linking him to the crime. Yet despite this, by March 2004, 12 months after the offence was committed, the CPS had still made no decision to prosecute. Gabrielle is convinced that had she not, during this time, lobbied her MP, the Metropolitan Police Commissioner, and crucially the District Crown Prosecutor of the CPS, the case would not have come to court. As early as June 2003, for example, she had to resist pressure from the police, who in a phone call asked her to consider giving up the case. She was so taken aback, that she initially said she would think about it. But 30 seconds later she recovered and rang back to say she would certainly not give up, but wanted her attacker dealt with properly. Thus, four months after the offence, the penny was beginning to drop – and she began to fear that unless she kept up the pressure on the officials concerned, Kendeh would not be brought to court.

Even so, little did she suspect that it would be over two years before he was tried and sentenced, which he finally was in February 2005. During this long wait her anxieties were further raised by the several changes of prosecuting counsel, each one planning a different approach to the case. Likewise, she was assigned three different police liaison officers, and as many changes in the person appointed to be her probation 'victim liaison officer'.

Before finally taking Kendeh to court, the CPS reduced the charge of attempted rape to the lesser one of sexual assault, which Gabrielle felt belittled what had happened to her. The CPS practice of reducing the seriousness of the charge is common practice whose purpose, according to Brian Lawrence, an experienced criminal court lawyer,[3] is to reduce the chance of a lengthy jail term and so reduce costs. Kendeh's sentence of four years imprisonment (in reality two years because of automatic remission) was a shock because Gabrielle had been told by the District Crown Prosecutor, "not to worry" over their decision to reduce the seriousness of the charge, because the judges "had the power to pass sentences of up to ten years for sexual assault". Coming as it did from a senior figure in the CPS, Gabrielle reluctantly accepted this assurance, even though she felt the lessening of the charge was wrong. It is difficult to accept that the District Crown Prosecutor thought such a sentence was likely. If she did, then it suggests she did not know that the average sentence for sex crimes in England and Wales, including the most serious such as rape and attempted rape, was then just five years.[4]

The lenient sentence Kendeh received for his attack upon Gabrielle meant that she was soon embroiled in discussions over the conditions of his release, which eventually took place in February 2007. (She later discovered that the prison gave Kendeh a copy of his release licence which stated what the conditions were, but failed to give a copy to anyone else). During an exchange with probation staff about these arrangements, she was made aware for the first time that the Home Office was considering deporting him. She learned that these proceedings had started in 2005, yet no one thought to tell her. She had been assured from the first his immigration status was absolute. Her probation contact told her, wrongly, that Gabrielle could not make enquiries about this because the matter of deportation was a private one between Kendeh and the Immigration and Nationality Directorate (now the Border Agency). This was despite the fact that two probation circulars directed the probation service to keep victims informed of this process at every step of the way. Gabrielle discovered this requirement in the relevant probation manual published on the web; it was she who then informed the management of the probation service that they were in breach of their duty in this respect, which was later acknowledged by the assistant chief probation officer for the Camberwell area.

Against the odds, she succeeded in getting the parole board to insert a condition into his parole excluding Kendeh from the Borough of Southwark, where all his many offences had taken place. Her reasons for wanting this were two-fold. First, Kendeh knew this borough like the back of his hand and this would make it easier for him to plan further crimes, and escape if, and when, he committed more offences within its bounds. Secondly, she travelled through it every day to get to her place of work, and she did not want to cross his path again. Yet despite the parole board agreeing to the necessity for the exclusion zone clause, Gabrielle was in constant conflict with the probation case manager who throughout, tried to get this requirement, vital for Gabrielle's peace of mind, removed from Kendeh's parole conditions.

Once alerted to the deportation proceedings, Gabrielle turned to her MP in March 2007, to seek her help in establishing Kendeh's deportation status. Later, Kendeh won his appeal and was allowed to stay by a judge who said "he had a right to a family life in Britain". He continued to offend and was acquitted from a robbery charge on a technicality, but was later recalled to prison, largely as the result of Gabrielle ensuring that the parole board was given the relevant information about him, as no official made any moves to do so.

Following his eventual release, he committed further robberies, and on 16 October 2009, he was sentenced to five and a half years imprisonment (two years and nine months in reality). The sentencing judge recommended deportation.

During 2010 and 2011, in anticipation of his further release, Gabrielle was once more in protracted discussions with the Home Office and the UK Border Agency, to seek assurance he would be deported. During these discussions, she realised they were updating her about a different offender – they had confused Kendeh with someone else. Gabrielle checked with the probation service who assured her that no mistake had been made. They were wrong. Further investigation by Gabrielle showed conclusively that all three authorities had confused Kendeh with another criminal. The Home

Office eventually agreed that this was so, and it was Gabrielle who supplied them with the biographical detail they needed to correct their documentation.

Two more deportation tribunals considered his case and on 1 of November 2009, they dismissed Kendeh's appeal and made a deportation order.

Finally, on 12 February 2012, Kendeh was deported to Sierra Leone, seven years after the deportation process had started, and almost 3,000 days (nine years) after he had ambushed and attempted to rape Gabrielle in Burgess Park. This crime has left its mark and has robbed her of her peace of mind. As with many other victims, Gabrielle experiences a measure of anxiety when faced with circumstances which remind her of the attack, and she is now more cautious in certain circumstances. She has also been made aware that lenient sentencing leaves violent, dangerous offenders free to roam the streets and parks of our communities. Following the assault, she continued her running, often with tears in her eyes, but determined not to let the experience of the assault rob her of her participation in the Marathon (which she completed in three hours 38 minutes). But she now never runs alone, (research by 'England Athletics' found almost half of the women included in their survey had fears for their safety when they were out running[5]), and 13 years after the attack it remains the case that much of the previous sense of freedom and joy this activity afforded her, has gone.

During this long ordeal, Gabrielle concluded that either she had been singled out for such maltreatment, or that the incompetence and lethargy she faced was systemic. In time, she concluded it was the latter, but it was small comfort to realise she was not alone, and that thousands of other victims of violent crime have suffered similarly at the hands of a department of government that frequently displays itself as 'not fit for purpose'.

Gabrielle, I suspect, was not alone in her natural and unquestioning acceptance that the criminal justice system would come to her aid. Most members of the public, who like Gabrielle, have no previous experience of violent crime, would, no doubt, maintain this rosy view of our justice apparatus – until the day they are subjected to a violent burglary, or their child is murdered, or their husband is kicked to death by thugs in the street outside his home. Then they will discover what Gabrielle discovered, which is that the justice system is incompetent, callous and disregarding of the victim, but almost fawning in its attitude to the criminal.

But why did the police and then the Crown Prosecution Service try to stop this case going to court? And why did they later reduce the seriousness of the crime? Why did the justice system drag its feet in dealing with this case? The following chapters attempt to provide answers to these questions. As stressed in the Introduction, the historical evidence quoted in this book, covering approximately 1950 to 2015, illustrates that only by examining its past performance can we begin to understand the extent of the justice system's deteriorating record in protecting the public from violent criminals.

# 2

## Violent Britain

Outside the Houses of Parliament in London is a statue of Richard I, a 12th century Plantagenet king of England. He was a member of one of the most violent dynastic families ever to rule this country, so much so that the Plantagenets have been described as 'a race much dipped in their own blood'. The position of this imposing sculpture is highly symbolic not just for historical reasons, but because it stands sentinel over a parliament building whose members preside over a nation that has become one of the most criminally violent in Europe. The argument followed in this book is that whether, according to the government, violent crime is rising or falling, the public should be protected from dangerous and violent offenders, with sentences that are sufficiently severe to stop them in their tracks. But the official record of violent crime in Britain shows we are far from enjoying such conditions. Many violent criminals are left free to roam the streets and the prevalence of their offending indicates that there are few places in our towns or cities where the public can be said to be truly safe, as Gabrielle Browne discovered (see Chapter 1). Comparisons of our violent crime rates, with those of other European countries, throws light on this problem.[6]

International comparisons of violent crime rates
per 100,000 of the population

| Crime | number per 100,000 pop Engl'& Wales | mean for 100,000 pop for Europe | England & Wales position | No. of Countries |
|---|---|---|---|---|
| All | 7079 | 4513 | 8th | 35 |
| Violence (assault) | 602 | 260 | 6th | 37 |
| Violence (aggravated) | 58 | 30 | 4th | 27 |
| Sexual assault | 79 | 33 | 6th | 34 |
| Rape | 29 | 12 | 4th | 36 |
| Robbery | 133 | 73 | 6th | 37 |

Source: European Sourcebook of Crime and
Criminal Justice Statistics 2014, 5th edition.

To have the fourth highest rate for aggravated (serious) violent crimes out of 27 countries is not something to be proud of and the other offence figures supports the claim that the people of 21st century Britain are a race 'much dipped in violent criminality'. In 2017 a 13% increase in crime was blamed on a surge of violence mainly in the Capital.[7] The violent crime rate in England and Wales is 15 times larger than that of Spain, (a country whose imprisonment rate is far higher than ours).[8][9] While any one of the thousands of violent attacks which occur in Britain every year would serve to illustrate this condition, one example stands out.

Just before midnight in January 2006, Thomas Rhys Price, a

31-year-old lawyer, left a London party and telephoned his fiancée to say that he was on his way home. He emerged from the tube station at Kensal Green about 20 minutes later and began walking towards their apartment. A few minutes later two teenage gang members attacked him. Eighteen-year-old Donald Carty kicked Pryce in the back, knocking him to the ground, and Delano Brown, aged 19, kicked him in the face. When Pryce tried to defend himself, the attackers stabbed him in the legs, hands, face and heart. Then they took his cell phone and his public transport Oyster Card, and ran off leaving him dying on the ground. The paramedics who strove unsuccessfully to revive him found his wedding vows strewn on the pavement.[10]

His attackers had carried out a campaign of violent robberies in London's tube stations over several months prior to their murder of Rhys Price, during which, the police estimated, they had committed at least 150 violent muggings. Carty had convictions for several of these offences in which victims had been stabbed and knocked near senseless before being robbed. Yet he had received nothing more serious than a conditional discharge. Brown had no convictions, but he, no less than Carty, enjoyed violence and both revelled in the power it gave them over others. The following graph puts this story into context and illustrates the increase in recorded robberies which has occurred in Britain since 1950.[11] [12] [13]

In that year there were two robberies per 100,000 of the population. A quarter of a century later, in 1975, there were 23. Another quarter century after that, in 2000, there were 162. By 2014 the number of robberies recorded by the police had fallen to 100 per 100,000 of the population, a number still 50 times more than the 1950 figure. (The fall in the number of recorded robberies may reflect, among other things, the increase in theft from online bank accounts. Robbers, no longer need to attack someone in the street, or hold up a bank, but can steal from the comfort of their own home. In 2015, at least over a million of these and other 'banking and credit fraud crimes' were notified but not included in the police crime statistics.[14] In 2016, the Nat West Bank account of Annette Jefferys, a North London business woman, was robbed of £17,500 in this way).[15]

Total robbery per 100,000 population England and Wales 1950–2014

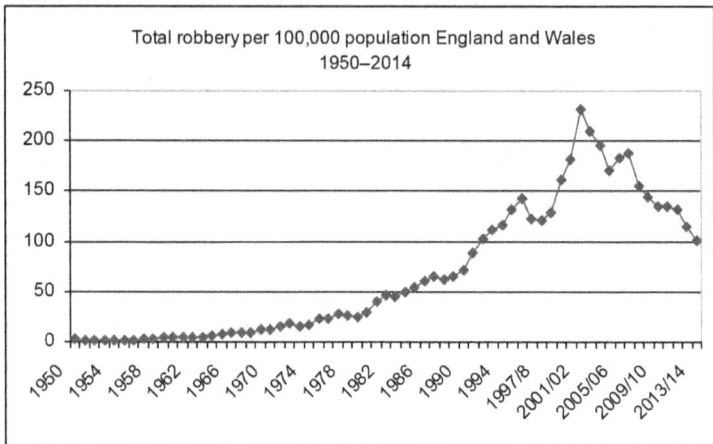

Sources:

Robbery figures for 1950–2001 in: Data.GOV A Summary of Recorded Crime Data 1898–2001

At: https://data.gov.uk/dataset/recorded-crime-data-1898-2001-02/resource/ b5b1c3fe-338e-472e-b844-75108c57436c

Robbery figures for 2002–2011 in: HO Stats Bulletin Crime in England and Wales 2010/11 HOSB: 10/11

At: http://www.cjp.org.uk/publications/government/crime-in-england-and- wales -2010-11-14-07-2011/

Robbery figures for 2012–2014 in: Home Office Statistical Bulletin Crimes detected in England and Wales 2012/13 HOSB: 02/13

At: https://www.gov.uk/government/uploads/system/uploads/attachment_data/ file/224037/hosb0213.pdf

National Population figures for 1942–1980:

British Historical Statistics, by B.R. Mitchell (Page 14)

https://books.google.co.uk/books?  id=Oyg9AAAAIAAJ&pg=PA1&source=gbs_
toc_r&cad=3#v=onepage&q&f=false

1980–2008 Annual Abstract of Statistics, No. 146, 2010 Edition

http://www.ons.gov.uk/ons/rel/ctu/annual-abstract-of-statistics/no-146--2010-
edition/index.html

2009–2011 Office for National Statistics, Population Estimates for England and
Wales, Mid-2002 to Mid-2010

http://www.ons.gov.uk/ons/dcp171778_288817.pdf

2012 Office for National Statistics Population Estimates for England and Wales
2012

http://www.ons.gov.uk/ons/rel/pop-estimate/population-estimates-for-england-
and-wales/mid-2012/index.html

2013 Office for National Statistics Annual Mid-Year Population Estimates, 2013

http://www.ons.gov.uk/ons/dcp171778_367167.pdf

2014 Office for National Statistics Annual Mid-Year Population Estimates, 2014

http://www.ons.gov.uk/ons/dcp171778_406922.pdf

As far as the absolute numbers of robberies is concerned, it is note-worthy that in 1969 the numbers of robberies for the whole of England and Wales exceeded 6,000 for the first time (6,041)[16] but as pointed out by Dennis and Erdos in their book *Cultures and Crimes*, in 2002 there were 6,500 in the borough of Lambeth alone. In the *one month* of December 2002 there were 282 robberies of personal property in Lambeth. This exceeds the figure for all robberies, personal and business, for the whole of England and Wales in any *year* between the two world wars, apart from 1932 when there were 342, and 1938, when there were 287.[17] These authors point to the fact that between 1893 and 1941 there were never as many as 400 robberies *a year* for the whole of England and Wales, but from February to December in 2001 the number of robberies *per month* in the borough of Lambeth never fell as low as 400.[18]

While large numbers of people are treated in hospitals as a result of street violence,[19] the highways of our country are not the only place where attacks occur. Available figures indicate, for example, that across 403 health boards, there were, in 2011, almost 58,000 physical attacks on medical staff in hospitals. This represents a rate of 46 assaults per 1,000 staff. But several health areas had rates of 200, and some 400 per 1,000 staff.[20] In January 2015, it was reported that large numbers of MPs had been the victim of violent attacks in their surgery and outside. Many were said to be frightened of leaving their home. In June 2016, Labour MP Jo Cox was shot and stabbed to death by a violent attacker on the steps of her surgery.[21] The Prime Minister and others of the ruling elite (including Hillary Clinton in the US) were quick to express their horror at her death, and MPs from all parties paid tribute to her from the floor of the Commons. But this killing was no more or no less a tragedy than the murder of hundreds of ordinary members of the public similarly struck down every year, but whose loss invokes no similar response.

History teacher and education researcher Robert Peal's graphic description of classroom anarchy and violence in many British classrooms suggest we may have some of the worst behaved pupils in the world.[22] The 'Progressive Education' methods introduced into schools from the 1970s onwards outlawed almost all forms of discipline. Formal control of the classroom was seen as authoritarian and repressive.

The fruits of this absurd philosophy have been bitter. Police officers now deal with thousands and sometimes tens of thousands of violent incidents in playgrounds and classrooms each year,[23] called to deal with attacks on staff and pupils, some involving knives and other weapons. For example, in 2009, 188,000 pupils were suspended from schools in Britain, of which 90,000 were for violence.[24] Two years later that figure had increased to 150,000.[25] It is known that six staff are attacked by pupils every week,[26] with one teacher a day taken to hospital,[27] of which at least 30 a year need to be taken by ambulance.[28] It can be no surprise that teacher stress levels have become unbearable in some schools. Examples of staff seeking damages because of ill-health brought about by dealing with 'nightmare pupils', are now not uncommon.[29] In one publicised case an exemplary teacher's career was destroyed because he threw a disruptive boy out of the class. Magistrates believed the boy's story that unnecessary force had been used. The teacher was fined £1,500 and made to pay £1,875 in costs.[30]

The disruptive pupil at the centre of this story was not hurt. While ruthlessly condemning this teacher for a form of violence that I suspect was more theatrical than real, the authorities bend over backwards to display their tolerance of real and repeated violence from pupils. The belief they will face little or no retribution from the courts has given children with a propensity for violence the go-ahead to attack teachers and other pupils where and when they like. In the summer of 2014 a 12-year-old boy hanged himself following a prolonged period of assaults and other bullying at the hands of fellow pupils. The perpetrators escaped any form of retribution.[31] In another school a teacher removed a violent 13-year-old boy from the classroom who was attacking another child. The staff member went off to look for a colleague trained to deal with such pupils. Meanwhile, the perpetrator broke away and went back to the now unattended class and continued his violent attack, hitting his victim over the head with a heavy wooden board. The boy was eventually removed from the school but no action was taken against him for the violent offence.[32] His disregard for any consequences he might have faced was perfectly justified.

The image of Britain as a violent place is not just built on anecdotes such as these. The official statistics for particular categories of violent crime tell a story that is hard to take in. For example, per 100,000 of the population, there are now 15 times more crimes in the category 'more serious wounding and acts endangering life' as there were in 1950. Similarly, there are 30 times more crimes of arson and, as previously indicated, 50 times as many robberies.[33]

In February 2013, the British Prime Minister visited India and described the massacre by the British Army in 1919 of 379 demonstrators at Amritsar as 'shameful'.[34] But this publicly expressed sensitivity to events which occurred almost 100 years ago, in a land far away, is in stark contrast to his silence in relation to the 2,348 homicides committed in his own country between 2010, when he came into office, and 2013 when he made the Amritsar speech. Many of these were committed by criminals allowed to roam because of lenient sentencing endorsed by his government, despite the violent histories of the killers concerned. Twenty of these homicides were by killers freed from a life sentence for a previous killing, courtesy of his government's policies. Can we imagine the Prime Minister announcing to the House of Commons that it is 'shameful' that the lives of many of those slaughtered by violent offenders in England and Wales would have been saved, if more severe sentencing policies had been in force?

In 2011, the British government expressed its 'outrage' over the killing of Libyans by their leader Gadhafi. They showed no inhibition about initiating a military response to protect the Libyan people from him, dropping bombs (some of which cost almost a £1 million each) from Euro-Fighter aircraft which cost billions to develop and keep in service. This is to be compared with their more miserly approach to spending money on prisons which would protect British people at home from dangerous criminals. Following the bombing in Libya the Foreign Secretary was interviewed on the radio by the BBC and aggressively questioned about the killing of revolutionary forces by the coalition air attacks. Mr Hague said that it was a matter of deep regret. But the interviewer pushed on and demanded to know what the minister and the coalition government in Britain was going to do about the fact that their actions had led to a loss of innocent life?[35] But BBC interviewers have never questioned British government ministers in this way, about those injured or killed in Britain every year at the hands of criminals allowed to roam free.

In 1950 there were 14 per 100,000 'violent crimes against the person' in Britain. In 2015 there were 1,437. [36 37 38 39 40]

Violence against the person crimes per 100,000 population, England
and Wales 1950–2015

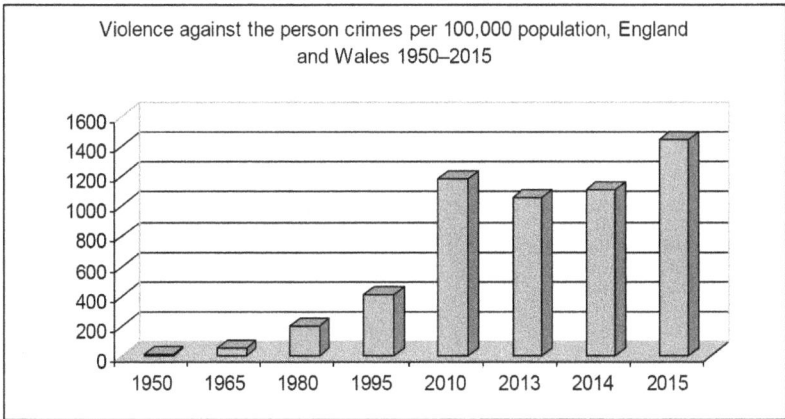

## Sources for violent crime data:

Data.GOV A Summary of Recorded Crime Data 1898–2001 at: https://data.
gov.uk/dataset/recorded-crime-data-1898-2001-02/resource/b5b1c3fe-338e-
472e-b844-75108c57436c

For 2001/02 to 2008/09

In: Home Office Statistical Bulletin Crime in England and Wales 2010/11 HOSB
10/11 at: http://www.cjp.org.uk/publications/government/crime-in-england-
and-wales-2010-11-14-07-2011/

NB: The VAP crime numbers for 2009/10–2010/11 are slightly less than later
figures provided in HOSB 01/14 below

For 2009/10–2013/14

In: Home Office Statistical Bulletin Crime Outcomes in England and Wales
2013/14 HOSB 01/14 at: https://www.gov.uk/government/uploads/system/
uploads/attachment_data/file/331597/hosb0114.pdf.pdf

For 2014/15

In: Home Office Crime Outcomes in England and Wales 2014/15, Statistical
Bulletin 01/15 https://www.gov.uk/government/uploads/system/uploads/
attachment data/file445753/hosb0115.pdf

## Sources for National Population figures:

1942–1980:

British Historical Statistics, by B.R. Mitchell (Page 14)

https://books.google.co.uk/books?id=Oyg9AAAAIAAJ&pg=PA1&source=gbs_toc_r&cad=3#v=onepage&q&f=false

1980–2008 Annual Abstract of Statistics, No. 146, 2010 Edition

http://www.ons.gov.uk/ons/rel/ctu/annual-abstract-of-statistics/no-146--2010-edition/index.html

2009–2011 Office for National Statistics, Population Estimates for England and Wales, Mid-2002 to Mid-2010

http://www.ons.gov.uk/ons/dcp171778_288817.pdf

2012 Office for National Statistics Population Estimates for England and Wales 2012

http://www.ons.gov.uk/ons/rel/pop-estimate/population-estimates-for-england-and-wales/mid-2012/index.html

2013 Office for National Statistics Annual Mid-Year Population Estimates, 2013

http://www.ons.gov.uk/ons/dcp171778_367167.pdf

2014 Office for National Statistics Annual Mid-Year Population Estimates, 2014

http://www.ons.gov.uk/ons/dcp171778_406922.pdf

2015 Population Estimates for UK, England and Wales, Scotland and Northern Ireland: mid-2015

https://www.ons.gov.ukpeoplepopulationandcommunitypopulationandmigration/populationestimates/bulletins/annualmidyearpopulationestimates/latest

Statistics by themselves, though necessary to give substance to the claim that Britain is a violent place, do not fully express the impact of these crimes, whereas it is examples which bring home the raw realities of violent crime, and its employment to resolve even sometimes trivial disputes, sometimes almost as a form of leisure pursuit. In 2010 the story of a plain clothes policeman who was stabbed in the stomach after tackling an armed robber in a betting shop in Bracknell, Berkshire, was reported in the press. As an indicator of how frequent these stories occur, it appeared in a column 1" by 2", several pages into the newspaper.[41] In the past, it would have been in large print and front page news. Another small paragraph reported that a 15-year-old boy had stabbed to death a former friend, 18-year-old Salum Kombo, in East London, over nothing more than a Facebook insult.[42] The use of mobile phones by thugs to film their attacks has added an extra element of shock interest to a public whose interest in stories of criminal violence has become jaded by their almost daily exposure to them. In one such case, a 17-year-old boy, Amar Aslam, was beaten to death in a park in Dewsbury, West Yorkshire, for his money, and while some of his attackers kicked, punched and then stamped on him until all life had left him, another one recorded the event on his mobile phone so they could enjoy their violence over and over again.[43]

Another story told of TV actress Charlotte Davies, who had appeared in popular TV programmes such as *Coronation Street* and *Hollyoaks*, who was blinded in one eye as a result of being attacked with a broken glass in a pub in Manchester,[44] following a row over a trivial matter. Her attacker, 21-year-old Sarah Harding was jailed for 27 months. There appears to be no shortage of hit men willing to kill for a price kept relatively low (about £1000 or less according to some reports) by the glut of criminals willing to take on such commissions. In 2013, two criminals, Ben Hope and Jason Richards, both in their thirties, were hired for a £1000 each to kill someone. They blundered and stabbed to death a different person, Aamir Siddiqi, 17, in front of his parents at the door of his home in Cardiff. The judge at Swansea Crown Court sentenced them both to life imprisonment with a minimum of forty years, a rare example of a sentence that comes close to recognising the malignity of the crime.[45]

David Grout, a soldier home on leave was left in a critical condition after an unprovoked attack in Eston, Teesside.[46] The 22-year-old father, who served with the Royal Signals Regiment, had been able to avoid injury from the bombs and bullets in Afghanistan, but not the violence in his own country. In 2009, police figures revealed that an 'honour' killing was carried out every month in Britain, and that the numbers of murders, rapes and assaults on people who dared to break strict religious or cultural rules was doubling every year,[47] (in 2017 it was reported that the Crown Prosecution Service was failing to prosecute some 'honour crimes' for fear of causing 'unrest' in Asian communities.)[48] In 2014 the police used Tazer guns 10,488 times, a 13% increase over the previous year,[49] an indication of the violence that criminals are prepared to use to resist arrest.

In December 2013, Radio 4s *Woman's Hour* reported that the number of women killed by partners or ex-partners went up from over 70 in 2009 to 120 in 2010,[50] while the number of notifications of domestic violence per year had risen to 800,000, with only 91,000 (11%) resulting in prosecutions.[51] Accounts of rape against women generally are rarely out of the press. As long ago as 1998, one newspaper reported that 18 British women on average were reporting being raped every day, approximately 6,500 per year.[52] Eleven years later (2009) it was reported as being nearer 47,000[53] while the number recorded by the police (in 2010) was 13,991.[54] The Stern Inquiry into how rape complaints are handled pointed out that only about 11% of all rape victims told the police about it.[55]

In February of 2013, a BBC news item brought to light concerns that numerous rape offences were not being investigated properly, and that the police were categorising many incidents as 'no crimes' in circumstances which warranted a charge being brought.[56] Despite this, it was reported in 2014 that over 22,000 rapes were recorded, their highest ever levels, representing a 29% increase over the previous year.[57] Press reporting of figures from the Ministry of Justice indicated that although there were over 5,000 extra sex crimes of all types for that year, there were only 77 additional convictions.[58] At the same time, the police inspectorate revealed that at least 68 rape cases had been incorrectly written off during the year under review by one police force in the north of England,

and that a quarter of rape allegations made to the police in parts of London were never recorded as crimes in 2013.[59]

We cannot hide behind the belief that violence generally is confined to our large cities and conurbations. Violent crime rates per 1,000 of the population in several smaller towns, chosen ad hoc from different parts of the country, such as Crawley in the south east, Launceston in the far west, Yeovil in the south west and Ashington in the north, were found to be among the highest, or often the highest, compared with the rates of other offences.[60] In 2015 the violent crime rate in the small market town of Tavistock in Devon increased by almost a quarter over the previous year.[61]

Violent crime is no longer a male preserve. The numbers of violent crimes committed by females, such as assaults, robbery and murder have increased over the last 30 years.[62] In 1995 the actress Elizabeth Hurley was violently mugged by a gang of young women[63] and by 2008 it was known that violence had taken over as the crime women most often commit; almost a quarter of all violent attacks are by women or girls,[64][65] and violent offences now make up a third of all their crimes.[66]

Some stand out for their viciousness: in one example two 17-year-old girls strangled a 70-year-old neighbour with a dog chain; in another, two other women tortured to death a 16-year-old girl in Manchester. Thirteen-year-old Louise Allen was set upon and killed by a group of girls described as acting like a 'pack of animals', after she left a funfair close to her home in Corby, Northants.[67] In 2013 the Home Office reported that a higher proportion of the sentenced female prison population was serving sentences for violence, than for drug offences, as was previously the case.[68][69]

Of even more significance is the marked increase in the number of women serving indeterminate prison sentences – in 2004 5% of all indeterminate prisoners were female, whereas in 2014 it was 12%.[70] Such disposals are an indication that they have committed very serious violent crimes and were thought to be dangerous, as was Ann Browning, who, in 2011 beat an elderly pensioner to death with a baseball bat before pocketing £250,000 from the sale of his house. The 54-year-old attacker stripped his corpse naked, bound his legs with a belt, wrapped his body in a shower curtain and buried it in the back garden of his home.[71]

In another example, three teenage girls, one of whom had attended an expensive private school, kicked a gay man to death. One of the attackers, Joel Alexander, aged 19, punched him with such violence that he crashed to the ground injuring his skull. The two 18-year-olds, Ruby Thomas and Rachel Burke then continued the attack with repeated and savage kicks to the head. He died from his wounds 18 days later.[72] The next day, one of the killers joked about what they had done on Facebook. These attackers had previous convictions for violence. The defence offered for one of the girls, when they were tried in court, was that her father had been a violent man, and this had somehow influenced her later behaviour. But to know what it is like to be on the receiving end of violence meant she had more than enough reasons to avoid inflicting it on others, and far from being a mitigating circumstance, it makes her behaviour all the worse.

Stories of knife robberies, violence and sex offences committed by young children are not uncommon. In 2012, the Home Office published a report which revealed that offenders aged 10–17 years committed 23% of *all* police recorded crime. This meant that this age group committed 1,064,000 offences in one year, of which 20% or 208,400 were for robbery, violence and sex attacks. Overall the under 18s were responsible for a half of all robberies, a fifth of all violent crimes and a fifth of all sex crimes.[73] [74] The degree of violence exhibited by the young often stands out. In 2009, two small boys aged ten and eleven subjected two other boys aged nine and ten to torture, violent attacks, and sexual abuse, only narrowly avoiding killing them.[75] In May 2010, two boys aged ten years, raped an eight-year-old girl, having first planned their crime and identified a secluded spot where they could carry out the attack.[76] In 2015 a six-year-old took two knives to school and threatened to 'chop his teacher's head off'.[77] The country's leading police officer on gang culture has warned that gang members are getting younger and that they are resorting to lethal violence much more swiftly even for the most trivial slights.[78] In Liverpool children are taught how to help friends who have been stabbed or shot, while in Birmingham, in 2015, a boy as young as 13, Petri Kurtin, robbed and murdered a 47-year-old woman. He knocked her to the ground and stamped on her face with such force that his footprints were left on her cheek.[79]

In 2010, Sir Alan Steer, a former government advisor, said that thousands of children were turning to crime because they had been expelled from school. He told a House of Commons Select Committee inquiring into behaviour in state schools, that many local councils had failed their pupils because they had allowed them to wander the streets and 'drift into crime'.[80] But in all my 25 years of working with offenders I never saw evidence of children 'drifting' into crime as if helplessly carried along by some invisible current. Neither did the young offenders become criminal *because* they had been ejected from their school. The children who choose to behave badly and refuse to work in the classroom are, in almost all cases, those who choose to offend. If the authorities have failed them, it is because they have taken no action to control them. In the past such criminal youngsters would have been sent to an approved school and would not have been allowed to roam the streets.

What also stands out is that many young criminals show no fear of the consequences of their violent offending. In 2010 a 15-year-old boy was stabbed to death in broad daylight by a rival gang of schoolboys at one of Britain's busiest railway stations.[81] The members of the gang were not in the least concerned that they had committed the most heinous of crimes in front of scores of commuters who could later identify them. Likewise, in the same year, a 15-year-old girl showed no hesitation in taking a 12" knife and a 'hit-list' of teachers and pupils into school with her to carry out a violent vendetta against them.[82] Another girl aged 13, who slashed a classmate across the face with a razor, causing wounds which required thirty stitches, was dealt with as if she had done no more than stolen an ice cream. Despite the life-threatening nature of this attack the judge gave her a two-year supervision order.[83] Such sentences give violent offenders both young and old permission to commit more violence. Fifty years ago, if a school boy made a stand against an order to do something he did not want to do, the most his protest would usually amount to would be a sullen silence and refusal to cooperate. Today, the protest can sometimes be a violent one, as illustrated by the 13-year-old boy who shot his rugby teacher in the face at point blank range with an air pistol because he did not want to take part in a game.[84]

Large numbers of crimes are also committed every year by offenders placed under probation supervision. To try and estimate how many has been made difficult because the government has published a bewildering variety of reconviction/reoffending rates over the last ten years. One of them, a 56% reoffending rate measured over one year, refers to those whose criminal backgrounds match those sent to prison.[85] This is of relevance because most offenders given community supervision fit this description. For example, almost 90% of offenders sentenced in this way already have serious criminal histories, as do 91% who are sent to prison.[86]

In 2015 there were 164,000 offenders under supervision in the community (*footnote*[1]).[87] [88] If we use the above reoffending rate, we can calculate that 92,000 (56% of them) reoffended at least once in a 12-month period but this gives no clue to the number

---

1    The total caseload of the probation service in *Offender Management Statistics Quarterly, July to September 2015* was given as 234,000 but 70,000 of these were in custody, leaving 164,000 used in the computation. The probation caseload figure for 2015 was revised upwards in *Offender Management Statistics Bulletin, England and Wales, Quarterly January to March 2016*, to 175,000 on supervision in the community. This results in an estimate of 1.5 million crimes committed each year by these offenders.

of offences they have committed. If, to estimate this, we make the modest assumption that each of them, on average, made three court appearances in the year and that at each court hearing they were convicted, on average for five offences, (three charges and two 'taken into consideration' – TICs) then we reach a total of 15 offences each (on average) per year, representing 1.4 million crimes, over 300,000 of which are estimated to be violent crimes (*footnote* [2]). Even if we use the 35% reoffending rate quoted by the government in 2014 for all adult offenders,[89] we arrive at an estimate of over 860,000 crimes per year (of which over 189,000 are estimated to be violent).

The assumption of 15 offences each per year on average is supported by several investigations which have found that offenders commit hundreds of offences in a 12-month period. For example, the Hertfordshire Police found that offenders under probation supervision in their area committed, on average 112 offences per year. But this was based only on vehicle and burglary crime, so the total of the crimes committed every year by them is likely to have been much higher.[90] The Halliday Report, published by the Home Office in 2001, estimated that the average offender carried out 140 offences per year.[91] In 1998, police in the south of England calculated that twenty young persistent offenders were responsible for thousands of crimes.[92] One notorious criminal had 175 offences dealt with as TICs at one hearing, while another, about to be sentenced for two burglaries, asked for another 225 further crimes to be taken into consideration.[93] While these numbers may be unusual, it is usually the case that the number of crimes 'taken into consideration', outnumber the current crimes dealt with when offenders are sentenced.

As serious as these crime numbers are for the public, they are likely to be an underestimate. Reoffending rates are based on just

2  Estimates from the British Crime Survey (BCS) suggest that violent crime accounts for 22% of police recorded crime and 23% of crimes reported by victims.

those crimes that result in a conviction or caution, and as most crimes are never cleared up, the real total committed by supervised offenders may run into several million. The government of course, should make this clear to the public in regular bulletins, presented in an easily understood format, as with for example, school exam results. But it does not. Reoffending data presented on the government websites is confusing. As already referred to, different failure rate measures have been used related to different time periods, and cover a variety of offender groupings (*footnote*[3]).[94] [95] [96] [97] [98] Members of the public consulting these records (should they know of their existence and where to find them), are likely to be bewildered in their attempts to fathom their meaning, and those unable or not prepared to spend the time required to do so, may give up in frustration. Is this their purpose? It goes without saying that the public have a right to be clearly informed about these matters so it can decide whether to support this sentencing policy or demand it is changed. Is this why they are shrouded in obscurity?

The evidence, accumulated over the last 50 years, of non-stop offending by criminals supervised in the community, means, in effect, that it is treated as a licence to offend. Surely, few officials, if any, faced as they are with the evidence of such obvious criminal intransigence, can truly believe that periods of formal oversight in

---

3   E.g. up to 2008 failure rates were measured as 'reconviction rates', since then the term 'reoffending' has been adopted using a different methodology for collecting data: before 2008 reconviction rates were measured over two years, but since then one year and three months time periods have been quoted: instead of just one heading i.e. 'offenders on community supervision' a variety of offender groupings have been introduced such as community supervision / a combination of community supervision and released prisoners / a combination of community supervision and suspended supervision orders / all offenders / adults only / juveniles only / a combination of released prisoners, those receiving a non-custodial conviction those cautioned, those tested positive for opiates / prolific offenders / 'matched pairs'.

the community have any meaning as a method of reform. In 2003, for example, serial offender Peter Williams, aged 19, was subject to supervision under the terms of a prison release licence and to an Intensive Supervision Programmes by a Nottingham Youth Offender Team, and at the same time, to a curfew order supported by electronic monitoring. Despite this multi-layered oversight, he took part in an armed robbery of a jeweller's shop in the Time Centre in Nottingham. Williams was armed with a crowbar. His job was to force open the boxes containing the jewellery, while another robber threatened the shop owners with a gun. During the robbery, the proprietor, 64-year-old Marion Bates was shot and killed as she shielded her daughter, Xanthe, from the attackers who were threatening her. Williams, who helped the gunman escape, was eventually convicted of her murder and sentenced to Life imprisonment with a minimum tariff of 22 years.[99]

As crime and violent crime has increased in Britain, so has the number of criminologists. At one time 'criminology' was thought not to be a proper subject, but today it is taught in almost every university. In the author's experience a minority of criminologists have stood out for the high level of their scholarship and for their contribution to our understanding of crime and its impact on the public. For example, the analysis by Professor K. Pease, which exposed the problem of repeat victimisation, particularly on the poorer sections of our community. But many other criminology departments collect crime data, pose questions and fashion theories, often with little practical relevance for the public.

For example, Professor M. Maguire in his paper *The Construction of Crime* posed questions about the 'meaning' of violence and suggested that this is not as straight forward as the public might think.[100] He warned that we need to understand the 'social and or the situational context' of violent crime before we jump to any conclusions about how to interpret it. For example, he points out that robbery includes actions as diverse as an organised bank raid, the theft at knife point of money from a shop till, or a street handbag snatch, and that the 'social context' of crime must be born in mind if we are to understand it. Violence, he says, must be seen against the back drop of the 'hierarchy of power' relating to the attacker and the victim, and that a punch can mean 'totally different' things in different circumstances. But this accepting, almost obliging attitude to crime, adds weight to the idea that some criminologists have long been to crime what Marshal Petain was to Hitler (see page 32 of *Spoilt Rotten, The Toxic Cult of Sentimentality*).

But I suspect that for the victims of violence it doesn't matter where they were attacked, whether by a robber in the street, behind a till in a shop, or in a bank, they would struggle to differentiate their injuries sociologically, or see the need to do so.

Since 1950, the ratio between police officers available to fight crime and the number of crimes being committed has worsened.[101] In 1951, there were 0.10 violent crimes per police officer,[102] [103] and in 2015 there were 6.55.[104] [105] If we use the British Crime Survey estimates for 2015 (based on interviews with victims), there were 11 violent crimes per police officer.[106] These pressures have increased with cuts in police numbers. They are now rarely seen on our streets, and police stations have been closed in their hundreds, and many of those still in existence are now closed to the public. The number of police officers per 100,000 of the population in England and Wales is now 248, compared with the European mean of 386.[107]

But logistic problems such as these have been just one of the many pressures the British police have had to face. For example, few events have proved so burdensome and destructive to the morale of the British police than the findings of the Macpherson Report of 1999,[108] written in the aftermath of the killing of Stephen Lawrence on 22 April 1993, in south-east London. The report criticised the police for the way the murder enquiry had been handled and furthermore said they were institutionally racist despite the fact Macpherson later contradicted himself by saying that "we have not heard evidence of overt racism or discrimination".[109]

Paragraph 6.45 of the report said that: "The over representation of racial minorities in the national stop and search figures led to the clear core conclusion of racist stereotyping." But his was a seriously flawed argument. In 2000, research by the Home Office showed that it was necessary to compare stop and search figures, *not* with the racial composition of the national population (or even the resident population), but with the racial composition of those *available* for stop and search, i.e. with those who hang around in public places, often at night, and who are therefore potential targets for police stops.[110] Miller's research concluded that based on stop and search data from five different areas of London, including Greenwich, where Stephen Lawrence was murdered, white people tended to be stopped or searched at a higher rate to the available population, while Asian people tended to be under represented and black people had a more mixed experience. Indeed, a year earlier a separate inquiry had found no evidence to support the assertion that discrimination between racial groups was responsible for the difference in arrest rates between different minority groups.[111]

In 2004, additional research findings based on Slough and Reading, replicated that of Miller and found that, compared to the 'available population', those stopped and searched were not disproportionately drawn from minority groups,[112] but demonstrated it was the whites who were over represented in stop and searches by the police.

Macpherson's misuse of the stop and search figures was highly damaging. In 1999, the year his report was published, the police stopped and searched over a million individuals. The following year this number had fallen by 20% to 857,000, and by 2004 it had been scaled down even further to 734,000 equating to thousands of fewer arrests and a reduced level of public protection from street violence and other crimes.[113]

But why, in the light of these results, did no one come to the rescue of the police and publicly proclaim that research results had repeatedly failed to find evidence that their stop and search activity was discriminatory against ethnic minorities? The Macpherson report had been received with uncritical approval by almost everyone. It made front page news and dominated the attention of the media. The claim that the British police were racist was made loudly up and down the land. Yet no one stepped forward to defend them, and rescue them from the burden of this false and damaging accusation. MPs, ministers, officials, academics and others have kept their heads down, and in doing so have cowardly betrayed the police and the public alike.

The Crown Prosecution Service (CPS) has further undermined their morale by closing the files on thousands of cases which the police have prepared for prosecution. Since its inception in 1986 no organisation could have done more to make the lives of criminals easier, safer and more rewarding. Before the establishment of the CPS the police were responsible for prosecuting the offenders they had arrested. The test they used to decide whether to take someone to court was simple – was there enough evidence to give a realistic prospect of a conviction? Their motivating principal was to ensure that as many as possible of those who were guilty were brought to justice and to protect the public.

But as pointed out by Brian Lawrence, a magistrate's court lawyer for 36 years, in his revealing book *They Call It Justice*,[114] the approach of the CPS was entirely different. Lawrence points out that its supposed purpose was to restore public confidence in the criminal justice system, to avoid miscarriages of justice and weed out (discontinue) 'hopeless cases'. It soon became clear that its main purpose was to save money by discontinuing as many cases as possible, sometimes even when there was sufficient evidence to proceed.

Lawrence argues that CPS prosecutors are rewarded not just on the basis of how many cases they can stop going to court, but also how speedily they can close the file. He revealed that at their meetings it was emphasised that if this route was not open to them, CPS prosecutors should make every effort to downgrade the offence, so that it could be dealt with quickly at a magistrate's court, and so avoid the costlier proceedings at the crown court. Not one word was said about justice for the victims.

In one year alone, 1992, the CPS threw out no fewer 193,000 cases that the police brought forward for prosecution.[115] In one example that year, the CPS closed the file on two armed robbers who robbed a minicab driver of his money and his car. There were no fewer than 11 strands of evidence which linked them to the crime, including fingerprints, and in the case of one of them, being seen abandoning the stolen vehicle. Although it is well known that forensic-type evidence is much more reliable than evidence based on human memory, when the cab driver failed to pick out the offenders in an ID parade, the CPS used this as a reason to drop the case[116] (the same tactic they tried with Gabrielle Brown, discussed in chapter 1).

By 1997, it was under fire because convictions had dropped by a third.[117] The government expressed its 'surprise' – but what did it expect? It set up an enquiry to 'investigate' this development (as if it did not already know the cause) but this changed nothing, and in 2008 it was reported that of the 693,250 crimes the police had cleared up that year, the CPS intervened to drop or discontinue 287, 250, i.e. 41% of them.[118] The effect on the police of this level of attrition can only be imagined. A former police officer with 38 years' service publicly declared that he despaired of the enormous number of criminals the CPS had allowed to escape from any form of justice.[119] In the last five years alone the CPS has refused to prosecute 345,990 cases presented to it by the police, (almost 70,000 per year) under the umbrella excuse that 'it was not in the public interest to proceed'.[120] [121]

It must also weigh heavily on the police to know for example, that in 1990 they detected 77% of violent offences,[122] but only 42% in 2014,[123] (the lowest level since records began in 1975 when it was 81%). Their awareness that thousands of violent crimes, such as wounding, grievous bodily harm, and assault, are committed without even a suspect being uncovered, let alone being convicted,[124] and the influence this had had on the way the public perceive them, has also doubtless affected their morale.

In *Explaining English Character,* a book written in the early 1950s, Geoffrey Gorer reported that his investigation found most British people had enthusiastic appreciation of the English police. Even those under 18, he said, looked up to them, and while they had no reason to fear them, they held the police in a certain amount of awe.[125] Contrast this with the attitude, in 2008, of two teenage girls who were asked by two constables to pick up litter they had just thrown down. They first mocked the officers and then violently attacked them, causing substantial injuries.[126] Violent behaviour towards the police is now common and 50 police officers a day are on sick leave due to injuries sustained in street attacks.[127] In one police district the police held a public meeting to see how it could 'better communicate with local people'. (Such meetings were not necessary in the 1950s.) No one turned up.[128]

To win back public confidence, many police authorities spend £100,000 a day on spin doctors[129] while the National Police Improvement Agency is known to spend £3,000 a day on consultants.[130] At least one force has resorted to allowing members of the public to ride in police cars while they are on patrol, to regain their support.[131] Yet money spent on spin doctors and consultants has done little to mitigate the fact that the public's admiration of the police generally, built up over more than 100 years, has in less than three decades, been seriously eroded.

While it remains true that the public acknowledge the bravery of rank and file officers who work hard to protect their communities, they have watched while they have been largely withdrawn from the streets, solved fewer crimes, and become embroiled by their senior managements in activities, such as the imposition of political correctness, that have taken them away from crime fighting.

For example, in 2009 the 200-year-old cheese rolling competition at Coopers Hill in Gloucester was banned by the council because of the number of injuries to locals who took part. The locals defied the ban and held the event again in 2013. The police were ordered to visit 86-year-old Diana Smart, a local woman who had for the last 25 years made the cheese used in the event. They warned her that she would be responsible if someone was hurt. The visit frightened her into stopping her cheese making activities.[132] Exactly what objective did the senior police managers think they were pursuing by instigating this visit? And indeed, what exactly was it to do with them? And why did they not send their officers to visit the manufacturers of boxing gloves or rugby balls and warn them that they will be responsible if someone who uses them gets injured? In 2012, a Devon woman was visited by the police because neighbours had complained she had 'disturbed' the owls located in a barn on her property. Examples such as these can lend a nightmarish quality to contact with the police because it means the public can no longer be certain what the limits are to their authority.

One serving police officer revealed that as many as one in five officers in his force were working on 'diversity, confidence, development, performance, community engagement, police pledges, and targets.'[133] A report by the police inspectorate confirmed this picture for the police generally. It revealed that overall they spend 22% of their time on 'support functions' such as finance, planning, catering and personnel matters, while for 47% of their time they were policing roads, and carrying out community work. Only 31% of their time was spent dealing with criminals, of which only 13% was devoted to investigating crime.[134] Three years later one chief officer, Nick Gargon, of the Avon and Somerset force area, admitted that his officers ignored swathes of 'petty crimes' (his description, not the victims') because to take action against them 'would block up the system'.[135]

This admission came just a few months before Dr Roger Patrick, a former senior police officer, gave evidence at the end of 2013 to a Commons Public Administration Select Committee, to the effect that the police had been manipulating their crime figures for years, and that their statistical returns could no longer be trusted.[136] He provided a detailed picture of the methods used by the police to make crimes 'disappear'. One involved treating complaints as 'false reports', made for the benefit of an insurance claim. For example, 15-year-old Reece Bahia was robbed at gun point in Birmingham on his way home from school. The police said they did not believe him and both he and his parents were threatened with formal police action if they persisted with their complaint. They were eventually vindicated and the police forced to apologise.[137] Another tactic involved the police in threats to both the victim and the assailant with arrest for 'causing an affray'. This usually frightened the victim of the violence into withdrawing his complaint.

The committee members were reported to have been both surprised and horrified by Dr Patrick's evidence[138] yet this was not the first time parliament had been told of these problems. In 2003, for example, a chief constable had described these procedures as 'administrative corruption' in his evidence to the House of Commons Public Administration Committee.[139]

In any case concerns over the manipulation of crime figures had already been brought to the public's attention by the press. One example headed 'street crime figures are fiddled' appeared as long ago as 2002.[140] In 2006 another one reported '11 million crimes left out of the figures'.[141] [142] In 2011 a London newspaper reported that the 'police are encouraged to reclassify crimes to keep numbers down'.[143] Is it likely that the MPs on this committee had not seen these press reports or others like them?

The committee members were reminded that in 2002 the police were directed to follow the National Crime Recording Standard (NCRS) rules to ensure that all police forces recorded crime in the same way. This meant that when a member of the public reported a crime, the police had to record it, unless there were reasonable grounds for doubt. But Dr Patrick pointed out that in 2004 they slipped back to their previous methods which meant that once again they decided whether a crime had been committed, not the member of the public who reported the incident. Following this there was a fall in the number of recorded crimes in some of the violent offence categories such as 'more serious wounding', robbery, arson, and 'threat or conspiracy to murder'.

The revelations of serious recording malpractice put the spotlight on chief officers, many of whom had already been suspended and or were under investigation for other matters. As reported by Andrew Gilligan in the *Telegraph*, no fewer than eleven English police forces, – almost 30% – have had one or more of their senior leaders under a cloud of suspicion for a variety of matters.[144] But who else, apart from police chiefs, is to blame for these corrupt recording procedures? The Chief Inspector of Constabulary, giving evidence to the Public Administration Committee in 2014, was reluctant to admit that these practices were as widespread as other witnesses claimed, or that they were driven by management.[145] But this did not sit easily with the admission by Chief Constable of Derbyshire, Mike Creedon, one of Britain's most senior police officers, that police crime figures could no longer be trusted. He said officers at every level were manipulating statistics because of the pressure to cut crime. He said measuring police performance in this way had become an obsession and left a legacy of 'unwitting corruption'.[146]

A short time later Sir Andrew Dilnot, chairman of the UK Statistics Authority, stripped the police crimes statistics of their official designation (i.e. withdrew the state's seal of approval).[147] Following this very public reprimand of the police, the police inspectorate admitted that at least 20% of all crimes go unrecorded – approximately one million.[148] However, Dr Patrick pointed out that the methodology, employed by the inspectorate in their investigation which arrived at this figure, was so badly flawed one would be forgiven for thinking it was designed to find nothing. Therefore, for the inspectorate notwithstanding to admit to almost a million unrecorded crimes supports the suggestion that the real figure is likely to be very much higher.[149]

Following this cautious statement by the inspectorate, even Sir Andrew Dilnot felt constrained to make what sounded like a confession, when he publicly expressed his regret that his committee had "not highlighted the major problems with police information earlier" and remarkably, said that he knew there had been concerns over the crime figures "for years".[150] This raises the possibility that he already knew or suspected what Dr Patrick had told the committee some few weeks earlier, namely that the police inspectorate reports had consistently played down the problem and put a generous interpretation on the evidence it had uncovered. None of them ever referred to these practices as corrupt, or held any chief constable to account.

One front line officer told the committee that he and his constable colleagues felt nothing but disgust for crime recording malpractices. He rejected the subtle hints made earlier to the committee by the chief inspector that the constables were responsible. He pointed out that senior police managers rule with an iron fist. He added that he had been bringing these problems to their attention for decades but nothing had ever been done about them.[151]

The possibility of collusion, between chief constables, the inspectorate and even the UK Statistics Authority, hinted at by these revelations, suggests that the government, no less, may have been turning a blind eye to crime recording malpractices which it may have known about for some time. Between 2006 and 2011, for example, it instigated three major enquiries into the reliability of police statistics (more than two years *before* Dr Patrick's revelations).[152] [153] [154] None of these resulted in any change, despite the concerns raised throughout this time about the crime figures, leaving the impression they were nothing more than public relations exercises to assuage public anxiety over these problems.

The target set by Tony Blair for the police to 'cut crime' was misconceived and encouraged this culture of accounting spivvery. It is not the police's responsibility to cut crime. The public expect them to catch as many criminals as possible and rigorously promote their prosecution. If Blair had set targets around these objectives a culture would have developed that was more in keeping with the protection of the public and less in keeping with the production of dubious, if not actually fictitious, crime statistics which those in authority find it convenient not to question too closely. In 2015, the commissioner of the City of London Police said that, "the notion of police recorded crime is history. It's dead in the water".[155]

All of this leaves the public in the dark concerning the true levels of violent crime perpetrated against them. Even the separate figures obtained by the Crime Survey of England and Wales (CSEW), based on interviews with victims, have come under serious questioning. These survey figures have always produced higher crime figures than those recorded by the police, but as far back as 2008 Professor Marion Fitzgerald, a former Home Office advisor, claimed that the survey was "very poor at picking up violent crimes"[156] and they were likely to be considerably understated. Seven years later in 2015, Professor Walby of Lancaster University, stated that her research had found that the survey underestimated violent crime by 60%.[157]

The government's preference for secrecy over these matters is further highlighted by the fact that for the last 14 years it has kept quiet about the results of two special studies it carried out in 2000, whose results showed beyond doubt that the crime figures made available to the public were little more than fiction. Although one was made the subject of a little-known report, at no time have the implications of either of these investigations been discussed publicly. Their silence on these matters was particularly noticeable during the period covered by Dr Patrick's revelations to parliament.

The first, Home Office Report 217, displayed its findings by showing the numbers of crimes committed in each of several sub-categories, but the box for the overall total was left blank.[158] It was as if the officials could not bring themselves to inform the readers that they had found there were at least *60 million* crimes committed in Britain, not five million, according to the police returns, or 12 million as reported by the British Crime Survey for that year. If the Home Office civil servants, responsible for the annual returns, did not know before, (which is so unlikely we can rule it out) these results told them that something was radically wrong with the crime recording procedures they had been using for years. This report should have shaken the Cabinet and parliament to their roots, and caused a wholesale rethink, not just about their crime recording methods, but about the ineffectiveness of the sentencing policies which lay behind these astronomical crime figures. But they kept quiet, and continued to rely on the crime returns they themselves had shown were not worth the paper they were written on.

For reasons about which we can only speculate, the then Prime Minister, Tony Blair, soon after this report was published, commissioned John Birt (now Lord Birt) to carry out another investigation to assess the number of offences committed in Britain each year. Perhaps Blair could not, or did not, want to believe the results of Report 217, so different were they from previous estimates. But whatever his motives, he was soon to receive one of the most profound shocks of his political life. John Birt's investigation found that there were not five million, or 12 million, or even 60 million crimes committed each year, but 132 million indictable crimes *alone* (of which at least twenty-six million are estimated to be violent offences).[159]

It is now known that Tony Blair's reaction was to lock the Birt report away in the Cabinet office, in a determined bid to ensure that no one ever saw it, particularly the public, to whom, of course, it was of most concern. (He had clearly forgotten the earlier promises he had proudly made in a White Paper entitled '*Your Right to Know*', intended, allegedly, to make government 'more open'.) And there it would have stayed, unknown to the world, had it not been for the determined efforts of an inquisitive newspaper journalist, who, no doubt, tipped off as to its existence, requested a copy under the Freedom of Information Act (FOI). This was refused at the first asking, and the second, but finally it was released, after four years gathering dust in a dark corner of a government office.

As with Report 217 mentioned above, the effects on the government of the Birt revelations should have been seismic. In the event, the news that there were over 130 million crimes per year, representing twenty-six times more than the police returns and ten times those of the BCS, caused not one stir in parliament or the government; all concerned chose to keep their counsel and their heads down. Likewise, there was practically no response in the media. The one journalist known to have responded to it said that having at last seen the material 'he did not know what all the fuss was about'.[160] Could it be that he really did not understand the dire implications for the public and the effect on their standard of life of this huge crime burden, now known to be much larger than anyone had dared imagine? Was it of no interest to learn that the government had known for years that their published crime figures were so inaccurate as to appear fraudulent? What would have served the public interest more would have been to have made this report front page news and highlight that the government's lenient sentencing policies, so actively supported by the pro-criminal lobby, were not only failing to control crime, but had changed Britain into a criminals' paradise.

For the purposes of research for this book, I requested an interview with the report's author, Lord Birt, in order to ask questions about his investigation (see Notes), and discuss, among other things, why a curtain of silence had been hung over his findings. He at first agreed, and then later withdrew his offer. He said that he had talked it over with a good friend who was a senior official and on further reflection he did not feel free to discuss it with me. But why, after 14 years, did they feel it necessary to maintain this veil of secrecy? What exactly was he afraid of? Why couldn't this report, containing information about the number of crimes committed every year in this country, be discussed openly? It was not as if he was being asked to reveal highly sensitive government data that, if known about, would have jeopardised Britain's security. The crime data I was asking about was public property in every sense of the word. They had paid for it. The salaries of those who worked on its compilation were paid for out of the public purse, and its subject matter could not be more central to the interests and safety of the public.

Lord Birt was assisted in the preparation of the report by a team of Home Office officials who presumably believed that the report's findings would never be made public. No one, inside or outside of the Home Office, at the time or since, has ever questioned the validity of its profoundly shocking assessment that each year there are at least 130 million *indictable crimes alone* committed in Britain. This amounts to a tacit admission that their published crime returns based on police and survey data, had been misleading the public for years. The pall of silence which has hung over the Birt report, and which officials still want maintained, is not because its findings were thought to be wrong and therefore of no value (if this had been the case it would have been criticised, not hidden). It is because officialdom recognised the story it told about crime and violence levels was, even then, far nearer the truth, and the senior official's advice to Lord Birt not to talk to me, despite the passage of time, indicates they are still terrified by it.

# 3

## Britain's Response to Crime and Violence

From the late 1950s Britain's official attitude towards crime began to change. Instead of being viewed as bad behaviour that needed to be punished and controlled, it was increasingly judged to be a symptom of a social or psychological malaise. The offender was seen as being forced into crime by poverty, inequality or other forces beyond his control, which society could, and should, alleviate. Greed, laziness, and the wish to dominate others, were no longer recognised as the motives for violent crime. Persistent violent and dangerous criminals, who spurned hard work and thriftiness as the route to a comfortable standard of living, were rewarded with state protection from prosecution whenever possible, and the guarantee of their human rights, even in the face of their violence and law breaking. What was required, our ruling elites argued, was the application, wherever possible, of non-custodial sentences (even for violent offenders), such as the supervision of offenders in the community, and to identify and alleviate the 'underlying causes of crime'.

Increasingly, the same expectations were placed on prisons, otherwise viewed as repressive, even harmful instruments that made prisoners worse. The route to the rehabilitation of violent criminals was to be sign-posted by leniency, concern and understanding. That there is and never was any evidence to show that prisons caused offenders to commit crime, or that counselling, therapy or other forms of help, can influence persistent offenders unmotivated to reform, has in no way dented the establishment's enthusiasm for such policies, which in the main do not affect them, but which have backfired seriously on large numbers of the public.

In 1959, the government signalled this change in its thinking with the publication of its report 'Penal Practice in a Changing Society'.[161] Its major purpose was, I believe, to prepare the public for the introduction of more lenient sentencing policies to confront what the report called the 'complex' dimensions of crime. It called upon universities to help identify its 'varied and complex causes', but nowhere did it offer any evidence to explain how it came to this view. Thus, it appeared to be calling for 'evidence' to support a conclusion it had already reached.

In the 1960s social scientists answered the call with a flood of theories concerning what they saw as factors associated with crime. These included psychological problems, the problems of adolescence, environmental pressures of schools, the influence of poverty and neighbourhoods, run down housing estates, the influence of criminal gangs, the rise of an anti-authority youth culture, lack of job training, the effects of rapid social change, personal insecurity, and broken homes.[162]

Thus, officials and those working with offenders could pick and choose which theory they liked best, depending on exigencies of the moment. These ideas, which lacked empirical evidence to back them up, nevertheless quickly gained ground among probation officers, social workers, academics, and others with specialist interests in this field, who showed no interest in, or were unaware of, the poor scholarship on which they were based. In one example, Howard Jones in *Crime in a Changing Society*, spoke of the need for the penal system to become an effective agency of treatment, promoting the idea that the criminal was a victim of a malaise not of his making, an idea which although now expressed with a different terminology, has underlined our approach to criminality ever since. Twenty-five years after the start of this cultural revolution, (for that is what it was), I met many students training for the probation service who had been brainwashed with anti-prison ideology to believe that criminals were victims of an oppressive society. Their university based courses taught groundless theories concerning the cause of criminal behaviour, and denigrated control and punishment as methods for dealing with it. Some criminologists went so far as to argue that criminals could be viewed as freedom fighters in the struggle against the 'power and domination of authority'.[163]

These courses provided an entry visa into the probation service for many militant Marxists who regarded crime as a function of the class struggle. They were more than prepared to soak up the pseudo-sociological slop presented to them by their teachers.

It was not long before some of these ideas found expression in our sentencing laws. Roy Jenkins, the Home Secretary, introduced parole in 1967 and championed tolerance towards offenders generally. But like many who shared his ideology and reforming zeal, his privileged lifestyle meant that he did not have to cope with its consequences. That was left to those less privileged than himself. The Bail Act (1976) allowed violent offenders to be bailed rather than remanded in custody. This has allowed large numbers of them ever since to terrify and intimidate witnesses and victims during the lead up to their trial. It has been reported for example, that as many as 30,000 court cases a year collapse as a result.[164] In one example, Jason Jones, a man in his late twenties with a history of previous convictions for serious violence, walked free from Manchester Crown Court. He had faced trial following a hammer attack in a street which left a 16-year-old boy seriously injured. The trial collapsed because the numerous witnesses were too terrified to testify against the defendant. Forensic tests had earlier found the injured boy's blood on Jones' T-shirt.[165]

In 1974 the Rehabilitation of Offenders Act stated that previous convictions could be ignored after a specified period. This meant in effect that criminals could deceive prospective employers by not disclosing all their previous crime record. Just a few years before, The Criminal Appeals Act, (1968) made it easier for criminals to appeal, and in 1974 (and again in 1979) Legal Aid Acts made it easier for criminals to get financial aid in mounting what often turned out to be a non-existent defence. Whereas in 1971 just 28% of defendants appearing in magistrate's courts were legally aided by the state, by 1989 it was 71%.[166] In 2011, one MP, David Davies, pointed out that the Human Rights Act was responsible for the rise in criminals taking legal action at the public's expense,[167] and by 2014 Britain's total expenditure on legal aid had reached £2 billion, the largest in Europe.[168] Numerous other criminal justice acts have increased the opportunity for judges to avoid giving a prison sentence, signalling the government was soft pedalling in its fight against crime and instead had declared war on prisons (*foot note*[4]).

The anti-prison organisations in Britain, such as the Howard League and the Prison Reform Trust, as well as some senior law lords,[169] have argued, along with many MPs and justice officials, that Britain sends 'too many criminals to jail'. This misleading propaganda which no government has challenged has been highly successful, as many now assume this is an indisputable truth.

But it is not a truth and never has been. The deception is created

---

4    For some earlier examples:
     1972 Criminal Justice Act (introduced Community Service Orders and Day Training Centres).
     1982 Criminal Justice Act (restricted the use of prison for under 18-year-olds).
     1991 Criminal Justice Act (ruled that previous convictions should not be taken into account when sentencing, and that fines should reflect the offender's stated income).
     2000 Criminal Justice Act (introduced Rehabilitation Orders and Community Punishment Orders, both to be served in the community).

by expressing the imprisonment rate as the number of prisoners in our jails per 100,000 of the population, which, as shown by the following graph, suggests our imprisonment rate has been rising.[170] [171] [172] [173]

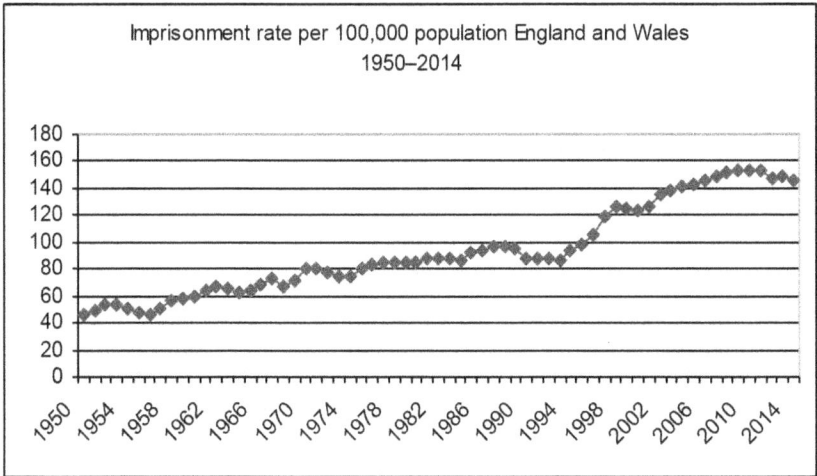

Imprisonment rate per 100,000 population England and Wales 1950–2014

Prison numbers:

1900–2008 Ministry of Justice Bulletin, Offender Management Caseload Statistics 2009 (Table 7.5 Prison Population) 1900–2008

2009–2010 Ministry of Justice Population in Custody monthly tables August 2010 (2009 and 2010 prison populations)

2011–2015 GOV.UK Prison Population Figures 2011/population Bulletin monthly December 2011

GOV.UK Prison Population Figures 2012/population Bulletin monthly December 2012

GOV.UK Prison Population Figures 2013/population Bulletin monthly November 2013

GOV.UK Prison Population Figures 2014/population Bulletin monthly December 2014

National population numbers:

National Population figures for 1898–1939 found in: Abstract of British Historical Statistics, B.R. Mitchell

National Population figures for 1942–1980 found in: British Historical Statistics, B.R. Mitchell

National Population figures for 1981–2008 found in: Office of National Statistics, Annual Abstract of Statistics no.146, 2010 edition

National Population figures for 2009–2011 found in: Office for National Statistics, Population Estimates for England and Wales, Mid-2002 to Mid-2010

National Population figures for 2012 found in: Office for National Statistics Population Estimates for England and Wales 2012

National Population figures for 2013 found in: Office for National Statistics Annual Mid-Year Population Estimates, 2013

National Population figures for 2014 found in: Office for National Statistics Annual Mid-Year Population Estimates, 2014

But a moment's reflection tells us that most of us do not commit crime and are not in that group of persons liable to be sent to jail. Therefore, this calculation tells us nothing about how lenient or severe we are in our use of prison for criminals. A more accurate imprisonment rate can be obtained by expressing the prison population against the number of crimes committed. The following graph shows that our imprisonment rate, when calculated in this way, has, since the 1950s, fallen not risen, and that we are not the 'prison obsessed nation' that the anti-prison lobby would have us believe. Since the turn of the millennium the rate has risen, but it is still far less than it was 60 years ago.
174 175 176 177 178 179 180 181 182

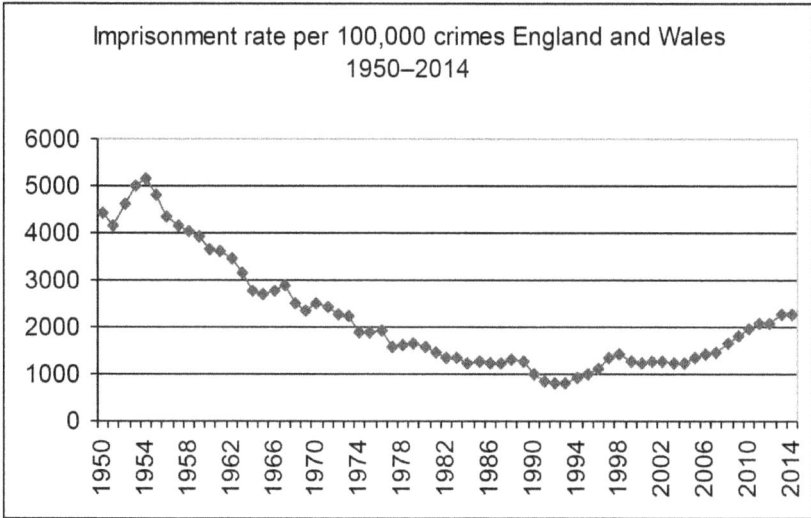

Imprisonment rate per 100,000 crimes England and Wales 1950–2014

Crime:

1950–2001 Data.GOV A Summary of Recorded Crime Data 1898–2002

2002–2003 Home Office Statistical Bulletin 07/03, Crime in England and Wales

2008–2009 Home Office Statistical Bulletin 11/09, Crime in England and Wales 2008/09

2005, 2006, 2010, 2011 Home Office Statistical Bulletin Crime in England and Wales 2010/11 HOSB 10/11

2004, 2013, 2014 Office for National Statistics, Crime in England and Wales 2014

2007, 2012 Crime in England and Wales 2013 (Table A4: Police Recorded Crime by offence, 2002/03 to 2012/13)

Prison numbers:

1900-2008 Ministry of Justice Bulletin, Offender Management Caseload Statistics 2009 (Table 7.5 Prison Population) 1900-2008

2009-2010 Ministry of Justice Population in Custody monthly tables August 2010

(2009 and 2010 prison populations)

2011–2015 GOV.UK Prison Population Figures 2011/population Bulletin monthly December 2011

GOV.UK Prison Population Figures 2012/population Bulletin monthly December 2012

GOV.UK Prison Population Figures 2013/population Bulletin monthly November 2013

GOV.UK Prison Population Figures 2014/population Bulletin monthly December 2014

The breakdown of the 86,000 prison population also undermines the notion that our courts are unthinkingly severe in relation to their use of jail. The courts had no other option but to pass a life sentence on the 7,576 prisoners convicted of murder. No one could say of the 5,809 serving indeterminate imprisonment terms that there were 'too many', as all have committed highly dangerous, violent offences. Similarly, who could say that 12,000 remand prisoners are 'too many', given that courts encouraged to bail almost everyone, considered they could not remand them on bail? On what basis can it be argued that the figure of 13,000 recalled prisoners, who have continued to offend following their early release on licence or after being placed on probation, is 'too many'? When all of these, plus the 10,512 foreign prisoners jailed for serious offences (and likely to be deported) are taken into consideration, it leaves just 37,000 'home grown' offenders sent to jail in circumstances where it could be said that the court had a matter of choice.[183] In contrast, there were, in 2015 almost four and a half times this number of offenders subject to community supervision by the probation service.

In the same way, reports put out, for example, by the BBC that 'England and Wales have the highest per capita prison population in Western Europe' are highly misleading.[184] When each country's imprisonment rate is measured against the number of crimes, we are, as shown below, 13th in an ascending order of 27 other nations.[185] [186] [187]

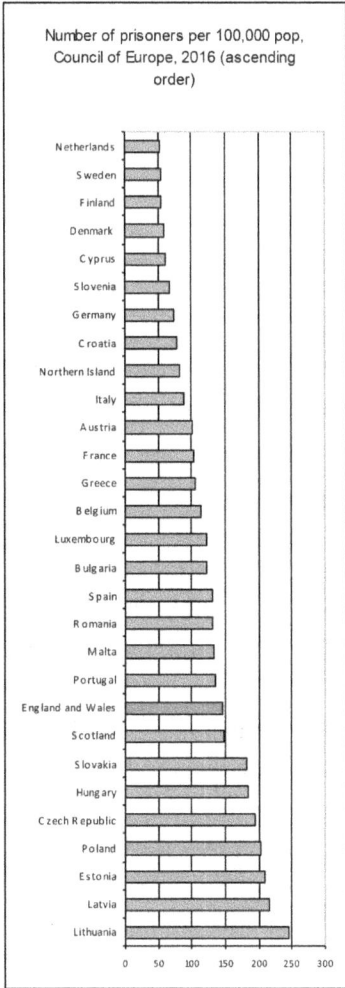

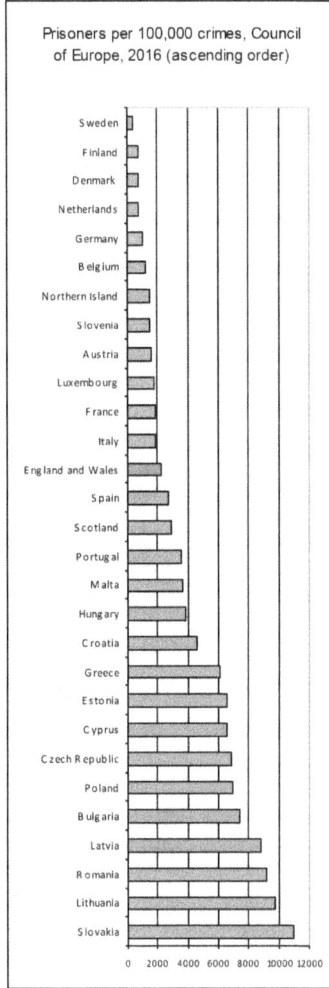

Sources:

Prison numbers:

Council of Europe Annual Penal Statistics Space 1, 2016 data

National population:

List of European Countries by Population 2015, United Nations Department of Economic and Social Affairs

Crime:

Eurostat Crimes Recorded by the Police, published 2014

Comparisons with Singapore, which has one of the best crime control records in the world, are even starker. Their imprisonment rate, per 100,000 crimes, is 32,304.[188] [189] For England and Wales, it is 2,261.[190] [191] Of interest is that in Singapore the rate for 'violence against the person crimes' is 71 per 100,000 of the population.[192] [193] For England and Wales, it is 1,437.[194] [195] Such figures speak for themselves.

In 2016, on a return flight from Dubai to Heathrow, 21-year-old Joshua McCarthy became violent after drinking several small bottles of wine. He abused Miss Hayley Morgan, one of the cabin staff, with foul language, spat at the passenger in front of him, and attacked another by biting him viciously on the arm. He threatened to kill other cabin crew who tried to restrain him. Despite the violence he exhibited, judge Sandeep Kainth sentenced him to a *suspended* prison term of nine months (two months for spitting, nine months for being drunk on an aircraft, and four months for the assault, all to be served concurrently).[196] Thus, McCarthy was freed, leaving Miss Morgan traumatised and unable to sleep, and anxious about how this would impact on her ability to do her job.

That McCarthy *thanked* the judge as he left the court is symptomatic of what now happens in Britain, with many violent felons viewing their experience in court as do satisfied customers exiting a department store. Twenty-year-old Daniel Phillips attacked 42-year-old Peter Davies outside a nightclub in Weston, Somerset. The attack was so violent it left the victim unconscious and with a fractured skull. Phillips was convinced he would be sent to prison.

But he told the court his mother had recently died, and this was one of the reasons why Judge Carol Hagen suspended his 12-month prison term for eighteen months. This signalled to the offender that the judge considered that beating someone senseless to the point of endangering their life was an acceptable way of expressing grief. Philips was later seen celebrating wildly with friends in the court corridor, and left as another satisfied and very happy customer.[197]

Government reports sometimes refer to criminals in the justice system as 'service users',[198] a term entirely in keeping with the results described above, and, in particular, with the experience of serial paedophile Michael James, 48. This offender, whose 15 previous convictions included an indecent assault on a boy, and gross indecency with a girl under sixteen, committed yet another offence while on licence, following his early release from jail. In July 2016, he exposed himself to a mother at a bus stop in Mapperley, Nottingham. Judge Timothy Spencer QC, asked James to *choose* his own sentence (despite the offence being committed while James was on early release licence) – did he want to go to prison or would he prefer his imprisonment term suspended? To no one's surprise, he chose the latter and left the court yet another satisfied customer of the justice system.[199] [200] A Singapore court would almost certainly have sent these offenders to jail.

In Britain, the percentage of those convicted of a serious crime who are given a suspended prison sentence (as in the case of McCarthy and Phillips) has increased from 0.7% in 2003 to 14% in 2015.[201] Likewise, only 28% are given a term of imprisonment.[202] In other words, the public is left to rub shoulders with the remaining 72%, except, of course, the justice elite, whose gated-communities in cities and country retreats provide them with a level of security not available to the majority. Likewise, only 35% of offenders proven to have committed a 'violent crime against the person' are jailed, while nearly a fifth are cautioned.[203] Government data has revealed that between 2011 and 2015 there were, on average, 19 cautions a year given for rape.[204]

In 2011, the Sentencing Guidelines Council indicated that criminals convicted of violence against the police should no longer go to prison but be sentenced instead to community orders, and hundreds more who commit lesser forms of violence against them should no longer be given community orders but fined.[205] This was despite the fact that earlier it had been reported that Britain's justice system was struggling to recover £1.5 billion in unpaid court fines, and had been criticised by the chairperson of the Parliamentary Public Accounts Committee for its poor record in fine collection.[206] The Police Federation expressed their astonishment that the government was more interested in keeping prison numbers down than protecting its members. And so it might. This was yet another warning of just how far the government was prepared to go in order to follow its anti-prison policy.

The government's anxiety over prison numbers can be seen for example, in their concern that the introduction (in 2003) of Indeterminate Sentences for Public Protection (IPPs), for violent and dangerous offenders, would substantially add to the population of British jails. Indeed, their forecast was that by 2008 there could be almost 85,000 offenders in prison, and by 2013 there could be as many as 107,000.[207] Was it therefore a coincidence that after 2003 (when IPPs were introduced), police cautions for violence against the person, robbery, sexual offences and burglary, as shown in two examples below, all started to rise?

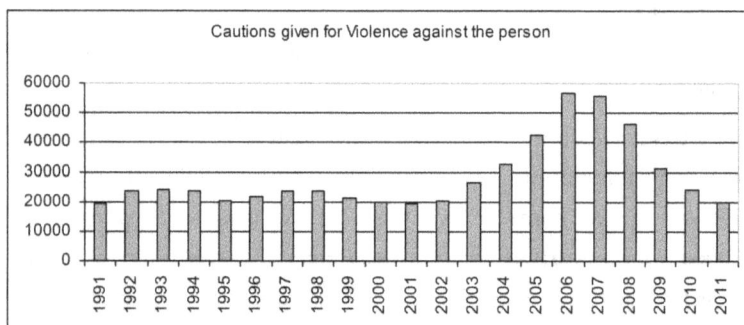

Cautions given for Violence against the person

Source:

1991–12001, Home Office, Criminal Statistics England and Wales 2001: Statistics
relating to Criminal Proceedings for the year 2001
2001–2011, Criminal Justice Statistics Quarterly Update to June 24th 2011,
Ministry of Justice, Statistics Bulletin

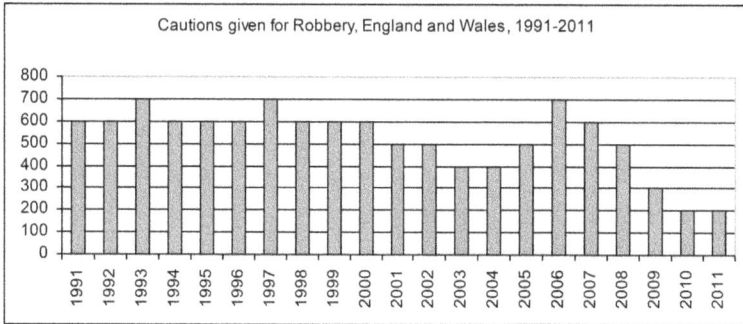

Cautions given for Robbery, England and Wales, 1991-2011

Source:

1991–2001, Home Office, Criminal Statistics England and Wales 2001: Statistics
relating to Criminal Proceedings for the year 2001
2001–2011, Criminal Justice Statistics Quarterly Update to June 24th 2011,
Ministry of Justice, Statistics Bulletin

But by 2006 the prison population was just over 78,000, and
by 2007 had increased to just over 80,000, making it clear that
the governments fears were not going to be realised. The 'End of
Custody Licence' introduced earlier on a temporary basis, which
was used to release thousands of prisoners before their sentence
had finished, no doubt contributed to this result. The numbers of
cautions for these offences then began to fall.[208] [209]

The chance that the police forces in the country decided,
independently of each other, to change their cautioning policy at
the same time, on two occasions, and regarding the same crimes,

must be regarded as a statistically remote possibility, which suggests that this mechanism may have been directed from the centre.

Furthermore, the average sentence length of those jailed for 'violence against the person crimes', is just 23 months,[210] which in practice means 11 months, because determinate sentences are subject to 50% remission. Such sentences frequently fall short of what the victims and their families expect. Consider 21-year-old Lewis Gill, a violent and convicted robber, who killed Andrew Young, aged 40, with a single punch. The attack took place in a Bournemouth street in November 2013, after Young had done no more than challenge a friend of Gill's for riding his bicycle on the pavement. Gill was convicted of manslaughter but Andrew Young's mother was astonished at the court's sentence of just four years in jail.[211] She was further stunned to learn that because, in 2008 the Criminal Justice and Immigration Act had provided that all determinate sentenced prisoners would be released automatically at the halfway stage, Gill will spend no more than two years behind bars.[212] Gill's mother praised the police but was unable to equate this sentence with the killing of her son, and publicly declared she felt the court had failed in its duty. I suspect few would disagree with her, particularly as the Court of Appeal later left Mrs Gill to chew on her grief by upholding the sentence, saying it was 'not unduly lenient'. It would be interesting to know what depth of malignancy must be displayed by a criminal before they thought otherwise.

To state the obvious, such lenient sentences allow persistent and violent criminals the opportunity to offend again and build long criminal histories. It can be no surprise therefore, that half of all those sentenced for violence have seven or more previous convictions, and nearly a third have 15 or more.[213]

It is now the case that 36% of offenders proven to have committed a 'violence against the person crime' are given a community penalty[214] (*footnote[5]*). In 2002, 32-year-old Mark Hobson pleaded guilty to grievous bodily harm, after he had stabbed a former colleague, William Brace, five times in the chest. Despite the life-threatening nature of the attack, which occurred in the middle of the high street, the court in Selby, North Yorkshire, sentenced him, notwithstanding Hobson's violent past, to just 100 hours community service. Few examples could illustrate so clearly the change which has occurred in the way British courts are prepared to view even the worst forms of violence. As is so often the case, it was the public, not the judge, who paid dearly for this leniency. Just two years later, in the village of Camblesforth, Yorkshire, Hobson murdered his girlfriend, Claire Sanderson, and her twin sister, Diane, by battering their skulls with a hammer. The following day he also murdered an elderly couple, James and Joan Britten while robbing them in their home.[215] It hardly needs to be said that had the Selby court provided proper justice for the stabbing offence, Hobson would have received a lengthy prison sentence, and these four murders would not have taken place.

But while courts have soft pedalled in their use of imprisonment for established and violent criminals, they can take a different attitude towards normally law-abiding members of the public. In 2009 a wealthy business man, 52-year-old Munir Hussain, returned from prayers with his wife and three children to his house in Reading, to discover that a violent burglar, 56-year-old Walid Salem, had broken into his house. Salem, armed with a knife, ordered them all to lie on the floor and threatened to kill them if they moved. But events moved quickly out of control for Salem. One of Munir Hussain's sons escaped and raised the

---

5   GOV.UK Criminal Justice System Statistics Quarterly: September 2015 shows that of the 33, 087 offenders proven to have committed 'violence against the person', 11,772, or 36% were given community sentences, i.e. 5,033 were placed on community sentence orders (to be supervised by the probation service), and another 6,739 were given a suspended sentence to be served in the community.

alarm. Salem fled but was caught and severely beaten by Hussain and two of his brothers. Salem, who had 54 previous convictions, was given a two-year supervision order. However, the courts did not hesitate to send Munir Hussain to prison for attacking the burglar.[216] While it is true that he committed a violent offence against Salem, surely understandable in the circumstances, why was he, as a first offender, sent to prison and Salem, a persistent and dangerous offender given his freedom?

Salem is but one example of thousands of criminals left at large in the community under the supervision of the probation service. In 1961, the courts sentenced 40,000 offenders to such orders;[217] by 1986 this number had reached 84,000,[218] and in 2014 it was close to 119,000.[219] The annual count of offenders under supervision in the community increased from 110,000 in 1965[220] to 164,000 in 2015.[221] These increases have occurred despite the justice system knowing of the continued and worsening reconviction rates of those sentenced in this way. (In 1979 they were 41%, measured over two years;[222] they are now over 50%.[223]) Whether crimes are rising or falling, their numbers matter because of the impact on the public of their continued offending.

In 1998 and again in 2008, the Home Office reiterated what they had assumed for years to be the 'risk factors' associated with crime. In an echo of the 1960s it listed poverty related factors such as accommodation problems, lack of money, and unemployment, as well as relationship difficulties, access to education, alcohol and drug misuse. As stated, these ideas had been the basis for dealing with offenders for years, but in a remarkably unreadable document, it re-presented them, and in the language of pseudo-science, it described how offenders should be 'treated' to overcome these problems along with their 'poor thinking skills'.[224] [225] [226] [227] It was also, I suspect, a rationalisation for the expansion of probation bureaucracy (England and Wales now have 33 probation staff per 100,000 of the population compared with a European mean, based on 30 countries, of eight [228]).

While he was justice minister, and again when out of office, Kenneth Clarke MP, made it clear he believed poverty to be a major factor determining criminal behaviour. He claimed that if we found ways to make offenders 'better off', then they would not need to offend. All they needed was 'a flat, a girl friend and a job'.[229] [230] If only it were so. In my contact with offenders, I found that many had jobs, a place to live and a girl friend, (often more than one, in fact), partners or wives, while for others being without a fixed address was not the same as being homeless.

The persistence of the idea that crime and violence represent some sort of crude reaction to poverty and inequality is all the more remarkable given that serious research and our own history contradict this view. In Britain during the first half of the 20th century, millions of people lived in real poverty. The absence of a male bread-winner due to the great loss of life in the First World War, high levels of unemployment during the great depression, little or no financial assistance, hunger, poorly constructed and damp housing, restricted access to medical services, overcrowding, no internal sanitation, access to water via one cold tap, or a shared pump in a courtyard, all represented the way of life for scores of communities. Yet in 1926, when degrees of hardship for working class people were beyond anything we could imagine today, the rate for 'violence against the person crimes' was 4.39 per 100,000 of the population,[231] a fraction of what it is today at over 1,400.[232]

R.A. Butler, who was Home Secretary from 1957 to 1962, noted that the marked increase in crime during this period coincided with the most massive social and educational reforms for a century. This was a period of distinct economic and social progress, with full employment and rising wages. Over a million new houses were built enabling a mass movement of people away from their previous slum accommodation. In 1961, as he pondered these developments, Butler said, "today the link between poverty and crime has been severed." Thirty-five years later research by both the Rowntree Foundation and the Home Office, came to a similar conclusion.[233] [234] Similarly, a detailed analysis carried out in 2011, based on 27 EU countries (including Britain) found, contrary to what many believed, that the countries with greater degrees of inequality and poverty had *less* crime than those who were wealthier, with better medical and welfare provision, and more equality.[235]

A seminal study of criminals on probation in 1969,[236] found that being out of work did not lead to crime or violence, because most them were in full time employment when they were reconvicted for further offences (similarly an analysis of Victorian and Edwardian crime found many offenders were in employment [237]). The 1969 study found most of these offenders did not *want* a job at a higher social class level than the job they currently held. They *chose* to stay in their lower skilled job. Interestingly, the study also found that overcrowding and poor home circumstances (despite persistent and contrary beliefs about this) were *not* correlated with reconvictions.[238]

But despite this our government remains afraid to act on the evidence, fearful, I suspect, of criticism from apologists for criminals, should it do so. Following the riots of 2011, (wrongly presented as being fuelled by poverty and inequality), it launched its 'Troubled Families' project. The aim of the programme was to help disruptive and damaged families raise themselves out of poverty, (which compared with circumstance in Britain eighty years ago, none of them have experienced) by helping them find work, and at the same time, cut their crime rates, truanting, drug abuse and anti-social behaviour.

That the title of their project was itself a lie (such families are not 'troubled' – why should they be when all is provided for them out of the public purse?) – can be seen from its results. After providing planned and consistent help to 20,000 families, (approximately 40,000 to 80,000 people), over a period of five years, it was found to be a lamentable failure. In 2015, the independent consultancy 'Ecorys' reported that despite the £1.3 billion of tax payer's money spent on the scheme, it had failed to have any effect on the crime and other problems mentioned above. The government locked the report away and it would have remained a secret had it not been leaked to the media in 2016. But even though these results gave them the grounds to do so, the government remain fearful of challenging the myth espoused by the pro-criminal lobby that criminals need 'help', and the programme is still running despite its failure.[239]

Although it is true that many criminals emerge from the poorer or less well-off sections of the community, it is wrong to interpret these conditions as factors which 'cause' crime. Criminals, I have found, *choose* to commit crime, and those who do are also the people who choose to live a life which results in most of them occupying the lower socio-economic class (e.g. failure to work at school, the constant demand for instant gratification, the use of violence to achieve this end, etc.) The fact that the majority of children from poorer home backgrounds go on to live decent law abiding lives, bears out this truth. Likewise, some from better off families whose backgrounds are free of those poverty factors said to be associated with crime and violence, nevertheless choose to become offenders. In 2014, 16-year William Cornick established his place among the infamous. He became the first pupil to kill a teacher in a British classroom. This young killer, who stabbed Ann Maguire to death in front of his classmates, came from a loving, well-off, middle class family.[240]

During my time as a probation officer I supervised and or wrote court reports on priests, politicians, young aspiring intellectuals, and other well-to-do middle class people all of whom had been convicted of offences. One well publicised former career criminal and violent robber, Bobby Cummines, once dubbed as Britain's most dangerous criminal, grew up in a comfortable middle-class home and went to a grammar school.[241]

Voices past and present have trumpeted the healing power of education on the criminal mind. In the Victorian era, social reformers such as Mary Carpenter and Joseph Fletcher among others argued that education would 'lead to a diminution in crime'.[242] Alas, hope springs eternal for penological liberals. How would they have coped with knowing that in the years following the Education Act of 1944, which made available free education for the whole nation, Britain's crime rate spiralled? In one prison where I worked for several years, there was a well-run school for the 14-17-year-old prisoners. Many of these young offenders were taught to read and write and were given basic proficiency in maths. While this was good in itself, it made not a jot of difference to their way of life and they continued to commit crime. It is a bitter pill for penal activists to swallow that education has no magical power of itself to reform those who do not want to be reformed.

In July 2015, the then justice minister Michael Gove criticised prisons because of the high numbers of prisoners who returned to crime on release, many of them violent. David Cameron echoed this criticism some months later in his call for a 'shake-up' of the prison system. Earlier, Justice Secretary Kenneth Clarke had said it was a national scandal that nearly half of all released prisoners reoffend within a year. All three of them noticeably failed to mention the even more serious problem of the high rate of further offending by those given community penalties – more serious because the public do not get a break from their continued crime, which they do if the offender is jailed. This appeared not to matter to them. They chose instead to denigrate prisons.

The reconviction rates of those given probation supervision, increase over time (for example they are over 50% for community supervision two years after the order was made, and almost 70% after nine years).[243] But significantly, longer prison sentences are associated with much reduced reconviction rates as follows: less than 12 months 60%, 12 months to two years, 39%; two to four years, 34%; four to ten years, 25%; ten years plus, 14%,[244] which Cameron, Clarke, Gove et al., never mentioned. The same is true generally for all previous justice and Home Office Ministers who have tended to speak of prisons as needing reform, while ignoring the failure of community supervision to come anywhere near the effectiveness of prison in protecting the public. But imprisonment does not only reduce crime. For the general population, the Standardised Mortality Ratio (SMR) for those in Social Class 5, aged 20–64, is 2.86. The SMR for the prison population is 1.4. Thus, on the assumption that most offenders in prison come from Social Class 5, imprisonment also saves lives.[245] [246]

In his speech, Michael Gove argued that the absence of educational qualifications is a major cause of former prisoners going back to crime.[247] This was a denial of reality, because prisons had been providing education for their inmates long before Michael Gove was heard of. Two months after his statement, a prison governor, during a radio broadcast, pointed out that an educational programme such as suggested by Michael Gove, would, in any case, have no relevance to large numbers of criminals now in British prisons, who were highly intelligent and already well educated, and who had *chosen* to use their talents to earn money from crime. Government data collected in 2003 indicated that 53% of prisoners already held academic qualifications of some kind,[248] and John Birt's earlier crime study estimated that 64% of criminals 'earn' over £100 per week from crime while almost a fifth make more than £1,000 per week.[249]

Many who work with offenders do so blinkered from reality, ignoring what history and evidence tells them about the futility of trying to reform offenders who do not want to change. In the early 1990s for example, a large 16-year-old girl with a history of violence, attacked a 14-year-old girl in a toilet. The victim was stripped, punched, bitten, and her money and some items of clothes were stolen. The social workers involved recommended that the attacker be 'sentenced' to a *second* tax payers funded holiday swimming with dolphins. The first followed convictions for previous violent offences.[250] In the same year, a male teenager, a violent and persistent criminal was sent on a one-month safari (at the tax payers' expense) 'to steer him away from crime'. No doubt Mark Hook, 'Safari Boy' as he was dubbed, enjoyed his holiday, but the authorities who sent him had to learn that he enjoyed committing crime just as much, if not more so. On his return, it was business as usual, and by 2012 he had committed at least another 113 offences, some of which were for wounding, aggravated burglary, carrying a knife and mugging an elderly woman.[251]

But stories such as these, widely reported as they were, did not stop other authorities from seeing deprivation as a cause of crime, which a show of generosity, with tax payer's money, could put right. For example, later in the 1990s another teenage criminal, Clinton Brown came to notice as 'Canal Boy'. As a reward for his crimes he was sent on a £12,000 barge holiday. The authorities concerned had to pretend to be surprised when, on his return, he picked up again on his suspended crime career, and successfully worked his way through large numbers of burglaries and muggings, some of which were committed while he was on parole from a prison sentence.[252] Yet another juvenile crime authority, going one better, sent a young criminal (Jason Cooper) on a £50,000 world tour to 'instil feelings of self-worth' into him, by 'broadening his horizons'. The youth crime workers involved in his case believed that his poor self-image (if he had one) was a by product of his disadvantaged upbringing, forcing him to rob in order to feel better about himself.[253] No doubt they were shielded from the inanity of the project by the fact that it was not their money paying for the world tour.

Once the holiday was over, he showed he had benefited from the rest and change of air, by throwing himself with renewed energy into his life of crime in which burglaries and robberies were prominent. These publicised examples are not unusual. As a senior probation officer I saw hundreds of court reports prepared by probation officers in which they fell over backwards to persuade the courts, often successfully, to sentence offenders to probation supervision with conditions attached directing them to attend some kind of community-based activity scheme, such as sailing, horse riding, a tennis course, or even driving lessons, again all at the tax payers expense of course, with the purpose of 'bolstering the offender's self-image', thought necessary because of his disadvantaged upbringing. Casey Brown was paid £60 a week by social services to give up his persistent offending. He took the money but his offending *increased* and in 2009, having been paid £1,560, he was sent to prison for five and half years for yet another armed robbery.[254]

It was George Orwell who said that, "some ideas are so foolish that only an intellectual could believe them, for no ordinary man could be so foolish." In the pantheon of foolish ideas none stands out so much as the willingness on the part of penological liberals to continue to believe (or pretend to believe) that criminals offend because of pressures not of their making and which are beyond their control. These wearisomely recycled arguments are at the heart of the ideological idiocy driving our crime policies.

This can be seen, for example, in the way the justice system views drug addiction as a disease which compels offenders to take them, and for which the offender needs 'treatment'. But offenders *choose* to take drugs. They are not compelled to take them by forces beyond their control, as made clear in *Romancing Opiates*, a book by an experienced prison doctor and psychiatrist, published in 2006.[255] Drugs, he points out, do not fly about the air and attack unsuspecting victims, for which they need 'treatment'. Drugs do not lay in wait and 'hook' unsuspecting criminals as they pass by. Criminals 'hook' drugs of their own volition – no one makes them and by the same token offenders who are motivated to give up drug taking will do so with or without help. They are entirely responsible for using them and, contrary to popular belief they remain responsible for their behaviour when they take them. The view often taken by the courts, that offenders under the influence of drugs are not in control when they commit crimes of violence (and other offences), and so should be 'treated' rather than punished, is seriously misguided.

This response to what is in effect irresponsible and self-indulgent behaviour, is now order of the day for governments, who appear too frightened by this problem to want to do anything but show how virtuous and compassionate they are to those who least deserve it. The Sentencing Advisory Panel, in 2009, for example, issued guidelines for courts, which said that, drug addicted burglars (even violent ones) should escape jail if they can show they are trying to deal with their 'problem'.[256] [257] Even Lord Chief Justice Igor Judge, thought to have had a tougher, more realistic approach to sentencing than previous holders of his office – even he announced that offending by some criminals 'was down to their addiction'.

It has been pointed out that 200 imprisoned addicts received approximately £16,000 each in compensation from the government because, they alleged, officials had forced them to undergo heroin withdrawal – a medically trivial condition – too quickly when they arrived in prison. Among them were a number of illegal immigrants: they probably couldn't believe their luck (or British stupidity).[258]

In view of the large amount of taxpayer's money involved, I asked, for the purposes of this book, for a transcript of the court hearing so that the public could be made aware of the Crown's response to these compensation claims. I was told that the Crown settled out of court. This means that it offered no defence, so there were no transcripts and no judgement available. In other words, it had all gone through on the nod. No one had the courage to raise objections on behalf of the public whose money was being given to those who could not deserve it less.[259]

An article 'Rewarding Bad Behaviour' published in the City Journal, New York, told of a patient who, in a hospital, pulled a gun and held it to the back of a doctor and demanded that she give him a heroin injection. She surrendered the keys of the ward medicine cupboard to him and told him to help himself. Then she alerted the authorities, who cleared the ward and called the police. By the time their armed response team had arrived, the man had injected himself with so much heroin he had fallen unconscious. He had to stay for a while in the hospital while receiving an antidote to the heroin. He recovered and the police then arrested him. Did this violent offender, who drew the gun on the doctor, also claim to have had been withdrawn from heroin too rapidly and demand his £16,000? If so, he could, the article suggests, write a guide book for others like him entitled, *Threatening Doctors for Pleasure and Profit*.[260]

Not everyone who takes drugs turns into a vicious thug but the false belief that it is heroin that causes offenders to be violent *against their will* means that much (and probably all) of the drug rehabilitation effort provided for criminal offenders is a chronic misdirection of money and other resources. Addiction to heroin cannot be blamed for a violent criminal propensity that was already present in the individual concerned, or the choice he makes to express it. Violent street robberies and other criminality existed long before illegal drugs became as available as they are today. Research studies have repeatedly demonstrated that drug-using criminals were criminals *before* they used drugs. For example, in the New Adams National Research Programme a significant minority of the 40% who reported a connection, admitted that crime came first,[261] A study in Leicester of almost 800 young people similarly found that for most of them crime came before their involvement in drugs.[262] A Home Office enquiry also concluded that drug abuse did not automatically trigger a life of crime.[263] Crime comes first, and drugs are just one more thing criminals spend their ill-gotten gains on.

Even if it accepted that some people might act in ways they would not otherwise do but for the powerful and sometimes paranoiac effects of certain drugs, they must bear full responsibility for their actions. Unless they were forced fed the mind-influencing substance, they are responsible for any crimes committed while under its influence. As pointed out, offenders take drugs (and drink alcohol) to excess voluntarily, no one makes them; they know full well their possible effects, and their culpability for each subsequent crime they commit under their influence is *doubled* because of that knowledge, not lessened as is argued so often by defence lawyers in pleas for mitigation.

We should not think that if criminals who previously took drugs and then stopped doing so, would then stop being criminals. If it was true that the drugs 'caused' the offender to commit crime against his will, then it follows he would, in the aftermath, be so horrified by what he had done, that he would never take them again. But the fact that drug-taking criminals are serial offenders, underlines once again the phoney nature of this excuse. If a previously law-abiding person committed his first offence after abusing drugs, we should expect a genuine sense of shame that would prevent any further drug taking and offending, whereas those with a criminal orientation suffer no such inhibitions.

In February 2014, 33-year-old Joanna Dennehy was convicted of stabbing to death Lukusz Slaboszewski, 31, Kevin Lee, 48, and John Chapman, 56, all of them known to her. She was a drug user and heavy drinker. But she was far from being a lonely 'no-hoper' with little or nothing to live for. She was educated, clever, good at sport and a keen musician. Yet in 2009 she was heard to say that she wanted to kill someone, something she failed to mention to the probation officer who was supervising her at the time.[264]

In 2013 her wish came true and she lured a friend to a house and stabbed him through the heart. If she had done this while high on drugs or alcohol, and if it were true that drugs were the driving force for this violence, one would have expected her, after the first killing, to be so overwhelmed with horror at what she had done, that she would never repeat such behaviour. But she was not horrified. In fact, she enjoyed the experience so much that ten days later she stabbed two other men to death. A short while afterwards she tried to kill two more, chosen at random, but they survived the stab wounds that she inflicted on them. She was arrested the same day and boasted to the police about her 'hectic week'.[265] Almost three years after these killings, a previously undisclosed report indicated that Dennehy was under probation supervision at the time of the murders, and that the probation service had failed to take notice of her failure to keep appointments.[266]

Medical evidence put forward in *Romancing Opiates,* indicates that withdrawal symptoms from heroin are no more serious than a mild dose of flu, and are exaggerated by drug using criminals. This has been assiduously ignored by the government and the 'helping' bureaucracies, whose livelihoods depend on a plentiful supply of drug addicts being referred to them for assistance. What stands out is that in the ten years since *Romancing Opiates* was published and despite its serious challenge to the activities (and reputations) of thousands involved in the drug support agencies, no one has attempted to refute it.

Similar evidence put forward by Booth Davies in 1992, in his book *The Myth of Addiction,* has also been ignored by the establishment. He demonstrated that drug users talked differently about their 'withdrawal symptoms' among themselves, compared with what they said to those who could prescribe more drugs for them. Pharmacological studies, he argues, reveal the mechanisms underlying the drug's pleasurable effects. But to infer from this that the person 'has to have the drug' is a step too far. There are no chemical properties of the drug to justify this inference. People take drugs because they *want* to – they enjoy the effect. Thus, he concluded that there is no cure for drug-taking, because there is nothing to be cured; no more in fact, than there is a cure for rock climbing, football or playing the violin.[267]

More recently Marc Lewis, a professor of neuroscience, has also argued strongly that addiction is not a disease but a habit. He points out, for example, that the thousands of American soldiers, who took heroin during their tour of duty in Vietnam, simply gave up this habit when they returned home, and survey research published over the last 30 years, indicates that most addicts eventually recover permanently and think of themselves as 'free', not cured.[268]

In one drug programme aimed at helping drug addicts become abstinent, psychologist Nancy Petry assumed that this could be achieved by rewarding them with vouchers (which could be exchanged for food and clothing) when they stopped. However, does this not imply that they are in control and could do so whenever they choose? [269] [270]

Even if this were not the case, this does not mean drug-taking offenders must commit violent or other crimes. The plethora of helping agencies, both social and medical, willing to support them with substitute prescriptions and other forms of help, rule this out. No one has died from opiate withdrawal, but since 1996, at least 3,000 addicts have died from methadone poisoning in Britain alone, the standard 'treatment' issued by the army of medico-social drug support-workers, as an opiate substitute. [271] [272]

Attempts to cure drug-taking offenders who do not want to change are a waste of time – and money. The enormous self-serving, self-perpetuating medical-social bureaucracy which has been set up to treat them, is misconceived and a waste of the millions of pounds spent on it. (Professor Lewis makes a similar point about the billions of dollars spent in this way in the USA.) Furthermore, our justice elite know this, because they have the data which shows that their sentencing tactics for drug-taking offenders, violent and otherwise, have never worked. For example, the early pilot courses run by the Home Office all failed to curtail the drug use and violent crimes committed by those offenders on these schemes. [273] [274] [275] [276] But they went ahead with them anyway. Offenders under supervision in the community subject to Drug Testing and Treatment Orders (DTTOs) were found to have reconviction rates of over 80% measured over two years. [277] [278] Our justice officials' answer to this failure was to change the name to Drug Intervention Programmes (DIPs) but their reconviction rates of 55%, were as bad if not worse, as they were measured over one year (not two as previously) and were for adults only. The scale of the failure is even more dramatic when we consider that this high reconviction rate is based on just the small minority of offences known to the authorities that these offenders commit.

Some trials have shown that heroin addicts commit fewer crimes when prescribed methadone than while still taking heroin.

But this is no more than we might expect. The fact that they were being *given* methadone meant that they did not have to steal as often as they did when they had to buy their drugs. Also, methadone would have sedated them and reduced their will to go out and steal. Nevertheless, despite the support they received on these trials, they still continued to commit crime.

To reiterate, those who inflict injury on others, either for money or for the sheer pleasure of it, or both, *choose* to do this, and nothing forces them to do so. The regular cries of drug workers for more resources to help offender addicts are hopelessly misdirected. Their call for 'rehabilitation – not prison' for criminal drug users is a denial of their criminal motivation.

During the 1990s the probation service embraced the idea that 'thinking skills' programmes, designed by psychologists, could identify faults in the way offenders made decisions and so help them avoid crime. Once again, the government ignored the failure of the early schemes based on these ideas, which showed failure rates of between 70–80%[279] [280] and decreed that thousands of offenders under supervision to probation staff, as well as offenders in jail, should attend these 'What Works' programmes.[281] [282] Probation staff excitedly applying these new methods became the order of the day. In one example, a 23-year-old dangerous criminal breached the terms of his prison release licence by violently threatening his parents. Instead of taking steps to see that he was recalled, probation staff gave him an 'anger diary' to fill in, seen as a method of re-programming his thinking, to control his violence. After a few weeks of this routine he once again assaulted his mother and violently beat a police officer, causing him severe injuries.[283] It is not known whether he made a note of this in his diary.

The Director of the National Probation Service, Eithne Wallis, earlier directed by the Home Office (2001) to implement this initiative, wrote a paper called '*The New Choreography*', in which she weaved her dreams of the probation service bringing about nothing less than a revolution in the reduction of offending.[284]

Probation trainees learned sections of it by heart as they knew they would be examined on it. Alas, the dream turned into a nightmare, when, between 2003 and 2004, the government's evaluation found these programmes to be a catastrophic failure, with reconviction rates of up to 80% for the 'cognitive skills' and 'substance abuse' programmes.[285] [286] [287] [288] [289] The probation service must have been deeply shocked by the results, as was no doubt its director, given the strength of her campaign in support of these failed programmes. A short time later, she resigned her Directorship of the Probation Service, and slipped quietly away to take up a post in the Islamaphobic Unit of the Home Office. That these methods should fail to influence offenders was no surprise to those who understood their deep-rooted criminal motivation, but what is surprising is that anyone should have thought that they would. None of the evaluations recognised the harm done to thousands of members of the public by the criminals on these programmes while supervised in the community.

It should be pointed out, lest anyone think this failure was due, not to the cranky ideas behind them, but to the faulty way the programmes were run in Britain, that New Zealand's offender treatment and management programme, run on similar lines, was also an expensive and disastrous failure. Their much vaunted 'cognitive based straight- thinking' programmes showed particularly bad results.[290]

The government's latest flirtation is with private companies, authorised to supervise lower-level risk offenders (legislated for by the Offender Rehabilitation Act 2014), in a system of 'payment by results' to reduce their offending-rate. They were set up in 2015, at a cost of £3.7 billion, but two years later, in 2017, a report by HM Inspectorate of Prisons and Probation declared they had failed to achieve any of their objectives, and had made no difference to the offending rate of the criminals concerned.[291] [292] The probation service maintains responsibility for the higher risk criminals, who continue to be supervised under the terms of the so-called rehabilitation programmes, 12 years after they were discredited by damning results described above. Nevertheless, they continue to refer to them as 'accredited' programmes (which might be funny if it was not so serious). The language used on their websites to describe them has changed. The label 'What Works Offender Programmes' has disappeared, and instead they are now called 'Transforming Rehabilitation Programmes' (TRPs). However, the content is the same and, under this umbrella term, they are running, as before, offender behaviour programmes, sex offender courses and anger management programmes, to name but a few.[293] [294]

Their annual reports speak brazenly of these as strategies to reduce reoffending, which ignores the fact that they are known to be useless in this regard. Despite this, the courts continue (or pretend) to believe in them. In 2012, Adam Strangward, aged 27, was convicted of assaulting a pensioner, Bob Savory. Strangward punched the frail 92-year-old man, during a row over the pensioner's Jack Russell dog. They had crossed paths while walking next to the river Nene in Peterborough.

Even though Strangward committed the assault while he was on an anger management course run by the probation service, District Judge Ken Sheraton said, "it was having a beneficial effect", and suspended Strangward's prison sentence in order not to interrupt it.[295] Given the fact of Strangward's conviction, on what basis did the judge make this assessment? And if he considers a vicious assault is a 'beneficial effect' of four months' anger management training, what would he judge as a bad effect?

One senior judge warned his colleagues that they should not automatically assume the reliability of finger prints when assessing evidence because its methodology, was not capable of robust testing.[296] Yet no similar warning has been issued to judges concerning offender-behaviour programmes that have been shown to have *no* reliability at all. In 2014 a judge awarded financial compensation to a convicted murderer and rapist who claimed his human rights had been breached because the prison had failed to provide him with rehabilitation courses.[297] Thus, he was compensated for being denied a course known to be useless.

Despite the harmful results of their offender programmes, (thousands have been victimised by criminals placed in the community on these schemes) belief in psychologists' skills in relation to their work with offenders continues. They have, for example, established powerful fiefdoms in prisons where they assess the suitability of dangerous lifer prisoners for release. The further violence and killings by these offenders granted their freedom after being assessed as representing an 'acceptable risk' to the public, has in no way undermined psychologists' self-belief, or the faith placed in them (or the parole board) by the justice establishment. A staff member from one jail was told by a prisoner that what you had to do if you had a bad sentence was to behave badly to begin with, and then 'improve', so that probation and psychology staff thought you had made progress, thus increasing your chances of being released.

In another, HMS Gartree, where so-called therapeutic work with violent prisoners serving life sentences for murder is carried out, an investigation revealed that these prisoners had long ago worked out exactly what was going on inside their jail regarding the role played by psychologists. One prisoner said, "Psychologists run the lifer units. No matter what, you have got to agree with them – if you do not you *stay.* They have got the keys to the gate – simple as that. They have got far more power than people imagine – one swipe of their pen and it's another 10 years."[298]

One senior psychologist in this jail admitted that her therapy amounted to getting the prisoners to express 'genuine remorse'. Another said, "most of the lifers here want to say they are sorry and to get involved in some form of restorative justice." If a prisoner convinced her on this point he gained a firm foothold on the release ladder. But is this not exactly what prisoners sentenced to life imprisonment, who want to be recommended for release, *would* say, and does it not also suggest that the lifer's assessment of the psychologists is far more accurate than is the psychologists of themselves? A member of the public might judge that even if a prisoner was genuinely sorry for the crime he has committed, this is no reason to release him. A truly remorseful killer will understand that he should stay in prison for a long time because of what he has done.

A former prison psychiatrist has pointed out that the 'redemption' of prisoners is now the aim of prisons, and illustrates how facile this is. By saying sorry and doing good works, criminals can be deemed to be 'cured'. It is as if, he argues, that good and evil were entries in a system of double–entry book keeping; by showing remorse the criminal can cancel out the violence and the killing he has perpetrated. The corollary of this is that if he did enough good works and showed active concern for the victims of crime in advance, he would have earned the subsequent right to torture and murder whomever he liked.[299]

The much vaunted 'restorative justice' programmes mentioned above, (which require offenders to apologise to their victims and sometimes provide some practical compensation) have all failed to stop offenders from committing crime,[300] [301] [302] [303] as has every other offender rehabilitation scheme used by the probation service – a finding laid bare by my 36 years of research into sentencing practices in Britain. However, there are a variety of other ways in which the justice system lets the public down, and the following are but a few examples. In 2016 it was revealed that nearly a half of the hundreds of repeat knife offenders dealt with in the previous 12 months had not been imprisoned despite the government's promised tougher approach.[304] In 2015, the West Midlands Police Federation stated that in the interests of cost-saving, cheaper, lower powered 'Panda Cars' without sirens, were being used for emergency calls, allowing criminals to escape.[305]

Basic errors in courts records have allowed violent criminals to avoid punishment.[306] A Freedom of Information request revealed that thousands of tagged offenders have tampered with their electronic bracelet[307] and half of the offenders wearing them breach their curfew conditions.[308] The private companies monitoring these offenders, Serco and G4S, have in the past ignored many of their violations and billed the government for large numbers offenders not on their books, and they have had to return millions of pounds paid to them.[309] Hundreds of dangerous sex offenders have gone on the run, despite supposed monitoring on the sex offender's register;[310] hundreds more have been removed from this list to protect their human rights;[311] and dangerous criminals escape in their hundreds from open jails every year.[312] [313] In one example a convicted murderer escaped twice from an *open* prison.[314] In 2006 the hunt for more than a thousand foreign prisoners released in error was wound down with hundreds still at large. The Home Office said they were no longer a priority, even though the Home Secretary had publicly declared he would move 'heaven and earth' to find them.[315] Thousands of arrest warrants issued every year when offenders fail to appear in court remain outstanding,[316] and government powers to stop dangerous jihadists and terrorists returning to Britain have never (at the time of writing) been used.[317]

There are also many examples to illustrate the readiness of our justice system to respond to what it sees as the needs of offenders, while trampling on those of their victims. I quote two that capture the spirit of its offender–friendly priorities. Former police sergeant, Richard Sainsbury, retired in 2011 after serving in the South Yorkshire Police for 34 years. When interviewed, he launched an attack on the Crown Prosecution Service:

"No matter how much evidence you put before them, they want more. They glibly dismiss evidence a jury should see and hear. There is not a bobby that submits files who does not have a horror story about a job that has been dropped. I can think of ten instances right now where bad men and women should have gone to jail and who in many cases never even went to court."[318]

In the late 1990s, Mrs Maureen Lawrence, faced what is probably the worst tragedy a parent could experience. Her 24-year-old daughter, Sharon was stabbed to death by her former partner,

23-year-old Anthony Greaves, in her home in Bacup, Lancashire. Some few months after Greaves was jailed for six and a half years for manslaughter, a letter was dropped through the letter box of Mrs Lawrence, then 50 years old, and struggling to come to terms with her daughter's death. Maureen Lawrence read it with disbelief. The letter was from the probation service and asked her if she would 'like to know how her daughter's killer was getting on'.[319]

# 4

## The Meaning of Violence

How are we to understand the malign behaviour displayed by criminals in their attacks on members of the public, frequently reported in the media? What is the meaning (if such exists) of, for example, the violence displayed by George McIvor, when, in 1997, aged 32, he burgled the home of 19-year-old Amanda Tanner? She disturbed him while he was looking for money in her maisonette in Barton Hill, Bristol. Instead of fleeing, he violently attacked her. Slightly built Amanda put up a fierce fight, scratching his face, but she was overpowered and killed by McIvor who stabbed her 47 times, beat her and finally strangled her. Amanda's unborn baby also died. Her body was not discovered until the next day, by her partner, Gary Gould, who could hear their 12-month-old son, Taylor, crying in the upstairs bedroom.[320] Or again, what is the explanation for the deeply malign violence displayed by a mother and stepfather who starved and tortured to death their four-year-old son, Daniel? The scale of the suffering deliberately inflicted on the child by his mother Magdelena Luczak, 27, and his step-father Marjusz Krezolek, 34, in their Coventry home over a period of months was truly horrific. At the trial, the court heard of harrowing details of the unimaginable acts of cruelty and brutality suffered by the boy, including water torture, starvation and being beaten around the head, and locked in a small, freezing, urine soaked box room. The judge declared the parents' motives 'unfathomable'. The police, likewise, could find no motive for the abuse, other than Kresolek's dislike of the child.[321]

From whence came the violence that resulted in the death in 2008 of the 18-year-old Harry Potter actor, Robert Knox, who was stabbed while protecting his younger brother from 21-year-old Karl Bishop, a criminal with a violent past? Bishop stabbed Knox five times outside the Metro Bar in Sidcup, Kent, and stabbed three other young men. Bishop had deliberately taken knives with him to the venue in the aftermath of a previous row with Knox and his friends. He had previously been heard to say that 'someone is going to die'.[322]

Two years later, in a taxi-rank in Fleetwood, Lancashire, on New Years Day in 2010, Jamie Perkes, 23, was stopped by a taxi driver from getting into his vehicle with a drink. Perkes responded with a sudden and unprovoked attack on 28-year-old Alan Taylor, who was standing nearby, but not involved in any way. Perkes, assisted by his girl friend, knocked Taylor to the ground and then repeatedly kicked him and stamped up and down on his head. In the weeks following, the victim was in constant pain and had trouble moving. He died of his injuries four months after the attack.[323]

Why did two teenagers, Leon Elcock, 16, and Hamza Lyzai, 15, think it was funny to spend time prowling the streets and attack elderly Asian men and women, in what were dubbed 'happy-slap' attacks, after their habit of running away laughing from the scene of an attack? On one such occasion, in August 2009, in Tooting, South London, they struck 67-year-old Mr Ekram Haque so hard he crashed to the ground and hit his head, dying seven days later of brain damage when his life support system was switched off.[324]

In 1989, the Animal Liberation Front (ALF) planted a high explosive bomb in Senate House at Bristol University to protest about their use of animals in laboratory experiments.[325] By chance, I saw and spoke with one of the bombers in the street opposite my house (though at the time I did not identify him as such). It was Wednesday 22nd February and he was keeping watch on the university which he could see, not far away at the top of St Michael's Hill, a well known Bristol location. He was agitated and asked me the time. When I told him it was about 12.40 pm, he protested that I must be wrong. He continued to pace up and down, frequently stopping to look towards the top of the University Senate House, just visible from his vantage point. He eventually cycled away, albeit very slowly, as if reluctant to leave. It was then about 1.15 pm.

At midnight on that day a large bomb exploded in Senate House. It had been planted in a bar on the fourth floor. Because it was empty no one was hurt. But things had not gone the way the ALF had planned. I suddenly understood the behaviour of the strange visitor to our street and informed the police of what I had seen, and hours of interviews and searching through photographs of possible suspects followed. He had been sent to observe the explosion intended for *midday*, when the bar on the fourth floor would have been filled with students and staff. There is, therefore, no doubt that the activists' purpose was to cause deaths and injuries on a horrific scale. Fortunately, the ALF had, by mistake, set the bomb timer for 12-midnight, not 12-midday. Only a moment's reflection is needed to imagine the carnage that might have occurred had their plan worked.

So how are we to respond to and understand the terrible violence the ALF displayed on this (and other) occasions, or the injuries and deaths inflicted on innocent people by violent criminals frequently reported on in the media? Are we to view it as the expression of deep-seated psychological or social problems for which they need help? Or is it the result of a choice freely made by otherwise normally functioning individuals willing to give vent to their violent propensities for the sake of stealing money, or imposing their will on others, or simply for fun?

Our helping professions find it hard to accept that criminals are violent, not because there is anything wrong with them in the form of an emotional or social malaise, but because it is their nature to be so. Observation of human nature tells us that most of us are, in varying degrees, born with a propensity for violence; we bring it with us into the world as part of our nature, but as with our conduct generally, we are free to exercise it or not. Except for those who are diagnosed as medically insane, nothing makes us act violently beyond our willingness to do so.

I suggest that there is a human spectrum, at one end of which are those with little or no propensity to violence. We have all met such people, gentle and vulnerable by nature, who could not use force against others even if their safety or lives depended on it. In one such example, a holidaymaker, who was viciously attacked by a migrant worker, had a knife in his back pocket which he could have used to defend himself. But he could not, and endured a horrifying violent and sexual assault.[326] In the middle of the spectrum are the majority whose capacity for violence increases as we move along towards the other end of the continuum, but it is kept in check, in the main, by legal and moral constraints leading to a healthy fear of retribution. When strict punishments are a certainty, many who would otherwise commit violent crime choose not to do so. When sentencing becomes more lenient, thus making violent crime less risky, they commit more of it. At the other end of the continuum are those whose propensity for violence is so great that no matter how draconian the punishment nothing will stop them, other than their own decision to desist. The case for these highly-dangerous criminals to be locked up for all or most of their lives, following a conviction for murder or other serious violent crime, should be beyond controversy.

But many psychologists reject this view, and argue that the drivers for murderous and violent acts are to be found deep in the psyche of the killer, and are often associated with early childhood or other developmental experiences. Stephen Griffiths is now in his early 40s; he has never worked and has always lived at the taxpayers' expense. Lenient sentencing had allowed him to build a long history of violent offending. At 17, he was sentenced to only three years imprisonment for cutting the throat of a supermarket security guard, who tried to arrest him for shoplifting. The security official was lucky not to have been killed.

During his violent criminal career, he attacked several women, and prison doctors diagnosed him as psychopathic. At one point, he managed to convince a jury that he was innocent of the charge of pouring boiling water on, and badly scalding, a sleeping girlfriend who had decided to leave him. Other girlfriends went to the police but were too terrified to testify in court, knowing that he would receive a short sentence at most. One girlfriend – whose legs he had cut with broken glass, whose nose he had broken, and whom he had knocked out – later told a reporter that he would attack her if she so much as looked at another man. When she left him, he hunted her down (despite court orders to stay away from her), slashed the tyres of her car, and daubed the wall outside her apartment with the word 'slag'. He was convicted of harassment in 2009.

Griffiths was highly intelligent and was chosen by the University of Bradford to pursue a doctorate in *homicidal* studies. It appears that either no checks were made on his background, or if they were, his violent past was ignored. Griffiths did not hide his violent tendencies. He kept hundreds of books about serial killers in his apartment, disclosed to his psychiatrist his intention to become a serial killer, and told a girlfriend that he skinned and ate rats alive, adding that his ambition was to become even more notorious than the Yorkshire Ripper, a man who killed 13 women in the 1970s. Nor did Griffiths hesitate to display his oddity to the public; he used to take his pet lizards, which he also fed with live rats, for walks on a leash. While following his doctorial studies, Griffiths killed and ate three women, two cooked and one raw, according to his own account. He later told the police he had killed other women.

In 2010 he committed his last murder in front of closed-circuit video cameras installed in his apartment block. According to the building's superintendent, who saw the video and called the police, the victim, Suzanne Blamires, ran from Griffiths' apartment with Griffiths wielding a crossbow in pursuit. She fell or was pushed, and he fired a bolt into her. Fully aware, even triumphant, that he was being recorded, Griffiths extended his finger to the camera, and then dragged the lifeless body by the leg back to his apartment. There, he later claimed, he ate some of her. When asked for his name in court after his arrest, he identified himself as the 'Crossbow Cannibal'. That reply assured him of the notoriety that he had always wanted. He was convicted of three murders and sentenced to life imprisonment. At the time (in 2010) it was thought he would probably be allowed to complete his doctorate – still at public expense of course – while in prison.[327] It is to be hoped that our justice officials will not allow him any time out of prison to conduct more field experiments. But, knowing their tendency to want to show compassion for wrongdoers, even those who kill others for a hobby, no one should bet against it.

Inevitably, explanations for his behaviour were sought. Psychologists discovered that he hated his mother, reputed to be sexually amoral, and so could point the finger at this aspect of his early family life as a possible determinant of his behaviour. But Griffith's brother, brought up by the same amoral parent, did not become a violent criminal. (Neither did Fred West's brothers, raised alongside him in the same home, become sadistic killers).

It has also has been suggested that violent behaviour may be brought about by stress linked to sleep-deprivation, or even addiction to chemicals excreted into our systems when we are violent. But I have yet to see a convincing case that the criminal thugs marauding on our streets, exercising violence for profit or pleasure or both, do so because they have had a bad night's sleep.

Dopamine, a drug associated with pleasure, is excreted into our system when we are violent, and some psychologists have argued that violent people may be displaying the fact they are 'addicted' to it. To suggest that this may cause some people to kill seems a thin case, but even if this were so, it does not absolve the perpetrator from any responsibility for his actions. For the excretion of this drug to take place, he would first have to be violent, and no one has demonstrated that its effect would be so strong as to make people behave in ways contrary to their own free will. Millions of men fought in two world wars and other foreign conflicts during the 20th and present century, but far from showing signs of 'addiction' to the violence they experienced, the response of large numbers of soldiers to these conditions showed the reverse. Our present knowledge of what constitutes 'war stress' suggests that the constant exposure to fear and danger may not be the only factor leading to post-war neurosis. Even some highly-motivated and trained professional soldiers have suffered nasty psychological reactions following their experience of killing their enemy. The fact that others remain unscathed serves to illustrate the point made earlier that we all (even soldiers) differ in our propensity for violence, one from another, and this may be the reason why at least some of the 100,000 British soldiers estimated to have deserted during the Second World War, did so.[328]

Michael Portillo, during his TV programme in 2012 which explored the meaning of violence, told of a Sudanese youth who became a child-soldier in the inter-faction fighting in the Sudan.[329] When he was seven years old his village had been wiped out by a Muslim militia and his mother had been killed while he watched. He wanted revenge and became a willing recruit into an anti-Muslim and anti-Arab military faction. He was submitted to brainwashing that told him that killing Muslims and Arabs was a service to his nation. He was a ready listener. But not all the African children forcibly recruited as child soldiers reacted like this, and many ran away. Even though their families had been, in some cases, butchered in front of them, they had no appetite for killing or revenge. Children vary, as do adults, in their propensity for violence.

Further support for this idea has come from a surprising source. The popular view of German SS men, Nazi officials and others associated with the massacre of Jews during the Second World War is that they were all equally violent and murderous. But research by Herbert Jager and others has suggested that this was not necessarily so.[330] It also supports the argument that ideologies that preach violence will only affect those who already have an innate capacity for it. They found, for example, that while many took part in the murder of Jews and Slavs, not all did with the same degree of willingness, and some even opted out altogether. Jager's research of official documents allowed him to classify Nazi war criminals into three groups. He found that 20% of the hundreds of SS men whose files he perused were 'criminals of excess'. By this he meant that they killed without orders and at other times exceeded the orders they were given. (These SS killers would be placed at the far end of the violence spectrum described above.) A good example is SS official Werner Brest, one of the chief architects of the 'final solution' from 1941 onwards. Brest developed hard line ideological views concerning the superiority of the German race and he accepted no limits to achieving the desired end.[331] He embraced Hitler's ideas and could not wait to put them into practice. He was the perfect example of Nazi propaganda falling on the ears of someone who was more than ready for it. This was the same Nazi propaganda, we must remember, that failed to influence millions of his fellow Germans, who remained opposed to Hitler.

The next 20% Jager described as 'initiative killers', meaning that they only killed within the limits of the orders given them, but they took place on their own initiative – for example those who volunteered for mass shootings. (These killers would be placed a little further away from the extreme end of the spectrum, because although their capacity for violence was high, it was slightly less so than the first group.)

Jager defined the remaining 60% as 'killers by order', who would only shoot prisoners when told to do so. But the research also found that about one in three of these SS men had problems carrying out these orders and some refused to do so. Based on these classifications, Jager ruled out the theory that these killers carried out these acts because they were terrified of reprisals if they did not obey. He concluded that pressure to obey against their will can be said to have existed only in a relatively small proportion of cases.

What was most influential in determining whether those involved obeyed orders to murder Jews in their custody was their capacity for violence – whether they had the stomach for it. If this was small or non-existent, they were likely to refuse. The behaviour of the infamous German Police Reserve Battalion 101, which, in June 1942, took part in the murder of thousands of Polish Jews, including women and children, showed that even among those prepared to kill, the capacity for violence and bloodshed varied considerably. On the day it started its 'special action' (mass murder) against the Polish village of Josefow, a minority of the battalion refused to take part, and they were allowed to step out and were given other duties. Some refused to go on after the first round of shootings. Others lasted a little longer before they stopped. They told their superiors they had had enough; they had reached the limit of their capacity for murder. Altogether about 20% of the battalion reacted in this way, i.e. refused to kill any of the villagers, or soon gave up. The remaining 80% went on killing until 1500 Jewish men, women and children lay dead in the forest close to where they had lived.[332]

Some of those who persisted with the shootings until the end complained afterwards of being 'sick of it'. This was not regret at having murdered fellow human beings, but a revulsion against an excess of exposure to blood and burst brains. To alleviate this problem those in charge of the next massacre arranged for them to share the killing with another death squad made up of SS men and Russian POWs. The battalion policemen involved in the next massacre, the cold-blooded shooting of 1700 Jews from the village of Lomazy (its entire population), did so without their earlier reactions. Experience had honed their capacity for violence; killing was something they could get used to. Whatever their reactions, nothing forced these men to murder. Their superiors had already shown there would be no reprisals against them if they refused. Thus, while some members continued to find a way of escaping these duties, sufficient numbers of the battalion showed willing and over a period of several months they not only increased their killing rate, but helped in the transportation of thousands of Jews to the death camps.

The Portillo programme, referred to above, explored the suggestion that ordinary people could become killers under certain stressful circumstances. To test this idea the researcher submitted himself to 60 hours of sleep deprivation while looking after two crying babies. A psychologist said post-experiment tests revealed he was, despite his normal non-violent personality, showing signs that signalled the onset of violent behaviour. But although lack of sleep can make us irritable and even angry (a common experience for millions of parents), most do not become killers.

A medical researcher recently revived the suggestion of a link between brain damage and the subsequent onset of violence.[333] However, no reference was made to the many thousands who have had accidents leading to such injuries, but who do not become violent. I have known many drug workers, psychologists and probation officers, for example, who are reluctant to believe that people are violent because it is their nature to be so. They prefer to see violent behaviour as the result of a physical or psychological condition, or related to stressful social conditions, which can be treated or ameliorated. But while their violence sets them apart – most of the law-abiding public would find it hard, if not impossible to injure someone, let alone kill them – many dangerous offenders also exhibit behaviour which makes them just like everyone else and it is this normality that those opposed to imprisonment find hard to accept.

Arthur Shawcross was probably one of the most dangerous

serial killers imprisoned in the US during the 20th century. In 1989 he was sentenced to 250 years in jail. He had killed at least 11 women. Interviewers who talked with him said that knowledge of his murderous record made him a frightening person to be with, but what really made their hair stand on end was his calm, matter-of-fact and normal manner. In 1972, he murdered an eight-year-old girl, who was later found with dirt stuffed in her mouth. At about the same time he raped and strangled a ten-year-old boy. The police who arrested him for these murders, aware of his physical strength and propensity for violence, would not stay in the cell with him on their own. During his sentence, he became a model prisoner, ingratiated himself with the welfare officer, psychiatrist and the church minister. He gained educational qualifications, and worked in the prison as a 'counsellor', and learned the language of psychiatry and psychology, which he used to persuade the authorities they could consider him for parole. After 15 years in jail he was released and started to kill again. In 1988, he strangled Dorothy Blackburn, a prostitute and mother of three children, and dumped her body in a river, and a short time afterwards he killed Anne Marie Steffan. Years later, when talking about these murders, he calmly explained that it took about four minutes to strangle his victim to death. He later spoke of experimenting by strangling others with his left hand.

He later admitted that he frequently went back to where he had dumped the body 'to clean up' and hide any links to himself. In 1989, as indicated above, his 20-year killing spree was finally ended by a jail sentence intended to keep him permanently behind bars, and several years later he died of a heart attack while still in prison.[334]

Faced with such an appalling record, the cry went up – 'What had made him such an evil person?' He became the focus of numerous psychological and medical examinations as the authorities assumed there had to be something wrong with him which drove him to such behaviour. His defence lawyers drew heavily on the ideas thrown up by these investigations, and tried to build the case that he had been abused and maltreated as a child, that he was brain damaged, and that he suffered from war stress following his tour of duty in Vietnam. They were all shown to be groundless. A medical expert opined that his ECG reading was abnormal and that "this neurological abnormality must be a factor in his drive to kill, rape and mutilate his victims". The ECG reading may have been a fact, but its link with his violent behaviour was just guesswork. His mother denied his allegations of abuse and no records existed to support his accusations. His army CO said he was a provisions clerk, and had not been sent on lone killing missions that, Shawcross maintained, had caused him stress. The claim he could not remember killing the women was easily refuted by his admission that he frequently revisited the sites at which he had left their bodies in order to destroy evidence.

After he was sentenced, further investigation suggested he might have a rare biochemical imbalance linked to a rare XY genetic disorder. But expert opinion is divided as to whether this could in part, explain his behaviour. Dr Kraus, who spent months evaluating Shawcross, referred to the millions of people throughout the world who have this disorder and who exhibit no anti-social tendencies whatever.[335] However, no one has claimed or demonstrated that the presence of a biochemical imbalance can cause an individual to act in ways contrary to their own free will. If this was ever established, it would indicate a lack of control that would make the individual doubly dangerous.

The difficult aspect to grasp about Shawcross was that, in parallel with his life as a killer, he led a normal life. He blended in with his locality, and was friendly with neighbours who viewed him in the same way they did other residents. He held down a job, and was said to be a loving father and grandfather. While in prison, Shawcross came close to explaining this conflicting aspect of his conduct, when he said with a chilling steadiness, that "people on the outside do not know what evil is". I suspect that he was telling us that such violent and depraved behaviour of the sort he exhibited, was truly evil when committed by those who are otherwise normal.

In Britain, the majority of convicted killers and those convicted of the worst forms of non-fatal violence are sent to prison, not to a psychiatric facility. Some of those who are hospitalised are later viewed as untreatable and either released or transferred to a prison. Many dangerous killers have been diagnosed as psychopaths, indicating, among other things, a lack of concern or conscience about harm done to others. But while psychopathic traits have been described and measured, no satisfactory case has been presented to show it is a 'condition', rather than, as is more likely, a description of how these dangerous people choose to behave. Thus, their capacity and enjoyment of violence apart, many violent offenders can behave like everyone else. John Birt's study in 2001 showed, for example, that over half of all career criminals had either vocational or academic qualifications; that many had jobs and a third of persistent offenders had high skill levels in relation to their occupations.[336]

Many in the criminal justice field misinterpret this normality as evidence that the offender has changed for the better or would be willing to reform if given the chance. Frequently, when passing sentence, for example, judges are reported as saying they are going to avoid a prison sentence because they want the offender to be able to keep the job he already has, or take up one he has recently been offered. They fail to see (or prefer not to see) that violent and criminal conduct of the offender can co-exist with the trappings of 'ordinariness', and that being in work will make not one jot of difference to whether he commits another act of violence.

Before the Second World War, the majority of the killers in the German Police Battalion 101 had never fired a shot; for the most part they were family men and held down regular jobs, (who, when the war finished, became non-violent and melted back into society). They were ordinary men living ordinary lives who had been given permission to express their violent propensities and commit murder, as have violent offenders in Britain, who have discovered that lenient sentencing has considerably reduced the risks to them if they kill or maim. Evidence published by the British Medical Association indicated that knife attacks, for example, had not only become more numerous but also more serious, with wounds that endangered life nearly doubling between 1995 and 2005, from 20 to 37 per 100,000 of the population.[337] Recorded figures for this crime category have since fallen to just over 31, but still far higher than 1995 and 15 times as high as the 1950 figure. In 2014, a BBC Radio 4 news item reported an increase in violent attacks against prison officers. The head of the prison department said that "this was because of the kind of person now coming into prison". 12 months later it was again reported that there had been a significant rise in the number of homicides by prison inmates and assaults against prison staff.[338]

Britain is a place where the casual use of violence has become an every-day occurrence, used by offenders as a solution to everyday irritations, minor problems and sometimes, as a leisure pursuit.

In July 2015, an argument following a road incident between two drivers was all that it took for a man to be later stabbed in the chest on a petrol station forecourt in Chippenham.[339]

For 24-year-old Christopher Monks,[340] a spoilt but apparently otherwise normal young man, hiring a hit man to kill his parents was the obvious solution to the annoyance they caused him by their constant fussing, a situation faced by many families at one time or another. But Christopher Monks senior, 58, and his 60-year-old wife Elizabeth fought off the knife wielding Shaun Skarnes, aged 19, who was hired to murder them. In another example, a 16-year-old boy dealt with a love rival by arranging for him to be beaten with baseball bats, and then stabbed and left to die.[341]

Frequently thefts occur in which the violence used was an embellishment, a little extra add-on for the criminals to enjoy. In 2009, a 61-year-old man, David Wells, was robbed by two violent thugs as he walked home. Gareth Law aged 21, and Samuel Cairns Spencer, 23, both from Bradford, demanded money and he gave them his wallet. They took the £5 it contained but then brutally beat him around the face and head, leaving him, in sub-zero temperatures, an almost unrecognisable heap on the ground.[342]

David Wells survived, but many assaulted in this way do not. A year earlier, Stephen Green, a former soldier, was similarly attacked by a gang of teenagers in an underpass as he cycled home from work in Dunstable. Nicholas Garland, 18, Shane Liddy, 19, Richard McNamara, 19, and Darryll Bennett, 18, stole £5 from him, before they beat him to death.[343] In another example, a 68-year-old church organist, Alan Greaves, was also beaten to death as he made his way to a midnight service on Christmas Eve, in 2012. He was attacked 200 yards from St Saviour's Church in High Green, Sheffield. The police stated the attack was unique in its viciousness. There were no suspects, no weapon was found, and the attack was without motive.[344] In 2008, a baying mob of youths hunted down and stabbed a schoolboy to death for no other reason than that he 'did not show them respect'.[345]

It was pleasure and excitement which motivated two boys from Doncaster, aged 10 and 11 to punch, burn, kick and stamp on their nine-year-old and 11-year-old victims, in a burst of ferocious violence in a disused brick field in Yorkshire.[346] One criminologist said that to behave in this way, the attackers could have no recognition of the harm they had caused and were unable to imagine their victim's feelings or distress. But this is yet another example of theoretical day-dreaming. Their behaviour makes it obvious that they knew exactly what was the effect of their cruelty, and that it was wrong. What other motive could they have for inflicting it – and in a deserted spot away from prying eyes? They had no difficulty in imagining what the pain and fear they were causing felt like. It was this that excited them, and enabled them to revel in the enjoyment and sense of power it gave them.

In 2011, Andrew Bayliss was in debt and owed £20,000. His solution was to kill and rob a taxi driver. He stabbed him fourteen times in the head before dragging him out of the taxi and dumping him in a ditch. This was not done on the spur of the moment, but was a carefully planned attack by a dangerous man. Bayliss used a false name when booking the taxi from a call box. He threw away his clothes and changed his appearance before going on the run.[347]

In 2010, 90-year-old Geoffrey Bacon, a Second World War veteran who was a driver for General Eisenhower in France, was murdered for his bus pass and £40. His killer, or killers, followed him to his flat on a south London estate where he had lived since he was six years old, and attacked him as he opened his front door.[348] The police stated that it was a particularly despicable crime because the victim was a vulnerable, elderly man. This implies that if the victim were younger and stronger, the crime would not have been so serious. As tragic as 90-year-old Geoffrey Bacon's death was, the crime would have been just as serious if the victim had been young, six feet tall and very fit. This killing remains unsolved.

Two years earlier four burglars battered a father of three to death, because he had the temerity to try and stop them escaping with their haul of property stolen from his house.[349] The possession of his wallet, DVD player, and a PlayStation was all that mattered to them.

Two burglars broke into the bungalow of an elderly man, and they tortured him for half an hour, eventually to his death, to find out where his money was kept.[350] The violence inflicted by Joby Barney, 25, and John James, 19, which left 75-year-old Mr Baker with 62 fractures to his ribs, a broken neck and back and extensive bruising and stab wounds to his face, was no more to them than a tool of their trade, a device for satisfying their criminal greed.

James Bullen battered his former headmaster, causing him severe injuries, to avenge a grudge he had held for 20 years since he was at school. The violence of the attack was such that the victim needed facial reconstruction.[351]

In 2009, a young bank worker was kicked to death in Sutton, South London, within yards of a police station, in a row over nothing more than his girl friend's Halloween hat.[352] A middle-aged man was kicked to death in Northfield, Birmingham in December 2009, because, it is suspected, he may have refused to give a gang of youths a cigarette.[353] A bus passenger was beaten and knifed repeatedly for asking a group of men if he could sit down near them.[354] A 23-year-old graduate was killed by thugs in a row over a half-eaten chocolate bar they had thrown into his sister's car.[355] A schoolboy murdered a former girlfriend after he was promised a free breakfast if he carried out the killing. He lured her to a remote forest and smashed her head with a rock after trying to break her neck.[356] Twenty-year-old Daniel Pollen and a friend, Andrew Griffiths, were waiting for a lift home in Romford, Essex, when they were suddenly set upon in a frenzied attack by three men. Andrew was stabbed, and punched in the face with such force that his jaw shattered, but he survived. Daniel was stabbed and died shortly afterwards.[357] There was no warning of the attack carried out by 17-year-old Michael Lynch, and his accomplices Michael Okonah, 25, and Timmy Sullivan, 19. The attackers were strangers to the victims. Their motive? From the witness box the killers said they had gone out to enjoy themselves. The violence they unleashed was their way of rounding off a good evening – one for the road you could say.

Scores of established criminals enjoyed several 'good nights out' during the summer riots in 2011. These provided an almost perfect laboratory demonstration of the fact that crime is not a disease and men are not by nature law-abiding. Most of the violence and looting was carried out by persistent offenders, who took advantage of the absence of any police effort to stop them at the outset of the trouble. Gordon Thompson, an established criminal, with previous convictions for violence, armed robbery and theft, seized the moment when it suddenly presented itself to him. He smashed shop fronts, looted, and finally set fire to a 140-year-old family furniture business, which burnt to the ground.[358]

Over half of those eventually arrested for taking part in the orgy of arson, criminal damage and theft, were rearrested within a year, for other offences such as rape, arson, robbery and threats to kill.[359] The youngest looter involved in the violent mayhem was sentenced to an 18 month 'rehabilitation order', and was told by the judge "you can't get away with this behaviour". But the sentence he had just given told the offender that he *had* got away with it, a point the young criminal rammed home when he was arrested again on other charges, only a week after his riot appearance.[360] However, some who took part in the violence and destruction were those who had, until then, led law-abiding lives. Indeed, some were prosperous and middle class and others were on the brink of promising and well-paid careers. Their normal fear of lawbreaking suddenly evaporated when they saw no one was trying to stop the violence and looting. And so they joined in. Yet there were others at the scene who were horrified and frightened by what they saw, and some, rather than smash shop fronts and plunder from them, tried to stop others from doing so.

The August riots were a shameful indictment of the weakness of our justice system that has fostered an expanding underclass of criminals ever-ready to take advantage of opportunities to steal, to be violent and cause mayhem. Several commentators referred to the pressures of poverty and inequality as possible causes. But, as far as is known, few, if any food shops were looted, and certainly no libraries or book shops were broken into.[361] The looters targeted clothes stores, TVs, computers and other electrical goods, some cramming their spoils into the boots of their cars to the point of overflowing.[362] Stores and buildings were set on fire for the sake of it. Some have even suggested that Thompson was making a statement about 'inequality', but this is pure fiction. This was no protest driven by hunger and deprivation. This was a demonstration of unbridled greed and violence by a criminal army-in-residence whose members have long discovered such behaviour pays and gets them what they want.

This was illustrated by a gang of ten men who, to achieve their ends, committed an act of unspeakable cruelty. They were arrested in 2008 for the gang rape of a 16-year-old girl in London. Following the rape, they poured caustic soda over her to destroy any evidence linking them to their crime, and it was feared at one point she would die from the terrible injuries which they inflicted upon her.[363]

During my secondment to a prison, I was presented, along with other members of the staff, with a baffling problem. A young prisoner, aged 17, with no history of self-harm or suicidal behaviour, began to cut himself. Over a period of weeks, he was regularly taken into the hospital where his sometimes-severe wrist wounds were bound and treated. He was then returned to his wing, only to repeat the act of self-mutilation. To begin with, he refused to say why he was doing this, but eventually he told us he had been targeted by violent bullies on his wing who were using him as a source of fun. They informed him that if he did not cut himself, and keep on doing it, they would do it for him. He was so petrified he did what they wanted. It emerged that these heartless thugs reaped as much enjoyment from this wounding by proxy as if they had cut their victim themselves, and this was their sole motive. It was not a revenge attack, nor was it associated in any way with gang rivalry. In fact, he was a stranger to them and represented no threat whatsoever.

Leisure violence can be purchased. Imagine a scene set in a crowded shopping centre. A man wanders in and puts on a frightening clown mask and produces a hand-gun. He then pumps a security guard full of bullets, and his blood is seen to be splattered over the walls. The gunman wanders on and heads for the cosmetic counter. The female assistant looks up and he shoots her in the head. Behind a shelving unit a woman customer is curled up and whimpering in terror and she too is shot at point blank range. And so, the scene goes on. In two minutes 11 people are killed. This is not a description of the Nairobi mall massacre in September 2013. This is a description of a scene from a video game called *Payday 2* – and the choice of who to shoot is in the hands of the player.[364] Hundreds of thousands, and possibly millions of people play video games of this sort, many of them children. Millions are spent on making violence more graphic and realistic in films. Many TV programmes and books are full of violent content.

Because the portrayal of violence has become so lurid, in 2012, some involved in the film industry, called for film-makers to rethink their approach, particularly in the wake of a series of school massacres in the US.[365] In Britain in 2012, Mark Bridger was sentenced to die in prison for the abduction and murder of five-year-old April Jones. A short time afterwards, Stuart Hazell was convicted of the sexual assault and murder of 12-year-old Tia Sharpe in south London.[366] Both of these predatory and highly dangerous paedophiles were known to have trawled the internet, repeatedly viewing sexually explicit images of teenagers and children. Inevitably in the aftermath, it was asked whether viewing such violent and pornographic images, wherever they were to be found, incited these two men to commit these acts of depravity. As long ago as 1997, the then Home Secretary Jack Straw was under pressure to tighten up on regulations covering the sale and distribution of videos in the wake of new suggestions of links between violence on screen and the behaviour of offenders. Research by Dr Kevin Browne of Birmingham University, suggested that violent and non-violent offenders react differently when shown graphic violent material, and these results have been supported by findings from Nottingham University as well as data from the US.[367] Studies into the effects on children of viewing violent material found that the younger the child the more likely they were to be affected by it, and that they can become more aggressive the longer they remain exposed to it.[368]

To return to the spectrum argument made earlier, children will differ in their propensity for violence, just as adults do, and those more likely to be influenced by violent images will be those who have greater propensities for violence to begin with. Dr Browne concluded that, "videos cannot create aggressive people, but they will make aggressive people commit violent acts more frequently."[369] Likewise, the images viewed by paedophiles such as Bridger and

Hazell did not make them violent men, but they dangerously excited a propensity that was already present.

Thus, violent and pornographic images are harmful, not because everyone who sees them will turn into violent killers and or predatory sex offenders, but because of their ability to incite such behaviour, perhaps for the first time, in people who already have a capacity for it, and because they encourage those with established violent records to commit more of the same. The availability of such images may help loosen, for some offenders, the restraints that previously checked their violent propensities. For such people, they may be as potent a trigger as lenient sentencing.

But is it not likely that the greater our exposure generally to violence, whether via the media or in cinemas and other entertainment outlets, the more likely we are to become inured to it? It is no longer the cultural antibody it once was. In June 2012, as part of an 'educational musical' focused on the Olympic Games, children in Abbotskerswell Primary school in Devon, were taught to sing a song promising extreme violence to rival competitors in the competition:

> *"You think you're really tough, but we don't give a stuff, we are going to kill you. I'll break your arms and legs, I'll make it that you'll beg, for me to stop the pain, think again."*

The school's head teacher, Viv Clare, apologised and ordered her staff to withdraw the song after parents complained about it.[370]

In another example, in July 2013 it was reported that a TV station had been fined for broadcasting a programme that urged Muslims to murder those who insulted their Prophet. It appeared in an article one inch high, and contained no comment. This was by any measure a serious offence and it would not have been unjust if it had resulted in arrests, tough sentences, and the closure of the station. Instead it was dealt with as a breach of broadcasting rules,[371] and the programme's incitement to murder was viewed as no more serious than if it had broadcast a misleading advert. Likewise, few parliamentary feathers have been ruffled by the large number of people killed in Britain by killers freed to kill again; no one in parliament or government seemed too bothered by the fact that our homicide rate doubled between 1964 and the turn of the millennium; apart from a small minority, there has been no serious demand from MPs for a change in sentencing laws which allow violent criminals generally, the freedom to roam and repeat their crimes, examples of which excite less and less concern, beyond a few moments of news media coverage.

# 5

## Released to Kill, Maim and Rape Again

It should not conflict with the principles of a civilised society for it to act on the precept that dangerous criminals who, having served a protracted apprenticeship in violent crime, and who eventually kill, or maim or rape, should be imprisoned either until old age undermines their ability and motivation to hurt anyone else again, or for the rest of their lives. Better still that repeat, violent and dangerous criminals are taken off the streets, before such dire events occur. Their criminal record speaks for itself and a confident, well ordered-society should have no qualms about locking the door on them.

But most of those serving sentences of life imprisonment face no such threat. Figures obtained by one MP showed that the average time served by all murderers is only 16 years, (17 years, according to the Prison Reform Trust[372]) while one in nine is freed from prison after serving fewer than ten years in jail.[373] Prisoners soon learn which boxes the prison system is required to tick for them to be placed on the equivalent of a moving conveyor belt that leads, sometimes even against their own expectations, to their freedom. Having negotiated the prison department's highly-bureaucratised yet arbitrary release system, once out in the community, many go on to rape, maim and kill again.

Between 1900 and 2014 there have been at least 203 *second* convictions for homicide[374] [375] [376] and we can approximate that at least 190 of these victims (those born after 1930) would be alive today and in most cases, would have had the opportunity to bring up families, follow their careers, and enjoy a full life, had they not been robbed of the opportunity. If an equal number of offenders had been executed (or even imprisoned) for killings they had not committed, there would be uproar from all sections of the population. But the injustice meted out to those robbed of their lives by violent criminals freed by the State, provokes the minimum of fuss, and is soon forgotten. Furthermore, as shown, the threat posed by killers who have gained their freedom, has increased, yet no one in the justice system, apart from recording the fact, has moved to do anything about it.

In the 25-year period after the abolition of the death penalty (1964–1989), the number of killers convicted of a second killing was, on average, 2.8 per year. Over the next 25 years it increased to 4.4 per year.

The numbers of those convicted of a second homicide has also increased per the population, as shown by the following graph.[377]

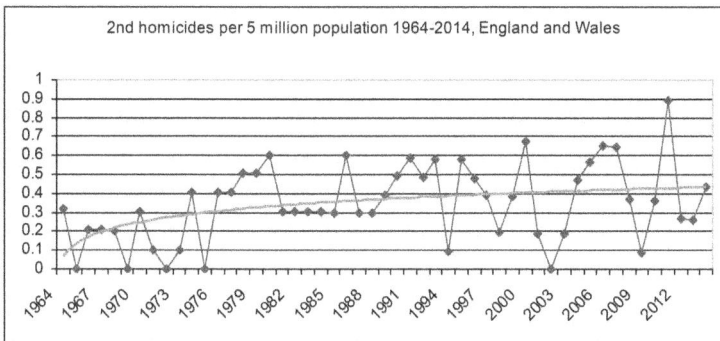

2nd homicides per 5 million population 1964-2014, England and Wales

Key: Trend indicated by Red line

Sources:

Period 1900–2011: This data has been compiled from Home Office bulletins and 'Homicide Firearm Offences and Intimate Violence; Crime in England and Wales Supplementary Volumes' for years 1900-2011 as well as newspaper reports for the same period.

Period 2012–2014: Office for National Statistics, Crime Statistics, Focus on Violent Crime and Sex Offences 2013/14

But whether the risk is going up or down is not the point. There should not be any. Was such a scenario ever imagined by those MPs who so zealously argued against the death penalty? And were the public warned that abolition might result in many killers being given the opportunity to repeat their murderous behaviour? Furthermore, did anyone at that time ever think that prison terms for killers would become as permissive as they now are?

In all likelihood, the majority of the public, no matter what their attitude is towards the sentence given for a first killing, would see no injustice in a whole life term of imprisonment being handed down after a conviction for a *second* homicide. Most would probably expect it. But a review of 183 cases of second killings, found only 11% were given a whole life term (based on 103 cases for which sentencing data could be found). The rest received life sentences with a minimum tariff, most of which were for 20 years or less. Most of the remainder, those who had escaped with manslaughter convictions, received terms of imprisonment of ten years or less, with some as little as four years.[378] Thus, even after a protracted history of violent crime, embellished by two homicides, the possibility of release was still being held out to 90% of these repeat killers, and for some of them it was a certainty. Their preparation-for-release courses which they followed in prison should have been re-named 'preparation-for-more-killing courses, as between them they brought a violent end to the lives of at least another 183 people.

It is sobering to consider that these second-time killers would have played the game and did what was required of them to be considered for release. In many cases their pre-release rehabilitation programmes would have employed psychologists and probation staff for hundreds of hours and copious files would have been collected on their response. This was certainly true of Clive Hayes a serial offender who, in 1973 was imprisoned for raping two schoolgirls aged 14 and 15.[379] Despite the gravity of this offence for which a life sentence would not have been unjust, he was sentenced to just three years' imprisonment. In 1975, within three weeks of his release he dragged another 15-year-old girl from the street into his car. He drove to his bedsit where he tied her up and raped her at knife-point. He was traced, arrested and this time the court imprisoned him 'for life', a formalised lie ritually intoned by judges because, unless otherwise stated, all such offenders are subject to release at the discretion of the parole board. At the trial the judge said that, "he could not see a time when Hayes would no longer be a danger to society". If this was so why did he not give him a whole life term? Such a sentence would not have been unjust.

Prison reports in 1991 indicated Hayes had made 'no progress'. For the prison psychologists and probation staff – and their assessment is the one that counts in this process – this meant he had shown no remorse, or gained any insight (or pretended that he had) into why he committed the crime. The concept of a dangerous prisoner's suitability for release being judged on this basis is both arbitrary and seriously flawed, and should be abandoned, because whether a prisoner is making 'progress' or not, whatever that means, should be held as irrelevant to the question of his release. He is sent to prison because of what he has done, (or should be) not because he has a problem that requires remedial help or treatment, or because he has shown no remorse. Later in that year, despite the 'no progress report', Hays' security rating was lowered to Category D, which meant he was transferred to an open prison. This put him on the moving staircase to freedom.

Only three years later, in 1993, a report by a probation officer said, despite knowing Hayes' offending history that "he was reasonably confident that Hayes would not re-offend." Probation officers are not the only victims of such self-delusion. Lord Phillips, a previous president of the Supreme Court, stated that "it was quite possible for an appropriate tribunal to reliably conclude that the risk of an offender carrying out further serious sex crimes could be discounted." Illustrating yet again that it is the foolishness of clever men (or those assumed to be so) that is of the most dangerous kind.[380] As stated above, the question of Hayes' release should never have been raised, but given that the system required him to say something, it would have been wiser for the probation officer to say that no one could say with any confidence that Hayes was no longer a danger to the public. Given his past crimes, it was entirely in the public's interest for him, without any fear of injustice, to stay in prison for ever.

However, this report had lit the blue touch paper for Hayes, who, against even his own expectations, suddenly saw the chances of release becoming a reality. Encouraged by this assessment, he attended probation run pre-release groups, aimed at developing 'thinking skills', then very much in vogue with psychologists and probation staff working in prisons. Furthermore, Hayes knew that it was essential that his attendance at these activities appeared on his prison CV before the authorities would consider giving him his freedom. Whether these programmes made any difference to him or not was not important (as reported in an earlier chapter their results, eventually published by the government, showed them to be useless). What mattered was that the prisoner should be made to jump through this bureaucratic hoop – which he did, willingly, in the same way a circus dog performs to win the approval of those that control him.

In 1995, Hayes made his submission to the parole board for his release, using the phoney language he had learnt on the probation programme. He told the parole board what he knew they wanted to hear when he said that he had offended because of his "distorted thinking, brought about by his abusive treatment as a child". He had learned, he said, "that this was the reason for his sexually violent relationships with women. I was a mixed-up person and I did not know my own identity. But that is all in the past, because I have now been taught to think properly." Hayes saved his best line till last, and crowned his performance with, "Now I feel happy in the company of women." While Hayes may well have done so, it is unlikely that the parole board saw the wicked irony in this last statement. Completely out of their depth, as they frequently are, the board members were persuaded by this stomach-turning nonsense and in 1996 they decided to release him. Not many cases could so clearly reveal their lack of judgement. This was not a complex case and it would have been clear to an alert 14-year-old that Hayes should have stayed in prison for the rest of his life. But parole board members all too frequently behave as if they are social workers operating a prisoner's aid charity, and like many others in the justice system, prefer to demonstrate their virtue as compassionate and understanding people, rather than do their duty. And the more dangerous the prisoner the more compassion they can show, and so the more virtuous they believe they are.

Carried along by a sense of their own goodness, the parole board released Hayes saying he was an *acceptable risk* to the public. But would the public agree? And why should they bear *any* risk? We can be certain that, because of their relatively wealthy and protected life styles, Hayes presented no risk to the parole board members. Certainly, Hayes did not kill any one of them, but he did kill, some years after gaining his freedom, a young Polish care worker living in relatively poor conditions in a bedsit on the outskirts of Bristol. Hayes' behaviour prior to killing her followed almost the same pattern demonstrated before his previous crimes when he abducted and raped three teenage girls. Did any of the probation, psychology or parole board officials involved feel some responsibility for this young woman's death? Were they shamed by it and the impact it had on her family, who flew from Poland to stand rigid with grief at their daughter's graveside? These officials have no excuse (except that of stupidity) not to have seen what was staring them in the face. They, more than most, should have known that violent offenders may well become more dangerous over time, not less, but they preferred to see what they wanted to see. While no one can predict an offender will *not* commit further offences, there are many whose violence is predictable, and Hayes fell into this category.

Thus, despite hundreds of hours of attention from probation officers and other staff in the prison, nothing had changed as far as Hayes was concerned. Furthermore, he had shown there was never anything wrong with his 'thinking skills'. With embarrassing ease, he had thought out and successfully executed a simple but effective plan to escape by outwitting those running the system, whose favourable recommendation he needed, thus gaining his freedom. This was, as with hundreds of similar cases, an officially sanctioned prison break. So much for the rehabilitation courses and the posturing of psychologists, probation staff and parole board members as experts in this field. Hayes had demonstrated that it was they, and not he, who needed help with their thinking skills.

Many others have used this method to escape from prison and analysis of the actual prison time served shows that the majority of second time killers serve less than 16 years.[381] Such liberality ignores the fact that dangerous criminals stay dangerous, but just as significantly, it reveals the State's refusal, or inability, to draw a clear line between right and wrong, and to judge that some crimes should be declared beyond the pale and the perpetrators locked away for the rest of their lives.

Violent men who kill are unpredictable. An analysis of 91 second homicides revealed that the average time between release from prison following the first killing and conviction for the second was five years, with a minimum of one year and a maximum of 16 years.[382]

Some kill again almost as soon as they are released, while others are convicted a second time after many years. For example,

John Slater was first convicted of murder in 1948. Over 40 years later, in 1989 he killed again. John Nixon served 21 years of a life-sentence that started in 1980. Four years after his release, he murdered again and on 2 March 2005, he was given another life sentence with a minimum tariff of 25 years. There was an interval of 19 years between Paul Brufield's first and second killing,[383] and David Cook, aged 66, strangled his neighbour with some wire in 2012, 24 years after he killed a Sunday school teacher. In contrast, Malcolm Green bludgeoned to death a young tourist from New Zealand only five months after being released from a jail sentence imposed for killing a prostitute.[384]

Ben Redfern-Edwards aged 21 was released after serving only half of his sentence for a violent armed robbery. On 30 January 2005, within 72 hours of being let out of prison, he battered to death a woman whose path he had crossed by chance, 'because her dog had barked at him'. His victim, 44-year-old Jacqueline Ross, who ran a local manicure and pedicure business, was the mother of two young sons, both under six years old. She had been walking her terrier dog, Rosie, along the Peak Forest Canal Towpath in Disley, a well-known beauty spot on the border of Cheshire and Derbyshire. Her half-naked body was found an hour or so after she was killed. She had sustained horrific head injuries inflicted with a rock.

Redfern-Edwards was sentenced to life imprisonment, but with a minimum tariff of only 22 years. Thus, the judge was still not prepared, even at that point, to throw away the key. In fact, he said that he would have given Edwards a thirty-year minimum tariff but he discounted eight years because of his age, but he made no reference to the fact that this had not prevented him from killing his victim. But he also reduced the tariff because the attack was instantaneous and not premeditated. Thus, although the family of the murdered Jacqueline Ross, and probably everyone else, viewed her killing as the most serious and heinous of crimes, the judge offered them the consolation that it would have been very much worse had Redfern-Edwards planned her death beforehand.[385] The victim's husband, Michael Ross, however, was far from consoled. He could not believe the leniency of the sentence and exclaimed that "the killer had been amazingly privileged".

Such a description could easily be applied to Ian McLoughlin, one of the most malignant of criminals to face trial in Britain in recent times. He killed his first victim in 1984.[386] He escaped with a manslaughter conviction and was given ten years in prison. He was released early and in 1992 stabbed his second victim, his landlord, to death. At this point, had he been given a whole life term no one would have been surprised or thought it an injustice. However, he was sentenced to 'life' imprisonment (the ritualised lie again) and given a 25-year minimum tariff. By 2013, despite him being a double killer, preparations to release McLoughlin were in full swing. He was allowed several temporary releases from prison, despite failing to return on time from some of them. These obvious danger signs were ignored.

In July 2013, McLoughlin was given a further unsupervised day out from Springhill Prison, near Aylesbury, in Buckinghamshire. He travelled several miles to the home of a released former inmate whom he had known, 87-year-old Frances Cory-Wright, a convicted paedophile, who lived in the secluded and beautiful village of Little Nettelden in the heart of the Bucks countryside. Knowing Mr Cory-Wright to be an Old Etonian and assuming he was well off, McLoughlin went with the express purpose of robbing him. He was in the process of filling a pillowcase with valuable possessions from the house, when the victim called for help. A neighbour, 66-year-old Graham Buck came to investigate and Mcloughlin dragged him into the house and slit his throat. It is significant to note here that many violent offenders are assessed as safe enough to let out for the day, as indeed was McLoughlin, as part of their preparation for release. How then does the justice system explain that when some fail to return, and go on the run, the public via the press are warned that 'they are dangerous and should not be approached' only hours after officials decided they were safe enough to be trusted with their freedom?

McLoughlin was eventually tried and convicted of murder, and given another 'life' sentence by the trial judge with a minimum tariff of 40 years. Despite being his *third* killing, it took an appeal by the Attorney General and an Appeal Court Hearing in a British court to get his sentence changed to a whole life sentence. Before the abolition of the death penalty, Mcloughlin, probably, would have been hanged after his first killing, had he been convicted of murder, but certainly after his second. But the price of human life has fallen and Mcloughlin was allowed three homicides before he was made to pay the ultimate price of complete loss of his freedom. How many will it be in another 40 years time?

The authorities said mistakes had been made in the decision to release McLoughlin for temporary parole. But I do not believe this. I do not think it was an 'error'. He had served 21 years of a minimum tariff of 25 years, and he was given parole because that is how the British system operates. It was part and parcel of the preparations that must take place for the parole board to later consider him for release. By this time, he was housed in a Category D prison, ostensibly for low risk prisoners, being considered for release, having no doubt been assessed as suitable for such a regime by psychologists. The system was doing what it was supposed to do. The error lies in allowing a sentence of 'life' imprisonment to be served as an indeterminate period with a minimum tariff that paves the way for these calamities, instead of a sufficiently long mandatory period, which in Mcloughlin's case, should have been for ever.

The forbearance shown to this triple killer and scores of other violent criminals can be compared with the law's ruthless pursuit of a British soldier who, while on active duty, shot and killed an Iraqi who had tried to take his rifle. Despite a number of military and criminal court hearings that cleared him of all blame, he was, over a 12-year period, hounded by legal threats of further prosecution, including an arraignment before the International War Crimes Tribunal. All of this wrecked his career and placed him under enormous strain.[387] He is not alone. There were, until recently, 1,230 public law claims against the Ministry of Defence and 700 private actions. In October 2015, the *Daily Telegraph* reported that British taxpayers were facing a bill of almost £150 million to defend British soldiers being sued by enemy fighters for breaching their human rights. As succinctly pointed out by the columnist Charles Moore, in such an atmosphere no one – soldier, sailor, spy, – who undertakes dangerous work for Britain's national security is protected from the aggression of his own country's legal system.[388] In 2016 it was announced that the firm of Public Interest Lawyers, responsible for bringing these actions, was to close, as hundreds of them were found to be without basis.[389][390]

In contrast, the probation service trod very lightly with Damien Hanson, a violent career criminal, convicted of attempted murder while robbing a man of his Rolex watch, and attacking him with a machete. He was released on licence after serving just seven years of a 12-year sentence, and so that he should not be too inconvenienced by this experience, he was placed on low level supervision by his probation minders. Only three months after his release from prison, armed with a gun and a knife, he and another criminal, Elliot White, also subject to supervision, posing as postal delivery men, tricked their way into the home of a wealthy business man, John Monckton. Monckton fought to keep them out, but he and his wife were overpowered. Their nine-year-old daughter partly witnessed the attack and hid upstairs in their Chelsea home. After the robbers fled, she saw blood all over the floor and walls of the entrance hall. Her mother, who had been stabbed twice in the back, was lying at the foot of the stairs. Her father, close to death, lay prostrate on the floor close by. John Monckton died, but Mrs Monckton survived, though she lost seven pints of blood, and now walks with a stick. The killer's haul consisted of a pair of earrings, two rings, a watch and a purse containing money.[391][392]

At Hanson's trial, his defence counsel said that not even the expertise of a consultant psychiatrist could explain his behaviour. But an expert's view was not necessary, because the killer explained his motives very clearly. He told a friend "I want to be a big man with lots of money". It was later established that the Moncktons were to be but the first of many victims, as Hanson and his co-attacker had researched and compiled a list of wealthy families whom they intended to rob, 'in order to get rich'. It would be interesting to know what his probation supervisors said of Hanson to justify their decision to put him on low level supervision. What happened to the Monckton family was a direct result of the concern shown for their attacker by the justice system that failed, when it had the chance, to lock him up for most of his active life, following conviction for his previous violent offence.

While these tragic events become no more than statistics to be recorded by our justice system, its sensitivity towards miscarriages of justice that disadvantage offenders, could not be more acute. For example, it was the wrongful conviction of two obscure poachers from a small provincial town in England that played an important part in the creation of the mighty apparatus of the Court of Appeal.[393] But when a judge, rather than sending him to prison, places a convicted criminal under probation supervision, or a violent prisoner is released early from a sentence that some might think was not long enough anyway, and he then goes on to rob, rape or kill again, is that not as bad a miscarriage of justice? These events occur many more times than those that disadvantage defendants, but no powerful legal or lobby apparatus has sprung into life to rectify this problem. Instead, communities up and down the country are required to live shoulder to shoulder with dangerously violent criminals released under probation monitoring, while their supervisors pretend they can 'manage' the risk they pose to the safety of the public.

Eighteen-year-old Opemipo Jaji, a violent sex offender, was given 18 months probation supervision in the community for making an indecent image of a child as well as robbing and sexually assaulting a 12-year-old girl. Questions concerning the sanity of such a lenient sentence immediately spring to mind, given the offender's crimes could not have more clearly signalled his dangerousness. To have made an image of this kind he would have first had to procure the child concerned – but from where and from whom – and how was this done? Did the seriousness of these questions not weigh on the mind of the judge? Six months later, Jaji made a visit, as instructed, to the probation office. Probably, by then, his visits had become routine. He would have sat with his supervising officer for about twenty minutes, and answered the usual questions about his job, if he had one, his accommodation, the type of friends he hung around with, and he might have been asked questions designed to elicit any behaviour which pointed to the risk of further offences being committed (not that the probation officer could have done anything to prevent them but he could record that he had raised the question and that would win him merit as an indication of good supervision).

All of this duly accomplished, Jaji left the probation office at about 4 pm. About five minutes later, probably just at the moment the probation officer was recording that all was going well with this case, Jaji fell in behind an 11-year-old girl walking home from school. He followed her, chose his moment and dragged her into a park and subjected her to a violent three-hour long assault.[394] While this attack was taking place, his supervising officer would have been putting the finishing touches to his record entry covering the interview. Probably, at the very moment that he closed the file and sat contemplating how well Jaji was doing and the wisdom the courts had shown in not sending him to prison, Jaji was repeatedly raping the terrified 11-year-old girl.

Yet despite examples of this kind many judges hang onto their almost superstitious belief in the recommendations made to them in probation reports. Barrie Compton, a criminal with 54 previous convictions to his name, was not sent to prison but placed on a community service order because the probation service persuaded the judge he was not a violent man. Just as his order was coming to an end, no doubt with all concerned anticipating recording it as a success, he befriended a 78-year-old widow living in the Chelmsley Wood area of Birmingham, and battered her to death with a crowbar and then sexually assaulted her.[395] This recommendation, like many others, was based on the naïve belief that the absence of previous convictions for violent crimes meant that the offender was non-violent. But the probation service has no special skills to make such predictions, and furthermore their own records make it clear that offenders, especially those allowed to stay in the community, and build long criminal histories, commit both violent and non-violent crimes. Fred West, in addition to being a mass murderer, had eleven previous convictions for theft. He had stolen all the seven video machines found in his home. In 2011, a schoolboy Santre Gayle was aged 15 when he was paid to murder Turkish-born Gulistan Subasi, a mother aged 26. The convicted killer, Gayle, had previously built a reputation as a petty criminal.[396]

The government's records confirm this conclusion. A Home Office analysis of the offending of persistent offenders revealed that whatever the offence for which they were sentenced, they are liable to be reconvicted for other types of crimes. Those convicted and sentenced for violence were later reconvicted for offences such as theft, burglary, fraud, drugs, motoring, criminal damage, as well as other indictable and non-indictable crimes. The same pattern was shown no matter what the original offence. For example, even those convicted of a minor offence, were likely to be later reconvicted for serious offences such as violence, burglary and robbery.[397] The further offending patterns of those sent to prison, and those placed back in the community under probation supervision, were highly correlated (0.75). This undermines the assumption made every day in British courts that some persistent criminals can be viewed as 'minor' or 'petty criminals', and therefore they pose a lesser threat to the public than others. All of them have a propensity to commit both serious and minor offences.

In the early hours of 7 May 2005, a crime was committed

on the streets of Britain that was so violent and depraved that it should have rocked parliament to the core and, at a stroke, caused the authorities to abandon their lenient pro-criminal sentencing policies. Sixteen-year-old Mary-Ann Leneghan, and another teenage girl aged 18, were abducted from the streets by a gang of six ruthless and violent criminals aged between 18 and 24, four of whom were on community sentences and subject to probation supervision.[398] The girls were taken by car to room 19 of the Abbey House guesthouse in Reading. The depth of depravity in the events that followed cannot be measured. In the tiny double bedroom, the girls were made to strip, and were tortured, repeatedly punched, kicked, scalded with hot water, stabbed and raped. Their ordeal lasted hours. Their attackers laid out towels on the floor to soak up the blood. Both victims were then bundled into the boot of a car and driven to a lonely spot in Prospect Park, Reading, where they were made to kneel and pillowcases were placed over their heads. They were told they 'were going to die slowly'. They were tortured again, with cuts, cigarette burns, more punches, and beaten with a metal bar. After being repeatedly stabbed Mary Ann Leneghan collapsed screaming to the ground and soon died. Her friend was shot in the forehead. The thugs then made their escape thinking both girls were dead and that they were safe. However, against all the odds, the 18-year-old victim survived and her evidence later helped bring her attackers to justice. Their so-called motive for this depravity was that the girls were associated with a rival gang, one of whose members, they claimed, had stolen drugs from them.

The setting for this vile crime was not Syria or Somalia, or some other country where the rule of law had collapsed and where psychopathic crime-lords ruled, but Reading in 21st century Britain. With an already formidable list of dangerous offences to their name, four of the six attackers, as indicated, were on the books of the probation service, a disposal which kept them out of prison whose further influence, the courts no doubt believed, would turn them into real criminals. The fact that one of them had previously abducted a 13-year-old girl, and subjected her to torture in which he had hung her upside down, beaten her, and had later been convicted of several other violent offences, was obviously not sufficient grounds for the courts to consider he had already earned this status.

The six attackers were all sentenced to life imprisonment with minimum tariffs ranging from 23 to 27 years. Adrian Thomas aged 20, Michael Johnson 19, Jamaille Morally 22, and Indit Krasniqi 18, were at large in the community thanks to the leniency shown them for their previous violent crimes. Joshua Morally and Llewellyn Adams aged 23 and 24 respectively, were the oldest members of the gang. If ever there was a case when 'life should mean life' I would argue that this was such an occasion – for all of them.

One year later the presence of a Home Office report identifying the scale of further offending by violent supervised criminals was leaked to the press. This had been deliberately kept from the public, and ministers fought for months to keep it secret. The Home Secretary personally intervened to block its release. At one point a senior probation official, in a statement argued that, "disclosure of the report would prejudice the effective conduct of public affairs."[399] The Home Office only gave in when it was pointed out that they were legally obliged to make it public. It reported that thousands of offences, many of them violent, were committed every month by those on probation orders.

This was no surprise to officialdom. As far back as 1997, the country was told that one in eight of those accused of murder was on probation.[400] It was reported that John Hicks, the then chairman of the Association of Chief Probation Officers, complained that these figures 'sent a misleading message to the public' and expressed regret at the way they had been released.[401] Does this mean he wanted them kept a secret, or published in such a way as to hide the truth? By the turn of the millennium the Home Secretary Jack Straw was promising a 'shake up' to deal with the problem. This turned out to be the usual hollow ministerial response,[402] because (among other serious crimes) killings and rapes, as shown in the bar charts below, continued unabated under the probation flag.[403] [404] [405] [406]

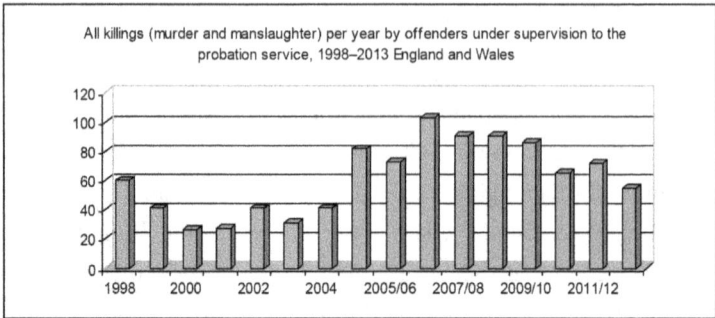

All killings (murder and manslaughter) per year by offenders under supervision to the probation service, 1998–2013 England and Wales

Sources:

1998–2002 Home Office Statistics England and Wales 2002

1999–2003 Home Office Bulletin 15/04 Offender Management Caseload Statistics 2003

2004–2011 Ministry of Justice 2012 Compendium of Reoffending and Analysis

2012–2013 Ministry of Justice, Proven Re-offending Statistics, Quarterly Bulletin, January to December, England and Wales

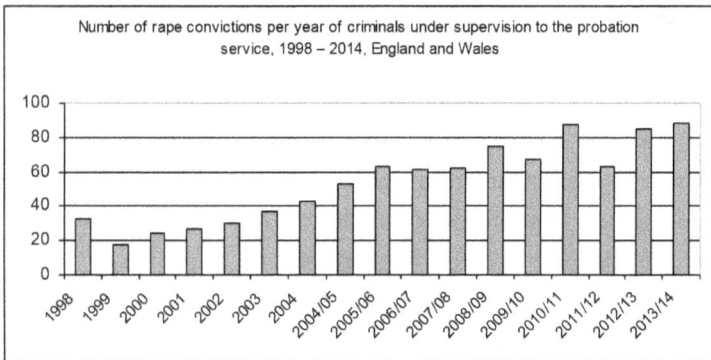

Number of rape convictions per year of criminals under supervision to the probation service, 1998 – 2014, England and Wales

Sources:

1998–2002 Home Office Statistics England and Wales 2002

1999–2003 Home Office Bulletin 15/04 Offender Management Caseload Statistics 2003

2004 2011 Ministry of Justice 2012 Compendium of Re-offending and Analysis 2012–2013 Ministry of Justice, Proven Re-offending Statistics, Quarterly Bulletin, January to December, England and Wales

Three years after Jack Straw's empty rhetoric, Peter Williams, (referred to in an earlier chapter), a young criminal subject to intense probation oversight by Nottingham Youth Offending Team, which included wearing an electronic tag, took part in an armed robbery of a jeweller's shop during which the manageress was killed.[407] One year later reports by the probation inspectorate also severely criticised both the Hertfordshire and the Hampshire probation services for the lax way they were supervising dangerous, high–risk criminals.[408]

In January 2003, PC Walker, a dog handler with the Nottingham Police, was killed by David Parfitt, a criminal who had been released from Ranby Prison a year before, after serving two years for robbery. Under post-release supervision to the probation service, his behaviour soon made it clear he was not to be trusted and he should have been recalled to prison. But warning signs that were not difficult to notice had been ignored in the lead up to the killing. He had regularly breached the terms and conditions under which he had been released early from jail. He had failed drug tests, and within weeks of being freed from prison, failed to turn up at the probation office as directed.[409] There was, as indicated, nothing difficult or hidden about these indicators. One did not need to be an expert to know what this behaviour meant. The office cleaning lady would have been able to interpret it accurately, yet nothing was done. Had these signs been acted on, PC Jed Walker would be alive today. Instead, allowed to stay in the community, Parfitt continued with his life of crime. He stole a car and PC Walker tried to stop him, but was dragged along a road for 100 yards until he was thrown into a concrete bollard and suffered fatal head injuries.

The chief probation officer of the Nottingham probation service nobly took full responsibility for the errors which led to this calamity, but then revamped the meaning of 'responsibility', by saying that he would not resign and neither would he discipline any of his staff. He blamed his service's heavy workload for the mistakes made.[410] If this was true, he should have made it clear to the Home Office at the outset that his staff were unable to exercise Parfitt's supervision properly. Perhaps he did. But if not, the public might well judge their interests were not served by him waiting until Parfitt killed PC Walker before making this admission.

Eventually, thanks to the civilising effect of penological liberalism, which teaches that while such killings are regrettable, it is nevertheless unjust to over-react to them by demanding severe penalties, the killer was sentenced to a token 12 years for manslaughter, (immediately reduced to six years by the 50% automatic remission rule) and his chief minder was left in post to run, what some may view, judging by its effectiveness, an out-of-its-depth *Dad's Army* type organisation.

Despite the widespread publicity given to the death of PC Parfitt and the attention drawn to the hazards of supervisors allowing dangerous criminals to slip off their radar, numerous similar examples continued to surface. In 2008, for example, a vicious criminal called Dano Sonnex, on licence following his early release from jail, murdered two young French students, allowed to do so because, yet again, the warning signs he exhibited prior to the killings were ignored, and in some instances, not even noticed by his probation supervisors. This had allowed Sonnex repeatedly to breach his release conditions, without the fear of recall procedures being instigated.[411] On this occasion, London's Chief Probation Officer David Scott resigned and blamed high caseloads, stress levels and sickness rates that had combined, he said, to undermine his staff's ability to supervise Sonnex more closely.

The Home Office inspection carried out a year later based on 276 cases across ten London boroughs, found that in almost a half of all the cases that they examined, probation officers had not learned the lessons highlighted by the previous killings carried out by supervised offenders in London and elsewhere. These included a failure to take breach action; failure to carry out home visits; supervising officer negligence; poor record keeping; no risk assessment or supervision plan; failure by managers to manage effectively; lack of communication; and no cover for supervising officers when they were sick or on leave.[412]

But whether probation officers are lax or follow all the rules associated with supervising violent offenders in the community, they can never offer sufficient safeguards for the public. Such offenders are not monitored twenty-four hours a day, and even if they were, a probation supervisor could not stop a determined and violent criminal from striking again. Furthermore, offenders who can be trusted to live in the community do not need supervision. Those who do therefore cannot be trusted, and should not be in the community, as clearly illustrated by double killer David Cook. He was monitored by the probation service, following his release from prison in 2009, having served 21 years of a life sentence for the murder of Beryl Maynard, a Sunday school teacher in 1987. In 2011, Cook's probation team, assiduously following the rules, visited him at his home. The record of their visit said that Cook behaved perfectly normally, offered them coffee, was relaxed and happy to talk to them. Unbeknown to them, the corpse of Cook's neighbour, Leonard Hill, lay in the bedroom directly above the room in which they were sitting. Cook had, two days earlier, strangled him to death.[413]

The probation service has been given an impossible task, and the chief crime of their senior management is not to have had the courage (or sense of public duty) to say so. The stress levels associated with this aspect of their work will be very high for those probation officers who genuinely believe they can prevent further violence and killing by those they supervise. Nothing could make nerves more taught than the conviction that avoiding another murder or rape hangs on their continued vigilance. Others who take a more realistic view and who know their supervision will make no difference to the violent criminal determined to strike again must nevertheless pretend that it can. For them, much of the stress, I believe, stems from this pretence and the knowledge they are colluding with a lie. The sense of shame this is likely to induce may well contribute to the pressure for them to conform to a system they know is wrong.

One probation manager in the south west, following an inspection of work carried out by her staff, summed up their impossible position as follows:

> "In the period under review, October to January 2004, there have been nine serious further offences (e.g. murder, attempted murder, manslaughter, rape, abduction, arson, false imprisonment, kidnapping, other serious sex and violent offences), committed by criminals currently under our supervision. The investigations of these crimes have revealed that:
> In none of these cases could we have done anything to prevent the crime.
> In all of them, the government's national standards, governing how we should supervise the offender concerned, were followed to the letter."[414]

I suspect she revealed more than she knew (or intended) by making this statement. But her next sentence provides clear evidence of how cut-off these officials are from the real world. She concluded by saying:

> "This is a good achievement."

So it might have been from the point of view of the blinkered probation bureaucracy, which first and foremost wants to avoid blame. But for the public in the real world nine of the most serious crimes such as murder, rape, and abduction committed in the space of just four months, in just one small probation area by criminals thought safe enough to be in the community, was anything but a good achievement. If this was a good result, what would a bad one be like?

Government statistics for all serious violent, and life-threatening crimes committed by criminals supervised by the probation service, including murder and rape already mentioned, provide, as shown in the following table, compelling evidence that the examples referred to above cannot be dismissed as anecdotal. They dash the myth that repeat, dangerous offenders can be managed safely in the community. For example, the total for the period 1998–2014 (for England and Wales) was 4,905 or 26 further serious offences committed every month by criminals on the probation service's books, or just to pick out two individual categories, almost six killings, and five rapes, every four weeks.[415] [416] [417] [418] [419]

| yr | at mur | mur | cons mur | un k | m/sl | ra | at ra | ar | arm r | rfimp | kid | oth | tot |
|---|---|---|---|---|---|---|---|---|---|---|---|---|---|
| 98 | 40 | 16 | 1 | 1 | 20 | 33 | 5 | 13 | 4 | 1 | 3 | 46 | 183 |
| 99 | 29 | 10 | 1 | 0 | 12 | 18 | 0 | 9 | 6 | 3 | 4 | 65 | 157 |
| 00 | 24 | 16 | 0 | 1 | 2 | 24 | 5 | 7 | 10 | 8 | 3 | 73 | 173 |
| 01 | 26 | 15 | 0 | 2 | 1 | 27 | 2 | 3 | 5 | 11 | 1 | 69 | 162 |
| 02 | 37 | 16 | 3 | 0 | 4 | 30 | 6 | 8 | 9 | 7 | 5 | 31 | 156 |
| 03 | 29 | 12 | 1 | 0 | 2 | 37 | 2 | 9 | 5 | 21 | 4 | 13 | 135 |
| 04 | 26 | 12 | 15 | | 15 | 43 | | 20 | | 0 | 8 | 100 | 239 |
| 05 | 60 | 16 | | | 22 | 53 | | 25 | | 0 | 13 | 137 | 326 |
| 06 | 56 | 15 | | | 17 | 63 | | 20 | | 0 | 20 | 158 | 349 |
| 07 | 74 | 14 | | | 29 | 61 | | 21 | | 0 | 38 | 368 | 605 |
| 08 | 66 | 15 | | | 25 | 62 | | 32 | | 0 | 57 | 415 | 672 |
| 09 | 62 | 18 | | | 29 | 75 | | 17 | | 0 | 19 | 367 | 587 |
| 10 | 56 | 15 | | | 30 | 67 | | 8 | | 14 | 0 | 81 | 271 |
| 11 | 49 | 8 | | | 16 | 87 | | 4 | | 2 | 0 | 55 | 221 |
| 12 | 59 | 9 | | | 13 | 63 | | 7 | | 12 | 0 | 50 | 213 |
| 13 | 41 | 9 | | | 14 | 85 | | 6 | | 13 | 0 | 55 | 223 |
| 14 | 52 | 13 | | | 22 | 69 | | 10 | | | 14 | 53 | 233 |

Key:

yr = year

at mr = attempt murder

mur= murder

cons mur = conspiracy to murder

un k = unlawful killing

m/sl = manslaughter

ra = rape

at ra = attempt rape

ar = arson with intent to endanger life

arm r = armed robbery

r fimp = robbery false imprisonment

kid = kidnapping

oth = other serious sex & violent offences

tot = total

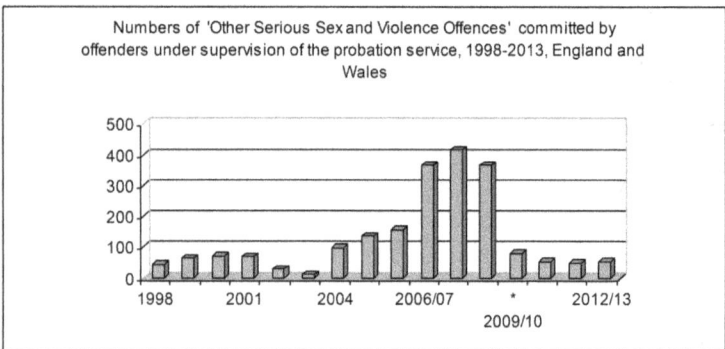

Numbers of 'Other Serious Sex and Violence Offences' committed by offenders under supervision of the probation service, 1998-2013, England and Wales

The government admitted that prior to 2006/07 there were serious faults in the way it had collected this data. Following the adjustments, their new returns reported a significantly higher total, particularly, as indicated above, in the category of 'other serious sex and violent crimes', which showed more than double their previous number.[420]

Sources:

1998–2002 Home Office Statistics England and Wales 2002

1999–2003 Home Office Bulletin 15/04 Offender Management Caseload Statistics 2003

2004–2011 Ministry of Justice 2012 Compendium of Re-offending and Analysis

2012–2013 Ministry of Justice, Proven Reoffending Statistics, Quarterly Bulletin, January to December, England and Wales

It would appear, from what followed, that the new higher figures revealed far more than the government wanted known. Their solution was to leave out Section 18 Grievous Bodily Harm (GBH) offences from the count, even though this crime is regarded as the most serious form of violence next to murder.[421] But this, it would appear, did not matter. Perhaps the officials concerned hoped that over time most would forget (if they ever knew) how this sudden reduction came about. The bar chart above displays the dramatic effects of this creative accounting introduced in 2009. Prior to this date GBH convictions had been included in the category 'other serious sex and violent convictions'. In 2008/09 the total of convictions for this group of offences was 367. In 2009, following the removal of GBH figures, the total was 81.

This was not the first attempt by officials to hide the true figures relating to these crimes. Earlier in 2006, they had released figures via the press, covering a 12-month period, which reported that 61 serious offences such as rape, murder, abduction, etc., had been committed by high-risk criminals supervised in the community following their early release from prison. But this was a highly misleading announcement, because this referred only to serious crimes committed by those offenders categorised as posing the most serious risk of further harm. They did not include those crimes committed by those in the medium risk or low risk range.

It is irrelevant to the victim of rape or the family of a murdered relative whether the attacker was labelled high, medium or low risk by civil servants. The futility of this bureaucratic labelling, (except perhaps as yet another way of confusing the public)

was clearly shown in the statement by Harry Fletcher, the then Assistant General Secretary of the Probation Service Union. He reported that, "the majority of these very serious offences are committed by offenders in the *lowest* risk category."[422] But the deception did not end there. The government's press release only referred to offenders released from prison, and those thought highly dangerous and supervised by Multi-Agency Public Protection Agency arrangements (MAPPA). It said nothing about the serious offences committed by offenders on other types of probation supervision. When these were taken into account, the total was, as shown above, 349, more than five times larger than that released to the press. In 2009, information obtained by a Freedom of Information request revealed that the government was still hiding most dangerous sex offences from the public, and that as many as 125 of such crimes in the previous year did not make it into official government figures.[423]

But who is the public to blame for this mayhem of violence committed against them by violent criminals, who, allowed their freedom, have, in the short space of 17 years killed almost 800 people, while supposedly being monitored carefully by the probation service? While it is the legislators who draft the sentencing laws, it is the judges who interpret them, but they do so shackled by 'advice' from the Sentencing Council. But this mysterious body is unelected, and its members are appointed jointly by the Lord Chancellor, one of the most senior members of the government, and by the Lord Chief Justice, in a process clouded in obscurity.

This single body has now taken over from two previous organisations, the Sentencing Guidelines Council (SGC), and the Sentencing Advisory Panel. The latter sent advice to the SGC, which in turn issued guideline advice, via the Lord Chief Justice, to the courts. But as the Lord Chief Justice was the chairman of the body issuing the guidelines and a member of the judiciary receiving it, and because a senior government minister is involved in deciding who sits on the Council, the true origins of this advice remain obscure. In fact, the structure determining the flow of the advice emanating from this quasi-legal cabal is reminiscent of that used by criminals, who seek to hide the source of their criminal money in a complicated network of bank accounts. For example, what source prompted the SGC to recommend, in 2003, that violent street robbers should not be sent to prison if their threats resulted in minimal harm to the victim?[424] Likewise, in 2010, who or what inspired the Sentencing Advisory Panel to issue guidelines which said that violent burglars who were armed or left their victims particularly traumatised could avoid prison and be given a community order instead?[425] In 2015, parliament ruled that 16 and 17-year-old offenders must be given at least 4 months in detention if convicted a second time of carrying a knife or using it to threaten someone. Less than a year later the Sentencing Council undermined this by directing courts to look for alternative sentences for under 18s convicted of these crimes. Where does their authority come from to oppose parliamentary law in this way and why does no one in government or parliament do anything to challenge such directions?[426]

The newly formed Sentencing Council claims it gives 'carefully considered and detailed sentencing' advice to the courts. But shouldn't these details be thrashed out in parliament and voted upon? The Council's so-called guidelines are based on the opinion of its fourteen members, (six of whom are non-judicial appointments), and therefore they will be arbitrary, a feature which is supposed to run counter to all aspects of British justice. A question mark hangs over its claim to be independent; it looks far more like an elaborately but poorly-disguised instrument of government policy, part of a carefully constructed network whose purpose, as mentioned above, is to hide from the public the origins of those ideas that seek to place ever more limits on the severity of sentences passed by the courts.

Furthermore, prior to 2009, the judges were technically free to ignore the advice issued by the Sentencing Guidelines Council. But His Honour Keith Matthewman, an experienced Nottingham

Crown Court Judge, remarked, shortly before he died in 2008, that Britain had the weakest judiciary for over a century. He observed that few judges were prepared to pass a heavier sentence than that recommended by the Council, for fear of being appealed, and the risk this posed to their chances of preferment. He regularly went against the Council's recommendations and was never promoted. Since 2009, however, the law has declared that judges must follow the guidelines, so in effect they are not guidelines any more, but instructions. But are they? This issue is fudged by a clause which says judges do not have to follow them if, in all the circumstances, they feel it would be 'against justice' to do so.

But even when such circumstances present themselves, few judges seem to want to take the risk. In 2012, for example, a judge dismissed the 34-month sentence he passed on a violent offender as 'pathetic'. The sentencing guidelines prevented him, he said, from handing down a more severe punishment. Samuel Evans, in his twenties, had unleashed an unprovoked assault on his victim, 33-year-old Matthew Edmunds, an aerospace engineer, which had left him paralysed from the neck down. Evans was on bail for a previous violent offence when the attack took place in the centre of Stroud. The exception which the guidelines allowed could not be more clearly demonstrated, yet the judge played it safe under cover of a public protest.[427] In another case, typical of many, a judge publicly declared he despaired of the guidelines which prevented him from sending a serial offender to prison. But, as he clearly felt justice was not being met by pursuing the rules, he could have ignored them – but chose not to.[428]

Thus, the law-makers appear to have given the judges, at least on paper, flexibility to decide on the severity or otherwise of the sentence, but, as argued, few will depart from what the Council directs. The public are frequently treated to a legal pantomime in which many judges complain of the restraints placed upon them and pass sentences they say they do not agree with, while officials point out that the law has left it up to the judges to decide what to do. When under fire, both sides can point the finger of responsibility toward the other. For example, a previous Lord Chief Justice, faced with criticism over guidelines issued by the previous SGC which said that young violent muggers need not go to prison if they only used minimal force, appeared, as head of the judiciary, to blame the advice sent down from the Sentencing Advisory Panel (of which he was chairman) to the Sentencing Guidelines Council.[429]

In 2014, a senior judge fumed at politicians after he was forced to hand a dangerous sex offender a lenient sentence. Only a few weeks after his early release from prison for child pornography offences, the criminal concerned offended again. But although he was sent back to prison to complete his original sentence, the judge complained that the law prevented him from sentencing the offender additionally for the new offence.[430]

It is highly probable that judges, valuing their independence, find 'advice' irksome, but rarely, as stated, does this result in them displaying their independence by passing a more severe sentence than that recommended to them. For example, even though the guidelines specify that judges should consider how dangerous an offender is before releasing him (or her) into the community, it was revealed, that in 2013, judges had bailed scores of convicted killers, paedophiles, rapists, and other violent offenders. Predictably, hundreds of these offenders disappeared and failed to turn up for the sentencing hearing. During the same period, large numbers of violent crimes, including rapes and unlawful killings were known to have been committed by criminals allowed their freedom by being remanded on bail (rather than in custody).[431]

This is a cancer in our justice system that the authorities will not cut out. A few MPs and sometimes ministers speak out against this practice but to no avail. In fact, in 2013, legislation was passed which prevented courts from remanding in custody offenders over the age of 18 who had a history of absconding, committing offences while on bail, and witness intimidation, unless the offence was imprisonable. Two years later at least one magistrate resigned because of the threats this posed to the public. Gone were the days when they could put the interests of the public first – the new ruling allowed, as an exception, a remand in custody only if it was in the interests of the *defendant's* safety.[432]

The justice ministry admitted that in 2014 there were 38 murders and 19 cases of manslaughter committed by those on bail.[433] At least one in five murder suspects are on bail at the time of the killing;[434] the answer to a recent Freedom of Information request has shown that between one and two killings a week are committed by offenders on bail,[435] while an earlier assessment had put this at two a week.[436] Patrick Sallabank was bailed for the alleged rape of a 16-year-old girl. While waiting for his trial, he raped another female teenager. In 2010 an ambulance technician Jonathon Vass was jailed for at least 30 years for the murder of his former girl friend while on bail for her rape.[437]

These are avoidable crimes, yet despite the extent of this problem the justice system has stubbornly refused to change course. In the 1990s the Home Office rejected calls from the victim's parents for an official enquiry after their 26-year-old daughter, Anna McGurk, was raped and murdered by Andrew Hagans, a dangerous offender awaiting trial on bail for a previous violent sex attack.[438] Hagans had originally been remanded in custody in Gloucester prison, but was released by Cheltenham magistrates to a bail hostel. Why? The victim's father was disgusted and perplexed by this decision. He pointed out that the magistrates knew that Hagans had at least twelve previous court appearances, and was a serial sex offender.

In 2008, the then Shadow Justice Secretary Dominic Grieve, publicly declared that the murders and rapes committed by offenders on bail was 'shocking' and the result of the government's reckless bail provision.[439] But less than two years later, when he was in government as the Attorney General he listened politely during a meeting with John and Penny Clough, the parents of a nurse, murdered by her former partner – once again an example of a killing by someone on bail at the time for a previous violent sex attack. As far as is known, he offered them no assurances that the conditions for bail would be tightened,[440] and no changes were announced following his meeting with the distraught couple.

The establishment regards the protests made by grieving families in these circumstances as so much emotional verbiage. Within a short while they can be disregarded and forgotten. It is much more concerned about keeping prison numbers down at almost any cost to the public. As the same time, there is no proper accountability for those judges and magistrates who make decisions that the public are left to conclude are cowardly or incompetent, or both. In one such example, a violent career criminal, Liam Kilroe from Billinge, near St Helens, Merseyside, was charged with two armed robberies. The police pleaded with the magistrates not to bail him because they knew he was dangerous. Kilroe had previous convictions for violence and other crimes going back nine years, and these included robbery with violence. Given the circumstances, the case for a remand in custody could not have been more obvious. But the magistrates remanded him on bail.

Did they go against all considerations for public safety because they took the view that Kilroe was someone in need of their protection against aggressive and unwarranted police claims, or were they responding to pressure to keep criminals out of jail? Whatever the reason for their decision the results were never in doubt. Within days Kilroe attacked a shop-keeper in Birleywood, Skelmersdale, with a knife in an attempt to rob him. A fight ensued during which the shopkeeper, Mr Singh, was wounded in the head, and Kilroe was killed by being stabbed through the heart with his own knife. In the aftermath, Mr Singh was arrested on suspicion of murder and the justice system preoccupied itself with whether he should face trial. It paid no attention to the near criminal incompetence of the court that had allowed Kilroe his freedom.[441]

In the same year 47-year-old Garry Newlove was kicked to death outside his own home in Cheshire by 19-year-old Adam Swellings and two other teenagers, when he tried to stop them vandalising his car. This was yet another example of a killing while on bail; at the time he committed the murder, Swellings was waiting to appear in court for seven separate offences, including violence.[442] Did the court that bailed him simply ignore Swellings long list of previous convictions and charges or think they were of no account? Although it is known that the magistrate responsible is a wealthy individual who lives in an up-market area, it is unlikely that even he did not understand the threat posed by Swelling if he were freed. We are again left to conclude that the magistrate must have known what the right course of action was but put it aside in favour of pandering to the establishment's wishes that he knew would put the public at risk. This was a cowardly response from a public servant who would have little to lose (except his self-perceived status) should he be sanctioned or dismissed for defying the guidelines by doing his duty and putting the protection of the public first. A law-abiding member of the public, Raymond Grange, wrote a string of campaign letters to his local paper warning against the folly of soft sentencing and urged a tougher approach 'before it is too late'. This was grimly prophetic. He was set upon by a gang of known thugs and stamped to death, simply because he happened to cross their path. One of his killers had been freed from jail just two days earlier, released on bail while awaiting trial on other violence charges.[443]

# 6

## Black Cap to White Flag: Killing, Violence

## and the Demise of the Death Penalty

Few subjects have stirred the hearts (but not always the minds) of the British as much as the debate over the death penalty. While it raised its head from time to time in parliament during the 18th and 19th centuries, it was during the period 1945 to 1964 that our soul-searching over capital punishment reached a dramatic climax. Throughout these years it dominated a great deal of time in both the Commons and the Lords, as those in favour of capital punishment tried to keep the small but powerfully organised abolitionist clique of MPs at bay. The verbatim Hansard reports show that many of the debates were largely dominated by emotive issues of individual conscience and personal ideology, and a failure to recognise (or refusal to admit) the influence of the death penalty in keeping our homicide rate as stable as it had been for a period of at least 75 years before 1965, when it was abolished.

Above all, the debates were dominated by the fanatic zeal of Sydney Silverman, an acid tongued and clever lawyer whose ability to verbally bully, reduce and intimidate opponents, did much to ensure many of those opposed to abolition, kept quiet. He made no attempt to hide his elitist contempt for public opinion which remained solidly in favour of retaining the death penalty, and it is beyond question that his influence and that of his small band of supporters was largely responsible for the eventual success of the abolitionists, when in 1964, parliament voted to suspend the death penalty for murder for five years, after which period it was finally abolished. No doubt he and his tiny group of followers believed in the virtue of their actions. But almost 50 years after this momentous change, we can only guess what their reactions might have been if they had lived to see the terrible price paid by the public for their victory.

A striking feature of the anti-death penalty campaign in Britain, going back as far as the mid-19th century, is that it has always been conducted against a background of solid public support for its retention. For example, in the 1860s, abolitionist agitation by John Bright, and a Royal Commission on Capital Punishment, found no support for it. The same was true of pressure from a minority group of Labour party activists in the 1930s.[444]

Although, since the early 21st century, there has been some shift in opinion away from the death penalty, most polls have continued to show a majority of the public in favour of its retention, in some form or other. Even in 1948, when the Commons finally voted in favour of Silverman's proposal to suspend the death penalty for five years, (this was overturned by the Lords) this was clearly in conflict with what the public wanted.[445]

Many in the upper house referred to the irony that it was they, and not their elected representatives, who were standing by public opinion. A high moralistic atmosphere was whipped up in the Commons during these debates with claims by many abolitionist MPs that the death penalty had no place in a civilised society which believed in the principle of the sanctity of life. In 1948 for example, MP John Patten said, "I believe capital punishment is a foul thing, an unmitigated evil, a centre of pollution." Another MP, Stanley Prescott, who had voted for suspension, felt more than a pang of conscience soon after. Following the vote, Prescott sent 39,840 reply postcards to his electors in Darwen, in Lancashire, asking whether they approved or disapproved of his action in voting for suspension of the death penalty. A third replied, (14,454) 718 approved, and 13,736 opposed what he had done. Prescott never again sided with the abolitionist cause.[446]

It is interesting to recall that it was not an MP, but Lord Salisbury, the Leader of the House of Lords, who during the 1948 debate, had put the case for the public, in his famous observation:

> "This (whether to abolish the death penalty) is a great issue. Only the people should decide great issues, unless they arise so suddenly that there is not time to consult them. In this case, there was plenty of time, but the advocates of abolition failed in their duty; they did not consult the people. There is good reason to believe that if the people had been consulted, they would have objected strongly. So, abolitionist Members are not only ignoring their electors, but defying them. The public must be trusted all the time, and we must be guided by their views when they are ascertainable, whether we personally consider them right or wrong. Anything else makes nonsense of our democracy".[447]

Sixteen years later, towards the end of the 1964 debate that resulted in the vote for abolition, Sydney Silverman stated that the test for keeping the death penalty would be that, "we have fewer murders when we have the death penalty, than when we do not have the death penalty." He added that, "this was the only rational ground on which the death penalty could be defended."[448] The steady increase in the homicide rate which began soon after abolition shows that by the terms of Silverman's own test the death penalty should have been retained. But no parliamentary or official voice dared utter this fact. It was ignored. On 16th December 1969, the House of Commons voted, 343 to 185 that the Murder (Abolition of the Death Penalty)

Act 1964, should not expire, thus permanently abolishing capital punishment for murder in Britain. On 20th May 1998. MPs, in a free vote during a debate on the Human Rights Bill, voted by 294 votes to 136 to adopt provisions of the European Convention on Human Rights, outlawing capital punishment for murder.

By then the homicide rate per 100,000 of the population had risen to 1.4, more than double what it was in 1963. But again, the legislators sealed themselves off from this reality – a cowardly omission by those whose job it is to represent the public's wishes and interests – and, eight months later, on 27 January 1999, the UK Home Secretary formally signed the 6th protocol of the European Convention of Human Rights in Strasbourg, on behalf of the British government, formally abolishing the death penalty in the UK. In so doing our ruling elite had made it clear that a public declaration of their doctrinaire principles was more important to them than the majority wishes of the public. In effect, parliamentarians had behaved as if they were members of a private club responsible only to themselves, concerned among other things, I would argue, not to be judged as uncivilised, and be seen by all as virtuous men and women, no matter what their private convictions may have been.

The following summary of poll results spanning over 60 years brings this point home, as they show the resilience of the public's view on this matter.

1948:

A *Daily Express* poll, a Gallop poll and a Mass-Observation poll, showed that 77%, 66% and 69% of the public respectively, disapproved of the 1948 Commons vote to suspend the death penalty. The strength of public opinion on this matter may be judged from the fact that despite the opportunity given by the Mass-Observation poll to respondents to choose middle-ground alternative answers, 69% of them still opted for the straight 'No' choice. No matter how the results were analysed, as between, for example, age, sex, income, or area, no differences from the main findings were found. While a majority of Labour MPs had voted for suspension, only 16% of the labour-supporting public did so.[449]

1953–1955:

The results of 3 Gallop polls, October 1953, July 1955, and December 1955, taken together, showed the public firmly in favour of retaining the death penalty, with 73%, 50% and 61% majorities respectively.[450]

1956:

Results from a Mass-Observation poll showed 49% in favour of the death penalty, with 18% against and 25% who had not made up their minds.[451]

2003–2011

More recent polling has continued to show a majority in favour of the death penalty in some form.[452] For example:

| | YouGov | Mori | Angus Reid |
|---|---|---|---|
| 2003 | 57% for murder<br>62% for murder of police officer<br>67% for murder of child<br>69% for a serial killer<br>63% would have hanged Huntley | | |
| 2006 | 49% for murder (1st time this has fallen below 50%) | | |

| 2008 | | | 50% for murder |
|---|---|---|---|
| 2010 | 51% for murder | 50% for murder | |
| 2010 | Certain cicumsrances 62% for child murder 70% in at least some circumstances 16% all murders | | |

In 2014, a YouGov poll reported 45% in favour and 39% opposed to the death penalty; in 2015 a NatCen poll suggested support for it was just below 50%.[453]

Contributors to the death penalty debates between 1945 and 1964, generally failed to appreciate or draw on the lessons of several hundred years of social, political and legal history, which showed that the decline in homicide rates from the 13th century was associated with the gradual establishment of a formalised system of law and order which increased the possibility of killers and other criminals being detained and facing retribution from the state.

There is now general agreement that homicide rates in England during the Middle Ages were significantly higher than they are today. Historians James Given[454] and T.R. Gurr,[455] (both found in Manuel Eisner, *The Long Term Historical Trends in Violent Crime*) for example, estimate homicide rates of between 15 and 20 per 100,000 of the population in the 13th century, dropping to around 10 in 1600, and eventually falling to approximately 1 per 100,000 in the 20th century.

The following table gives an overview of these figures.[456] [457] [458]

| Period | Homicide rate per 100,000 of the population |
|---|---|
| 13th | 20.0 |
| 16th | 5.4 |
| 17th (1st half) | 5.9 |
| 17th (2nd half) | 3.5 |
| 18th (1st half) | 2.1 |
| 18th (2nd half) | 1.5 |
| 1800–1824 | 1.2 |
| 1825–1849 | 1.7 |
| 1850–1874 | 1.6 |
| 1875–1899 | 1.3 |
| 1900–1924 | 0.8 |
| 1925–1949 | 0.8 |
| 1950–1974 | 0.7 |
| 1975–1994 | 1.2 |
| 1995–2011 | 1.4 |

Improvements in medical care have also influenced the number of homicides, as modern techniques have saved the lives of many who would otherwise have died from injuries sustained as the result of violence. However, at the very moment these medical improvements began to make an impact, that is, from the 1970s, our homicide rate started to rise for the first time in hundreds of years. In fact, between 1950 and the turn of the millennium it doubled, despite these medical advances.

Of course, it is also likely that extreme poverty may have been a factor contributing to violence and killing for some at various stages in our history. But, according to historians J. A. Sharpe,[459] and Clive Emsley,[460] poverty was not the only motivation for crimes committed between the 16th and 19th centuries; likewise, the records of those transported to Australia in the 18th century show that while hunger and the need to survive may have been a factor in the crimes of some of them, many of those sentenced were persistent criminals who had chosen criminality as a way of life.[461]

Our homicide rate started to rise in 1974, not because of poverty or hunger, as such conditions no longer existed, but, I would argue, when the effect of lenient sentencing policies and the absence of the death penalty began to make their impact. While the penological liberals might not like it, it is difficult to argue against the broad conclusion that the dramatic falls in the homicide rate in England between the 13th and 20th centuries were associated, as previously argued, with the gradual imposition of law and order, with eventually, an organised constabulary increasing the possibility that those who killed would be caught, tried and if found guilty, face the threat of the ultimate punishment – death by hanging at the hands of the State.

Those in favour of the abolition of the death penalty argue that it is morally wrong to execute offenders because it as an offence against the principle of the 'sanctity of life'. They have also argued that it is arbitrary, inconsistent in its application, that it is open to error, irreversible and cruel. Furthermore, they claim that evidence shows that the death penalty does not act as a deterrent. To support their view, they cite countries such as the US, that have retained the death penalty but have high homicide rates. But the evidence from several American studies contradicts this conclusion.[462] [463]

The statistics from the numerous studies on which this latter possibility is based are impressive and together they conclude that between three and eighteen lives are saved by the execution of each convicted killer.[464] [465] Thus the 'sanctity of life' argument can be turned on its head, and therefore, because it saves lives, the death penalty can be viewed as morally obligatory – a disturbing conclusion for many.

The United States, following its Supreme Court ruling, suspended capital punishment in 1972. This ruling was reversed in 1976. The US execution and homicide data for the periods before, during and after the suspension of capital punishment is highly instructive. As the number of executions came down between 1930 and 1972, so the homicide rate went up, and it noticeably increased during the period when there was no death penalty.[466] When the number of executions started to rise after 1976 the homicide rate began to fall. In 1980 it was 10.2 per 100,000 of the population; by 2000 it had halved and was 5.5. It is now 4.5.[467]

Likewise, in 1980 the homicide rate in Texas was 16.9 per 100,000 of the population, and by the turn of the millennium it had dropped to 5.9, following its reinstatement of the death penalty in 1982, despite a population increase of 32%, from 14 million to almost 21 million. It is now lower still at 4.4.[468] [469] US criminal justice statistics indicate that violent crime and homicide rates have continued to fall for the United States generally, well into the second decade of the 21st century and places as far apart as New York and Los Angeles can claim that they are now much safer places to live in than they were in the late 1980s.[470] [471] This trend continues. Figures published in 2017 for New York, showed that the numbers of homicides for that year were a sixth of what they were in 1990.[472]

The other familiar objections to capital punishment mentioned above, do *not* argue in favour of abolition, because the world of homicide suffers from those same problems in even more acute form and in larger numbers. To state the obvious, the loss of life at the hands of a killer is irreversible; and such deaths will forever be seen by the victim's families and the wider public as wrong, arbitrary, and cruel.

In Britain, wrongful executions were a rarity. In the US, according to the Death Penalty Information Centre, there have been since 1976, perhaps 13 executions in which there was evidence of innocence.[473] This is less than 1% of the 1,359 executions that have taken place during the same period.[474] In contrast, the equally wrongful deaths in the US of those killed by criminals over the same time span, amounts to approximately 70,000, a figure that would probably be higher if it were not for the presence of the death penalty.

A similar argument can be applied to England and Wales. Since

1976 there have been approximately 22,000 criminal homicides, which the following analysis strongly suggests would have been considerably fewer had the death penalty not been abolished. The following graph shows the number of homicides (per 100,000 of the population) per year in England and Wales from 1950 to 2016. This reveals a remarkable period of stability with the homicide rate staying between 0.5 and 1 (available data indicates this stable trend stretched back to at least 1898). In 1974 it began to rise, an indication, I would argue, that it took ten years for the abolition of the death penalty in 1964 to influence the number of killings.[475] [476] [477] [478] [479] This long period of stability in the homicide rate may have encouraged those who disagreed with the death penalty to believe that its presence had no effect on would-be killers. The threat of the hangman's noose, they could argue, did not cause the number of homicides to fall.

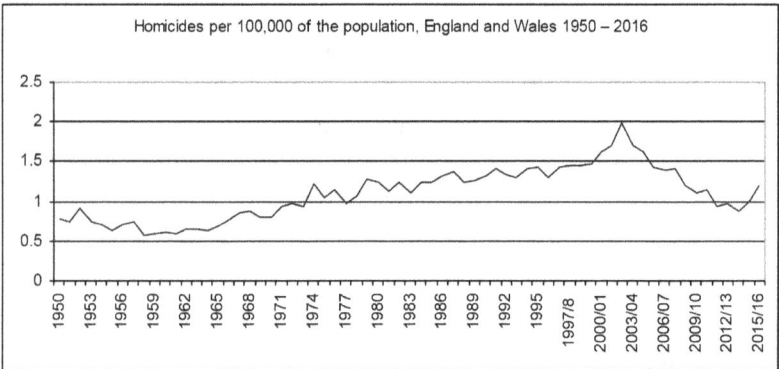

Homicides per 100,000 of the population, England and Wales 1950 – 2016

Sources:

1898–2001: Data.GOV A Summary of Recorded Crime Data 1898–2001

2002–2011: Home Office Statistical Bulletin Crime in England and Wales 2010/11 HOSB 10/11

2011–2012: Home Office Statistics, Crime in England and Wales, 2012.

2012–2014: Office for National Statistics, Crime in England and Wales 2014

2014–2016 Office for National Statistics, quoted in 'Murder increase sparks warnings from police chief. *The Times*, 20 January, 20

Even the respected Sir Ernest Gower, in his report to the Royal Commission on Capital Punishment in 1953, had misinterpreted the previous 50-year period of stability in homicide numbers as indicating that, "there was no convincing statistical evidence that it was a deterrent".[480] While, as stated, this belief may have shored up the convictions of some MPs, who later argued against capital punishment, this was a misreading of the data. As long ago as the 1880s, Samuel Romilly, in his famous treatise on the death penalty, pointed out the hidden factor in the homicide statistics as being those whose propensity to kill was held in check because of the presence of the death penalty.[481] His warning was prophetic, because following its abolition in Britain, the homicide rate had, as indicated earlier, doubled by the turn of the millennium.[482] Such a statistical fact makes it difficult, to say the least, to hang on to the old doubts concerning its influence. But this understanding has come too late in the day for the hundreds killed by violent criminals every year, many by killers freed from prison to kill again since the death penalty was abolished, and it has meant little or nothing to post 1964 governments and most MPs, who, to this day, have refused to stir on the matter.

Thus, what the graph illustrates is that the increase in the number of homicides involved violent people who were previously restrained from killing because of their fear of the gallows, and who were sane and knew what they were doing. This interpretation is supported by the fact that there has been, since abolition, a significant fall in the proportion of homicides committed by insane or disturbed individuals whose troubled state of mind and conscience about what they had done led them to commit suicide after they had killed their victim. The absolute numbers of these homicide-suicide cases have not changed a great deal, but as a proportion of all homicides, their numbers have noticeably dropped. Before abolition in 1964 a third of murders were followed by suicide,[483] but by 2014 they had fallen to 4%.[484]

On the other hand, the proportion of killers formally diagnosed as insane (who rarely commit suicide after killing) has remained consistently low, and for over twenty years has stayed between 0.1% and 0.9% of all homicides.[485]

This, I suggest, explains why the homicide rate remained stable for so long. A larger proportion of killings during the period 1889 to 1974 were carried out either by those who, as discussed in the previous chapters, were so dangerous that no form of punishment, no matter how draconian, would deter them from killing, or by sane individuals experiencing a period of instability for whom, likewise, the presence of the death penalty made no difference. (Of note is that multiple killers, who fit such a profile, were found by US research, not to be deterred by the threat of the death penalty, although single killers were).[486] To restate, the noticeable increase in the homicide rate since abolition reflects that far more homicides are now committed by violent criminals, often with long criminal track records, whereas previously, offenders with such profiles were prepared and able to control their violent propensities and stop short of killing because of the fear of the hangman's noose, but who, with this threat removed, felt it much safer to give them full vent.

In an example, which can be replicated in hundreds every year, Mark Hampson, in 2002, was sentenced for the murder of a 26-year-old woman. He had stabbed her 81 times and smashed her skull into fragments.[487] As is often the case, he was found to have had a long history of frightening violent criminality pre-dating this murder, going back more than twenty years. He had been in and out of prison for 15 years and his previous crimes included slashing the face of a man with a knife, and attacking someone with a brick. When he killed his young female victim, he was on bail for serious firearm offences. As argued, his violent profile is typical of many of the perpetrators who now make up the homicide statistics, those who have no conscience about taking someone's life, and who enjoy violence and the rewards it brings them; it is their numbers which have substantially increased since hanging was abolished. For those with the propensity for it, killing is much less risky than it was before 1964 – because hanging has not been replaced with a sentence providing the same deterrent value.

Over recent years the cement has hardened over the politics surrounding this issue; pressure from the European Court, the fear of derision at the hands of abolitionists who remain fiercely intolerant of further discussion, and an understandable fear of wrongful convictions, have effectively stopped any further debate on the subject. No one has dared to argue, even in hindsight, that the death penalty was an effective deterrent, or that, in its absence, we need a sanction that is viewed with similar dread by violent criminals. As matters stand, we abandoned a system which between 1900 and 1964, saw, on average, just over 11 hangings and 300 homicides per year, for one with no hangings, fictitious sentences of 'life imprisonment', that, generally, last no more than 16 years, and close to twice the number of criminal homicides every year.[488] Likewise, there has been little notice taken of the fact that the number of policemen deliberately killed every year by violent criminals has on average, doubled since the death penalty was abolished.[489]

Many violent offenders, born for example, in the 1920s, 1930s, and 1940s were, in 1964, of age to notice the difference abolition made to their chances of survival if they killed someone, and the figures show, as suggested, that it took ten years for this to begin impacting on the public, when the homicide rate started to increase in 1974. What Britain has witnessed is the effect of two post-abolition generations of violent offenders with no awareness of the threat of the hangman. If we accept the idea that children under ten years do not generally think about such things as capital punishment, and therefore have no real awareness of it, then this concept would encompass not only those children born after abolition in 1964, but those born after 1954. Thus, by 1974, when the homicide rate started to accelerate, those with the propensity for violence would have reached their 20th birthday, fully able to exercise their violent capacities, free of the restraints imposed on earlier generations through fear of the hangman's noose. For example, in 1957 those under 21 years of age represented 14.7% of all males convicted of murder. By the early 1970s this figure had more than doubled to 32%.[490]

But many have argued that the increase in murder convictions since abolition is not due to an increase in violence, but is the result of the juries being more prepared to convict for murder since the death penalty was abolished. This long held myth is undermined by the evidence. If, as alleged, the increase in murder convictions reflected a change in the attitude of juries, freed from concerns that their decision might lead to the defendant being hanged, then we would have expected to see, after abolition in 1964, a fall in the percentage of homicides resulting in manslaughter convictions. But far from falling, they increased, and the number of murder convictions, (for all ages) as a percentage of all homicides, did not start to rise for another 16 years (in 1980).[491]

As indicated earlier, the recorded homicide numbers started to decline in 2009/10, but this fall was arrested in 2015 with a 14% increase to 574. This was 71 more than the previous year.[492] In 2016, the homicide numbers increased again to 695.[493] Whatever other factors may be at work behind these variations, one important influence on the homicide figures has been, as touched upon earlier, the improvements in medical care.

A report published in the British Medical Journal in 2002 highlighted that technological developments had helped to significantly depress homicide rates, because doctors were saving the lives of thousands of victims of violent, life threatening attacks, who four decades ago would have probably died, thus converting homicides into serious violent assaults. The lead author of the study pointed out that although the research was US-based, there was every reason to expect a similar trend in other developed countries.

The report stressed that these changes were particularly noticed after 1972, on the heels of the US involvement in the Vietnam War which triggered big advances in trauma care.[494]

This being the case, we would expect to see an increase in the numbers of the most seriously violent and life threatening crimes (short of homicide). The following graph for the period 1950–2013 (the last date for which this data could be found) shows that this is what has occurred, thus providing support for the contention that doctors are saving increased numbers of those subject to extreme violence.[495] [496] [497] [498]

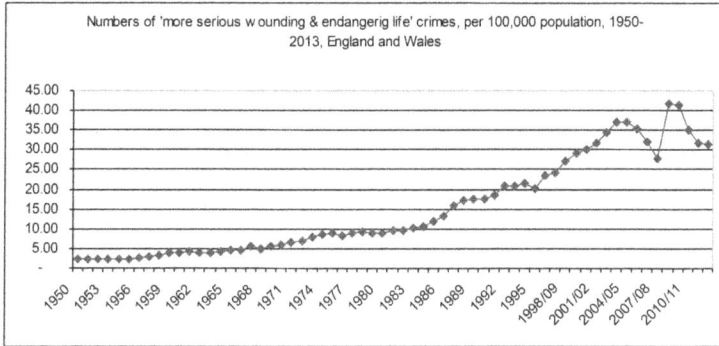

Numbers of 'more serious wounding & endangerig life' crimes, per 100,000 population, 1950-2013, England and Wales

Sources:

Data.GOV A Summary of Recorded Crime Data 1898–2001

Home Office Statistical Bulletin, Crime in England and Wales 2010/11, HOSB 10/11

National Statistics Crime in England and Wales, year ending June 2012, Appendix tables A4

National Statistics, Crimes detected in England and Wales 2012/13, Data Tables: Crimes detected in England and Wales 2012/13

In 1950 there were 2 of these crimes per 100,000 of the population, and in 2013 there were 31.[499] [500] [501] [502] In line with the developments outlined in the British Medical report, the increase can be seen to have been particularly noticeable from the early 1970s onwards.

Medical researchers have estimated that homicide numbers would be up to five times higher than they are if it had not been for the improvements in trauma care,[503] as illustrated by the graph below for England and Wales 1950-2015[504] [505] [506] [507] [508]

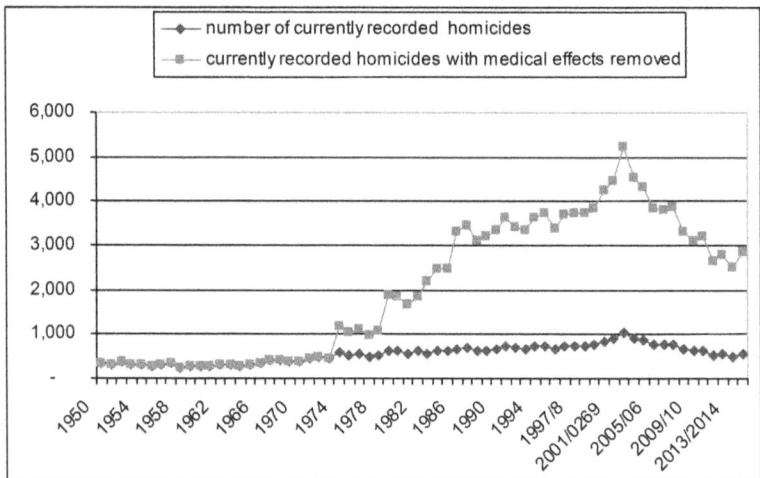

Source for homicide figures:

1950–2001: Data.GOV A Summary of Recorded Crime Data 1898-2002

2002–2011: Home Office Statistical Bulletin Crime in England and Wales 2010/11 HOSB 10/11

2011–2012: Home Office Statistics, Crime in England and Wales, 2012

2012–2014: Office for National Statistics, Crime in England and Wales 2014

2014–2015: Office for National Statistics, Crime in England and Wales 2015: see also 'Homicide in England and Wales up 14%' the *Guardian* 21 January 2016

In 2015, for example, there would not have been 574 currently recorded homicides but 2,870. Thus, medical science has masked the full effects of the rise in violence. Had it not been for the skilled intervention by physicians, for example, Mrs Monckton (referred to in chapter 3) may well have died, in addition to her husband, following the violent assault on them in their Chelsea home by serial criminals Damien Hanson and Elliot White, leaving their nine-year-old daughter to face life as an orphan.

Yet despite the importance of these medical advances and the serious qualifications they make to the homicide figures, they have never, in the author's knowledge, been referred to in any official criminal justice document. Homicide is arguably the crime of deepest concern to the public, and should therefore be of the highest concern to government officials and the factors affecting it should be reported on extensively to those they are supposed to represent. But no government statistical bulletin displaying homicide statistics has, as far as I know, referred to the influence of medical advances on these figures, even in a footnote.

Homicide numbers may also be under-recorded because some of the thousands who disappear every year and are never traced, may have been unlawfully killed. According to some police sources 275,000 persons go missing every year in Britain, the equivalent of the population of Plymouth.[509] Most are found within a day or two, but some have vanished without a trace. Many of those who have never been found were known to be ordinary people with no more than the usual pressures of everyday living, endured safely by millions, and so suicide or some other voluntary act can be reasonably ruled out. For example, three years ago, 60-year-old Susan Grey went for a walk with her dog and disappeared. In 2003, a seven-year-old boy, John Fletcher simply vanished. Likewise, in 2009, a 14-year-old Glasgow schoolboy inexplicably disappeared and has never been seen since.

The official line is that cases of this kind represent only a tiny number of all of those listed as missing, but sources nearer the police rank and file indicate that every year as many as 20,000 are still not traced after one year. If only a small minority, let us say 5%, of these were the result of violence and their bodies never found, it would add another 1000 homicides per year to the official total. Figures from the National Crime Agency put the annual missing persons total, for the year 2012–2013, as 306,000, with 97% found safe and well, most within 48 hours.[510] This meant that over 9,000 were *not* found. If we assume once again that in the overwhelming majority of these cases there were no suspicious circumstances to consider, but in 5% there were, this leaves, for the year in question, 459 persons for whom foul play was the likely cause of their disappearance, but which were not included in the homicide figures.

The Home Office view of this problem is, as one might expect, far more conservative. They conclude that of all those that go missing 2,000 people are still missing after one year.[511] If only 5% had been murdered this would add another 100 to the homicide total. Figures provided by ten police forces in 2012 for the number of fatal outcomes arising from their missing persons data, enable us to compute an estimate of 614 fatalities for all 42 forces, associated with missing persons. The source of this data, the UK Missing Persons Bureau, gives four possible explanations for these deaths as suicide, accidents, natural causes or violent crime.[512] On that basis, if we assume one quarter of the 614 total was due to violence then this would add another 154 to the homicide total for the period concerned (2010–2011). On the other hand, a quarter of the National Crime Agency figure of 9,000 persons still missing after one year in 2013, would add over 2,000 to the homicide figure for that period.

Double killer Christopher Halliwell murdered 20-year-old Becky Goddard in 2003 and he buried her body in a field in Gloucestershire. At Bristol Crown Court the judge sentenced him to a whole life term and said that had it not been for Halliwell's confession, he had no doubt her body would never have been found. Had this been the case she would have remained a statistic on the list of missing persons, following her disappearance from her home area in Swindon in 2003.[513]

Weight is added to this argument by the discovery of over 60 dead bodies, all of them hitherto missing persons, over a five-year period in the canal systems around Manchester.[514] Some of them bore the marks of a violent attack. It is highly improbable that this will be the only place in Britain where bodies have lain undetected. Experience has shown how effectively a corpse can be hidden and impossible for the police to find, even when they are given clues to its whereabouts, as was the case in the search for the body of 12-year-old Keith Bennett murdered by Ian Brady and Myra Hindley in 1964. They carried out the notorious 'Moors murders' between July 1963 and October 1965. Their victims were five children and young people aged between 10 and 17. Three of the victims were discovered in graves dug on Saddleworth Moor, near Manchester. But, as stated, the body of 12-year-old Keith Bennett was never found, despite extensive excavation by the police after Brady had guided them to the part of the moor where he claimed the boy was buried.

In the process between the finding of a dead body and the conclusion it is or is not a homicide, there are several decision points. Research spanning more than sixty years has consistently found numbers of errors made at the original site by the police and later by coroners, and, further down the investigation chain, by both non-forensic and forensic pathologists' examinations. D. Harvard's research in 1960 concluded 'many homicides are missed each year' and referred to a 1958 investigation which found that one fifth of 1,404 cases, certified as natural deaths, were found to be wrong. In another albeit smaller example, seven out of eight exhumations were found to be missed homicides due to inadequate investigations.[515]

In 2015, an audit by the Forensic Pathology Unit of the Home Office found that out of the 32 cases which, in 2012, had been referred from non-forensic to forensic pathologists for further examination, the latter had made serious mistakes in 15 of them, or 47%. Ten (later) confirmed homicides had been missed as well as five cases showing 'suspicious circumstances'.[516] No extrapolation can be made from this to deduce what this might represent as a percentage of all 'investigations of unexplained deaths', but at the very least these results indicate there can be a gap between the number of dead bodies classified as homicide, and those which actually are.

The report also identified that many of the 'non-homicide' decisions were based on whether the dead person was elderly, or known to be a drug user or an alcoholic. This could, potentially, be another source of error, if no further investigations were carried out, to determine the cause of death.

In 2009 it was reported that someone was attacked by a stranger every 30 seconds on British streets.[517] The increase in the number of 'stranger homicide' indicates that over the last 40 years street violence has become more freewheeling – any victim will do. In the five-year period 1967–71 the average percentage of homicides committed by strangers per year, was 5.2.[518] [519] For the period 2009–14 it was 25.6.[520] [521] [522] [523]

The percentage of homicide victims under 16 years old who were killed by strangers or unknown assailants has doubled in the last 21 years.[524] [525] In one chilling example, in 2013, a 14-year-old girl ordered the fatal stabbing of a 15-year-old boy. (Only forty years ago, such vengeful and malignant behaviour was generally the prerogative of mafia bosses and other hardened criminal gang leaders). The soon-to-be-dead 15-year-old boy had argued with her because she had interrupted his game of football on the estate where they lived. But these youngsters had grown up in an era of unstinting state leniency towards wrongdoing, and with such reduced risks for its perpetrators, violence is now turned to as the remedy for even trivial hurts and insults. As a true child of her time, the 14-year-old girl, requiring an immediate remedy for her hurt feelings following the argument, called her boyfriend, and she was heard to tell the victim, Junior Nkwelle, that she had arranged for someone to stab him. A short time later, the killer, 17-year-old Marc Anthony Tulloch, stabbed Junior through the heart. There was no history of previous contact between these two boys; there was no quarrel between them; they were strangers to each other.[526]

In the autumn of 2009, in an example of a killing that is not unusual on our streets, 30-year-old Ben Gardner was walking home with his girlfriend, 28-year-old Allana Devine, from a club in Sutton, South London, where they had been celebrating Ms Devine's birthday. En route, they were confronted by a gang of thugs, one of whom snatched the hat from the young women's head, and spat on it. The couple did not react and went on their way. A little later, they again encountered the same group, Daniel Ransom, 21, Ross Collender, 21 and Jordan Dixon, 18, all from Carshalton. Ms Devine asked them to return her hat, whereupon Collender, 'suddenly and unexpectedly', according to a witness, attacked Ben Gardner. Both Collender and Dixon punched Ben Gardner to the ground and then kicked him to death. A witness described it as if Collender was taking a 'penalty kick'. The attack was captured on CCTV and the trial judge noted the look of pleasure on the faces of the attackers after their onslaught.

All three were convicted of murder and given a life sentence, but as previously pointed out, this is a customary lie practised every day by British judges without falter or hint of embarrassment. Even though this attack was entirely unprovoked, Collender and Ransom were given minimum terms of 16 years and Dixon, 14 years. So, given their ages and the propensity of our parole board to believe that such people have, in many cases, a right to a normal life, no matter how malignant their crime, the likelihood of their release at or near their minimum terms is highly likely.

Both Collander and Dixon had between them at least 23 previous convictions, many for violence, including offences of ammunition and knife possession and several breaches of community orders. This case could not be more illustrative of the central point argued in this book, which is that had they been stopped in their tracks earlier with severe custodial sentences, this murder would not have taken place. But the court's lenient approach towards these offenders for their past crimes, (seen by them as a weakness which they could exploit), was such that on that fateful October night in 2009, they were out roaming the streets, free to kick Ben Gardner to death solely for the pleasure it gave them.[527]

Similar examples in which the victim's head is kicked repeatedly as if it were a football have been recorded on CCTV cameras or mobile telephones, and posted onto the internet. These brief film clips of life on Britain's streets are so violent and degraded of humanity that they are almost unwatchable. The scale of the increase in this problem can be seen from the fact that the average percentage of homicides brought about by hitting and kicking for the five-year period 1967–1971 was 2%.[528] [529] For the five-year period 2009–2014 it was 19%.[530] [531] It is often reported that many of the attackers had been drinking, but not everyone who drinks to excess becomes violent. Violent drunks have a violent propensity to begin with. Drunk or sober they are responsible for their behaviour, and drinking associated with violence is an aggravating factor, not one of mitigation, as is often argued by defence lawyers. In 2010, research published by the University of Manchester, reported that perpetrators of homicide under the age of 25 years were more likely to use hitting or kicking to kill their victims, who in turn, were more often young, male and a stranger to their attackers.[532]

Weapons are also used by assailants to inflict what frequently amounts to life threatening and sometimes fatal violence to resolve arguments or to what amount to no more than minor disputes. While the government figures indicate there has been a fall in the use of firearms by criminals, from over 24,000 in 2004 to 7,866 in 2015,[533] there has been a rise in the number of serious violent crimes in which knives were used. There were, in 2014, 200 homicides resulting from knife attacks, (in 2013 the figure was 195). The numbers of attempted murder involving knives also rose to 248, from 198 the previous year. Likewise, the number of other serious violence offences in which knives were used, such as assaults with injury with the intent to cause serious harm, rape, and other sexual assaults, all increased in 2014,[534] and again in 2015.[535]

From 1979 the numbers of 'threats to kill or conspiracy to murder' crimes started to rise, a trend which was to continue for a quarter of a century, until 2004, when they started to fall steeply, until 2013, when they once again substantially increased.[536] [537] [538] [539] [540]

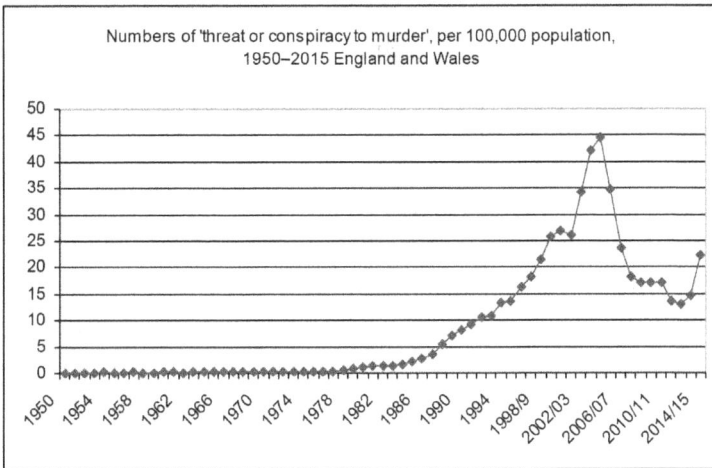

Numbers of 'threat or conspiracy to murder', per 100,000 population, 1950–2015 England and Wales

Sources:

1950–1996: Data.GOV A Summary of Recorded Crime Data 1898-2002

1997–2007: Crime in England and Wales 2010/2011

2008–2012: National Statistics Crime in England and Wales, year ending June 2012, Appendix tables A4

2012–2013: National Statistics, Crimes detected in England and Wales 2012/13, Data Tables: Crimes detected in England and Wales 2012/13

2014–2015: Statistica: The Statistics Portal

But did the numbers of these crimes *actually* fall? It is difficult to believe that large numbers of criminals would all agree at the end of 2004, to control their urge to threaten people with murder. Indeed, it is known that violent intimidation generally remains a serious problem for victims and the courts in their efforts to bring violent offenders to justice. Does the decline, from 2004, show an increased willingness by the prosecution authorities to reclassify this offence and call it something else? And or, are we looking at an example of those changes in police recording tactics discussed in an earlier chapter, in which more offences of this sort are declared 'no crimes', or are downgraded to a lesser charge, or made to disappear in some other way? It was in 2004, we must recall, that the police reverted to their previous crime recording practices which included various ways of 'losing crimes', to meet crime reduction targets. Despite this, (if this is what occurred) in 2013 the number of these crimes started to rise again, and of significance is that the number of threats to kill in which knives were used also increased by 11% in 2014.[541]

Available data strongly suggest that immigrants to Britain now commit a significant proportion of homicides as well as other serious violent crimes. A Freedom of Information Act request revealed that immigrants to England and Wales make up almost one in every five people charged with murder or rape.[542] This data supplied by 43 police forces showed that the suspects came from all over the globe, and that in total 91 foreign nationals were charged with murder (17% of the total murder charges for that year) and another 406 immigrants were put before the courts accused of having carried out a rape attack (18% of the total rape charges).

In London alone, of the 547 people charged with rape, a total of 174, or more than 30%, were non-UK citizens. These included people from Afghanistan, Angola, Ghana, Macedonia, Russia, Zimbabwe and Chile to name but some. The nations whose individuals were charged the most frequently for rape in the capital were Jamaica (19), Nigeria (11), Poland (10), Australia (9), Bangladesh (7), Italy (7), Romania (7), and Somalia (7). In

London, a total of 197 people were charged with murder and 40 of these were immigrants (20%), including five people from Jamaica, four people from Pakistan and four from Poland, and three from Somalia and three from Bangladesh.

In addition to the capital, other police forces had a major multinational dimension to their investigations of serious violent crimes. These included:

Thames Valley: a total of 21 out of the 97 people, charged with rape, were born abroad (22%). These included four from India, three from Romania and two from Iraq and two from Zimbabwe.

Sussex police, who charged five non-UK nationals with murder. Three were Poles, one a South African and one a Lithuanian. Of two charged with rape, one was from Kazakhstan and the other from Uzbekistan.

South Yorkshire police: of the 22 people charged with murder, six came from outside of the UK (27%); two from Bangladesh, one each from Somalia, Iraq, Afghanistan and the Czech Republic.

Hertfordshire: Out of the 30 people charged with rape, a total of eight were born outside of the UK (27%), including one from Venezuela and one from Nepal.

Gwent: Police charged ten people with murder, six came from the UK and the remaining four came from Poland (67%).

Kent: Five out of the 17 people charged with murder came from Afghanistan (29%) and four of the 76 charged with rape came from Lithuania (5%).

Avon and Somerset: The police charged 13 non-UK nationals with rape from a total of 98 (13%). These included people who were born in Togo, Sierra Leone, Tunisia, Ghana, Somalia, Zimbabwe, Nigeria, Poland and Lithuania.

But while foreigners may be responsible for anything up to 20% of the worst violent crimes in our country, they only make up just over 6% of the 48 million adults in Britain. Why is this? It is not because foreigners are generally more violent than we are, but that over the last twenty years, we have imported into our country a tidal wave of other people's gangsters, career criminals and violent thugs, along with law-abiding immigrants. Eight years ago, (in 2008), a Lithuanian police chief claimed that the entire underworld of Vilnius was now in Britain, (no doubt an exaggeration but nevertheless, a pointer to a serious problem) and because they are EU citizens we cannot deport them, even on occasions when they are convicted of crimes, as our liberal judges frequently rule in their favour, allowing them to stay.[543] Could we conclude from this that one of the reasons so many foreign criminals want to live in Britain is not only due to our generous benefit system, which they can take advantage of when their criminal earnings are low, but because they have heard that our courts are prepared to be tolerant even when dealing with life-threatening violent crimes?

In 2011, 33-year-old Kuba Dlugosz, a career criminal on the run from authorities in Poland, broke into the home of an 83-year-old Miss Kelmerson, in Stamford Hill, north London. He tied her up, robbed her and then left her to die from hypothermia. He had twice been arrested by British police in the weeks before the burglary, but his fingerprint records were not checked against those of his home country, an omission that was to cost Miss Kelmerson her life.[544] Despite this, Dlugosz was given an indeterminate sentence but with a minimum tariff of only seven years.

Another Polish criminal, Damien Brauer, 21, on the run from jail in his home country, slipped into Britain under the noses of Border Control officials. Sometime later, in Ipswich during the early hours of 27 May, 2007, he stabbed 19-year-old Matthew Buckman several times in the back and neck following an altercation.[545] The Home Office later admitted they did not even know he was in the country. Brauer also received an indeterminate sentence but with a minimum tariff of only 27 months.

A recent analysis by Robert Rowthorn, from Cambridge University, of the benefits and costs of immigration to this country, concluded that the benefits were not only modest, but overwhelmed by the costs in terms of strains and stresses on our infrastructure, such as housing, land, schools, hospitals, water supply, and transport systems.[546] However, his analysis left out the economic and social costs of the crimes committed by immigrants. This is a significant omission, given, as indicated, that the figures from the Freedom of Information question concerning non-British suspected of violent crime, suggest that, even if not all of them were convicted, they are responsible for many of the worst kinds of violent crime, namely killing and rape.

Home Office data indicates that as a generalisation, killer and victim belong to the same ethnic group. Figures published in 1999 indicated that 92% of white homicide victims were killed by white perpetrators and the majority of black victims, i.e. 70%, were likewise killed by black assailants; and 66% of Asian homicide victims were struck down by Asian attackers.[547] Data published 14 years later showed small changes to this picture. For example, fewer white people were involved in the killing of black victims, 13% as opposed to 24%, and also in the killing of Asian victims, 19% as opposed to 28%. Whereas in 1999 there were no black suspects associated with the killing of Asians, the later figure indicated that 10% were. The percentage of Asian homicide victims killed by Asian people remained the same, i.e. 66%.[548] The same data also indicated that for all three ethnic groups referred to here, knives were the most used weapon in killing, and that 'hitting and kicking' was the second most used method. Black homicide victims were far more likely to have been shot than whites or Asian victims, and a greater percentage of white victims were kicked to death than was the case for black or Asian homicide victims.

While the increase in violence and killing that has taken place since the 1960s has, generally, touched most parts of the country, the capital has become a particularly dangerous place, with a higher homicide rate than for the country as a whole. In 2015 for London, it was 1.4 per 100,000 of the population,[549] and for the whole country was 1.0.[550] [551] In that year, for example, if the homicide rate for the whole of the country had been the same as that for London, there would have been 810 homicides instead of 573. London, for example, is now more dangerous and crime ridden than New York, with more rapes, robberies and other violent offences.[552]

An analysis by the police of 125 homicides showed that in 28% of the cases, the victim was the same nationality as the attacker, a lesser proportion than indicated by the statistics for the country generally, suggesting a higher rate of inter-race killings in the Capital. The youngest killer in this sample was only 14 years old and the eldest was 78 years.[553]

Separate data covering the period 2005 until 2013 indicates that the number of teenagers convicted of murder in London (in which a variety of weapons were used) has fallen since 2010. But does this reflect the hard work of the police in opposing gangs and disrupting their use of weapons, or is it the result of some of the killings being downgraded from murder to manslaughter? According to figures from Operation Trident, the police operation which concentrates on firearms use in black communities, the number of people shot dead in London (by both teenage and adult killers) has been falling since 2002. Nevertheless, between 2005 and 2015, published figures indicate there were, overall, no fewer than 185 teenage murders alone in London during that period, an average of 18.5 every year. Sixty-nine per cent of these victims were stabbed to death and 17% of them were shot to death.[554] [555] The police claim that the number of shooting incidents is generally falling. But such claims are overshadowed by observations of street workers closely associated with criminal gangs. These workers claimed that, "the number of shooting incidents reported is only a fraction of what is taking place. Gun crime has never gone away. Firearms are being discharged daily, in some parts of London. Those using guns have got younger. These children are unpredictable, they have access to guns and they are willing to use them."[556]

For many years, it has been suspected that much of this gun crime was associated with London's black Afro-Caribbean community, but few dared speak of it because of the embargo on free speech imposed by the fear of accusations of racism. Indeed, the writer Rod Liddle had earlier suffered this fate when in 2009 he voiced the view that much of the street violence in London was associated with young black men. But in 2010 these facts broke through the surface of such restraints when police data was published which showed that the majority of men held responsible by the police for gun crimes, robberies and street violence in the capital are black. The data showed that of more than 18,000 men and boys proceeded against by the police for gun crimes in London for the period 2009–10, 67% of them were black; for robbery offences it was 59%, and for street crimes which include muggings, assault with intent to rob and snatching property, the proportion was 54%.[557] The figures also showed that black men are twice as likely to be the victims of gun and knife crime, meaning that much of this is black-against-black violence, thus casting doubt on these being casualties of racism.

Many teenage killings arise out of inter-gang rivalry, often involving those from the black community. In 2013 for example, a 15-year-old boy, Sofyen Belamouadden, was hunted down and stabbed to death in broad daylight by a 20-strong gang of youths at the entrance to Victoria Tube Station in London. The attack arose out of a clash between rival gangs based on two schools. Three teenagers, Obi Novokeh, Christopher Ouroregtie, and Sampson Odegbune were each jailed for life and given a minimum tariff of 18 years each. Others, including Junior Bayode who was only 16 years old when he joined in this attack, were given lesser sentences.[558]

However, the membership of these violent teenage gangs can often be spread among white British, black British as well as non-British immigrants. Furthermore, the link, which some observers are quick to make between the violence they display and the often poorer, run down areas of London in which they live, is misleading. For example, while the analysis of all murders in London for the period 2006 to 2012, showed that the four boroughs with the highest number of murders per 100,000 of their population are among the poorest (Newham, Southwark, Hackney, and Lambeth), not all boroughs regarded as poor had high murder rates .[559] It would be wrong, as previously argued, to interpret this apparent connection to mean that poverty was the driver for crime and violence. As discussed earlier, different studies carried out over several decades have failed to find any evidence to support this nevertheless widely held belief. It would be more realistic to interpret this association the other way around, i.e. most people who choose to be violent and commit crime (whatever their ethnic origin) are the same people whose life choices generally keep them in the lower classes of our society, e.g. they refuse to work at school, are violent, ill-disciplined, demand instant gratification, and fail to plan for the future. This is not to say that they do not have access to money – crime and violence brings many of them a good income and their social station in life can be seen as an indicator of how they choose to live and spend their ill-gotten gains.

Likewise, these same four boroughs have, compared to others, very high percentages of non-British in their populations. But again, it would be wrong to over-interpret this, because data also shows that other boroughs with high numbers of immigrants in their populations are not associated with high murder rates. This suggests that the boroughs with the highest number of these violent crimes have a greater concentration of violent *criminals*, whether black, white, British or Non-British. The presence of large numbers of immigrants (most of whom are law-abiding), can be seen therefore to be independent of the high murder numbers, and, in general, be explained by the cheaper housing costs in these poorer districts. The figures from Tower Hamlets support this possibility. It is the second poorest of the London boroughs, has a very high number of immigrants (almost 50%), but its murder rate is less than half of Lambeth's. Likewise, Redbridge has an even higher percentage of non-British in its population (54%), is in the middle range on the poverty/wealth score, and has one of the lowest murder rates. Almost half of Hounslow's population is non-British, it is also midway on the poverty/wealth score and has a low murder rate. At the same time, not all non-British people live in the poorer areas. Kingston upon Thames for example, with relatively few murders by comparison with others, is one if the better off boroughs and almost a third of its population are immigrants.

Thus, in summary, although overall, the murder rate and the percentage of non-British in the borough's populations are correlated with each other and with poverty, closer examination suggests that this may be because criminals, of whatever ethnic or racial origin, tend to be found in the poorer districts, and it is the cheaper living costs found in these areas which, independently, may explain their association with immigrant populations. The varying murder rates across the London boroughs is more likely to reflect the numbers of violent criminals in these districts, (of whatever race or ethnic origin) although it is now strongly suspected that almost one in five violent crimes is committed by those who are non-British.

A separate review of 131 of the killings that took place in London in 2009[560] showed that there was more than one killing every three days. Almost half of them (47%) were committed in eight out of the 32 boroughs. These were Greenwich, Hackney, Harringay, Lambeth, Lewisham, Newham, Southwark and Tower Hamlets. It also revealed that killings took place on every day of the week, and that most took place on a Sunday and the least on a Wednesday. February, in the depth of the winter, was the safest month as far as homicide was concerned, with three no-killing-days which were a Monday, Tuesday and Wednesday. March and September were the most dangerous periods with the highest number of killings in a month with 15 each. Twenty-five homicides occurred on a Sunday, making it, as stated the most dangerous day overall. The second most dangerous day was Thursday with 21, and Saturday was the third most dangerous with 20.

The nature of the violence can be deduced from the fact that anger and revenge was the motive for 81% of these homicides and in these cases the victim was beaten and kicked to death. A quarter of all the homicide victims were killed in this way. The fact that a large proportion (34%) of the homicides were downgraded to manslaughter, with murder convictions for only half of them, may help explain why so many of the victim's families leave the court angry and alienated from the justice system. Their complaint that justice has not been done, either because the killer was not sent to prison for life, or that the justice system's requirement for speedier and cheaper disposals, has dominated the proceedings, seems well justified.

In one such example in 2014, 15-year-old Kariton Burton knifed a London street trader to death. He was angry that his victim, Rashid Naeem, had earlier offered him some trivial slight. Burton, accompanied by 16-year-old Javauntee Campbell, approached Naeem and deliberately provoked him by stealing two watches from his stall. A confrontation followed in which Campbell knocked Naeem to the ground and Burton then stabbed the victim through the heart. This murder, which occurred on a Sunday, was carried out in broad daylight in front of scores of shoppers. Burton was convicted of murder and sentenced to life imprisonment, but then he laughed out loud, no doubt with relief, as he heard the judge say it would carry a minimum tariff of 15 years. He knew that despite his cold-blooded killing, he would eventually be released while still young enough to enjoy his freedom, even though the judge made a point of saying that in killing Naeem, Burton had passed a life sentence on all the members of the victim's family. Campbell was convicted of manslaughter and sentenced to ten years in a young offender's institution.[561] But would it not be more just to take the view that if the attackers intend to harm their victim, as certainly was the case in this example, and if the harm results in the death of the victim, then that is murder, whether or not they 'intended' to kill? On this basis, Campbell was also guilty of murder.

# 7

## A New Sentencing Code: Keeping Britain Safe

The death penalty was not abandoned because it failed to protect the public, who have paid a heavy price for its removal, but because it offended the ideologies of many of our ruling elite, and others who were uncomfortable with the idea that the state had the right to take life. The fear of wrongful executions was another powerful and understandable component in the argument against its retention.

What capital punishment demonstrated was that the majority of would-be killers can be deterred from killing, whereas the present half-way house system falls lamentably short of this. Our sensitivities towards wrongful deaths at the hands of the State should be matched by a rejection of a system which results in the far more numerous, equally wrongful, and in many cases, avoidable deaths at the hands of violent criminals. Would-be-killers (and serious repeat, sex and violent offenders) need to know the price they will pay for their crimes will be the certain loss of liberty for all or most of their lives, consequences so dreadful for most of them that they will avoid it.

As illustrated by the experience of Gabrielle Brown (see chapter 1), the Attorney General does not always allow victims to appeal against what they consider to be a too-lenient sentence. But, even when he does, the Appeal Court's intervention makes little difference. An analysis of 103 cases referred to them in 2007 showed that a third of the sentences remained unchanged. These included a sentence of community supervision for robbery with a knife, one of 18-months imprisonment for two convictions of rape and two indecent assaults, a deferred sentence for aggravated assault, and several robbery offences dealt with by means of conditional discharges or community sentences. In one case, the rape of a child for which, I suggest, twenty years would not be inappropriate, the original six-year sentence, (in reality three years) was left unchanged.

The increases in the remaining two thirds were minimal. The average original sentence (for such crimes as rape, attempted murder, serious violence, robbery) was 2.9 years, which the Appeal Court raised to 4.6 years (an increase of just 1.7 years). In one example a sentence of child rape was doubled from two years to four years, but I suspect few in the public would have questioned it had it been changed to twenty years.[562] Earlier, in 2006, it was made known that the Appeal Court had substituted a community rehabilitation order for an absolute discharge given to an offender who had admitted indecently assaulting his niece, and that they had doubled the five-year sentence given to a man who had raped and sexually abused his daughter over a period of 16 years. But in both cases, they had in effect replaced a lenient sentence with another lenient sentence, particularly as, in the case of the latter, the offender will only serve half of it.[563] In 2010, they added ten years to the minimum tariff to be served, bringing it to thirty years, for a man who had killed a woman in cold blood with a bolt gun, but this was unusual.[564] It is also the case that the Appeal Court has upheld Whole Life Terms for the 'worst' murderers – often multiple killers – but what grounds could they have used to justify doing otherwise?

Given these results we might well ask whether they were in the public interest or worth the expensive Appeal Court apparatus. The Lord Chief Justice and President of the Queens's Bench Division thought it was, although he may have wished, in retrospect that he had chosen his words more carefully. He said: "The right conclusion to draw from these statistics is that the system is working as intended."[565] So it may be from the point of view of the justice elite, but is it likely that the public who pay for the justice system to protect them would agree? A survey of public attitudes carried out by the Ministry of Justice in 2013 suggested many would not. Almost 50% of the 74,000 respondents indicated that judges were too lenient with cases of violence and other serious crimes.[566] An earlier poll suggested that 70% of the public wanted a life sentence 'to mean life'.[567]

But as noted, a life sentence now means on average, no more than 16 years, and an investigation by Philip Davies MP revealed that 1 in 9 murderers is freed after serving fewer than ten years in jail.[568] Yet few may know that after the abolition of the death penalty in 1965, judges argued for the right to decide on the sentence for murder. But the 1965 Act denied them this and made the sentence one of mandatory life imprisonment.[569] The judge's feathers were truly ruffled, and as a sop to them, and for no other reason, a clause was slipped into the act which gave them, for the first time, the discretion to recommend a minimum term or tariff. But to begin with they used it sparingly and then only to indicate a long period of incarceration for what they considered the worst murders. Between 1965 and 1972 there were only forty-five such recommendations (about 1 in every 12 convictions for murder). In other words, in the early 1970s, judges used their discretion to ensure as far as possible that those they regarded as the worst offenders should not be released too soon. But today they seem more concerned to ensure the murderer is not kept in jail too long, as 83% of the minimum tariffs for life sentences are under 20 years and a third under 10 years – all supposedly substitutes for the death penalty.[570]

Had 'life imprisonment' meant a whole life term, as the public, in 1965, were led to believe, those murdered by killers and rapists freed from their so-called life sentence, would, to state the obvious, be alive today. Anthony Rice, for example, would not have been at liberty to strangle and stab 40-year-old Naomi Bryant, a sufferer from multiple sclerosis, to death in 2005. Rice had multiple convictions for violent sex attacks going back to 1972. He was released in 2004 after serving 15 years of a life sentence for the attempted rape of a five-year-old girl. At the time of the murder, Rice was on licence and living at Elderfield Probation Hostel in Otterbourne, near Winchester, Hants. At the inquest following Naomi Bryant's death, for which the victim's mother fought tooth and nail, in the face of resistance by the justice system, the jury found that the probation service, the police and the prison service were all guilty of a string of errors which contributed to this tragedy.[571]

But, as previously stressed, this is the wrong emphasis. He should never have been released in the first place. To stress the point yet again, once out on the street, no amount of supervision by the police, or the probation service could have prevented Rice from further attacks of this kind. The coroner expressed the hope that this case would be a wake-up call for all concerned. But our justice elite do not need a wake-up call. They know the results of their policies, and choose to do nothing about them.

In 2007, a judge underlined this. Andrew Mournian, a violent criminal, was released early from jail, and five days later, battered his girlfriend, Amanda Murphy, to death.[572] In the face of criticism of the early release scheme which followed, the judge in the case said, he did not believe that Mournian's early release had led to Miss Murphy's death… "he would have carried out the attack whenever he was released". Is this not a tacit admission that Mournian should have been locked up forever or at least until old age rendered him harmless? But the judge had nothing to say on this point. After all, with rare exceptions, it is not members of the judiciary or justice elite and their families who are slain by dangerous, violent offenders freed to strike again, but those members of the community who lead a less privileged and protected way of life.

The way to ensure that men like Mournian and Rice do not get a further chance to exercise their violence is for us to adopt a '2-strike' sentencing system. This would mean the imposition of a whole life term of imprisonment, following a second conviction for a serious violent crime, identified on a list of qualifying 'strike' offences legislated for by parliament. Its tough punishments would be aimed, not at the first-time offender of previous good character, who killed or injured someone, – unless circumstances suggested otherwise – but at repeat, violent and dangerous offenders, for whom violent crime has become a habit or even a way of life. But a first strike offence which was clearly premeditated, such as using a firearm against a police officer, would attract a severe penalty, even if the perpetrator was a first-time offender.

Otherwise there could be a more lenient approach, as shown in the table below, towards (probably very few) offenders convicted of a first-strike offence, who had no previous convictions for violence. If two such men fight and one is killed, and the jury are persuaded that the killer genuinely did not intend the death of his adversary, then a conviction for manslaughter could follow and the judge could be given discretion to be merciful, and, as suggested below, pass a sentence according to the circumstances of the offence within the limits set by parliament. Likewise, leniency could also be exercised when deaths or injury occur following genuine cases of self-defence, extreme provocation, or other circumstances provoking a sudden, albeit uncharacteristic outburst of violence.

But these were not the circumstances surrounding the violence shown by 21-year-old Lewis Gill. In 2014, he was sentenced to four years for the manslaughter of Andrew Young, a 40-year-old male, suffering from Aspergers syndrome.[573] He killed him with a single punch, delivered with great force, to the head, in an unprovoked attack outside a Tesco Metro store in Charminster Rd, Bournemouth, the whole affair being captured on a CCTV camera. Andrew Young had just challenged a cyclist for riding his bicycle on the pavement and Gill intervened with a sudden and deadly attack on the unsuspecting and defenceless Young, who was sent crashing to the ground and as a result suffered fatal head injuries. This was not an act of self-defence or an 'out of character' rush to the head, or loss of control. Lewis Gill was a violent man and was serving a suspended six-month prison sentence for a previous violent robbery when he killed Young. The sentencing code I am putting forward here would have stopped Gill in his tracks long before he crossed paths with Andrew Young, by ensuring at the very least, a ten-year prison sentence, without parole, for his earlier violent robbery.

A second and more severe tariff would operate against first strikers who had previous convictions for violent or sex crimes. Such offenders convicted of murder, would be locked up for the rest of their lives and would not be able to go on to commit a second strike offence. Others convicted of violence short of murder would be told they faced imprisonment for the rest of their lives if convicted of a second strike offence. An offender who reached this stage would have made it abundantly clear he was very dangerous and that no sanction, no matter how severe, would stop him murdering, raping or maiming again. The case for locking up second strikers for life should be beyond argument.

For those who are not in sympathy with such long prison terms, it must be emphasised that they reflect the very high level of threat presented by repeat, violent offenders, which sets them apart. However, such details could be decided upon by parliament, following a protracted consultation with the public. If the majority supported it and parliament voted for it, a tough 2-strike system could be introduced and judges would have no choice but to impose the sentences fixed by legislation. They would no longer receive directions from the Guidelines Council because it would be abolished. Any changes thought necessary to the way violent criminals were sentenced would be debated openly in parliament and voted upon giving the public the benefit of knowing what was the reasoning and evidence behind such developments. If parliament agreed, some variations in the sentence could be built in for criminals who were juveniles at the first-strike stage. Courts would no longer be able to give discounts against the sentence for early guilty pleas. Instead, defendants accused of a first-strike offence would know that they were at risk of additional time being added for a late abandonment of a not-guilty plea.

The suggested terms of imprisonment are shown in the example below, to be served without parole. These may be too severe for some or too lenient for others, but the crucial point is that the new arrangements should have public support, and not be based on the views of a minority of officials and so-called 'experts'. Not all crime types have been listed; nor are their descriptions necessarily exactly as they would be found on an official list, but are put in as general examples of how the system might operate

Key:

PCs = Previous convictions for violence:

GBH = Grievous bodily harm.

| Offence | 1st strike no PCs | 1st strike with PCs | 2nd strike offence |
|---|---|---|---|
| Murder | 4–20 years | whole life term | |
| Attempted murder | 3–12 years | 18 years | whole life term |
| Manslaughter | 2–12 years | 20 years | whole life term |
| Wounding (GBH) | 2–12 years | 17 years | whole life term |
| Using firearm against police | 11 years | 14 years | whole life term |
| Crime with a firearm | 10 years | 14 years | whole life term |
| Kidnapping | 15 years | 18 years | whole life term |
| Burglary with violence | 12 years | 20 years | whole life term |
| Robbery | 10 years | 18 years | whole life term |
| Aggravated robbery | 14 years | 19 years | whole life term |
| Rape | 15 years | 26 years | whole life term |

| | | | |
|---|---|---|---|
| Attempted rape | 10 years | 15 years | whole life term |
| Sex act with a child | 14 years | 17 years | whole life term |
| Threats to kill | 10 years | 14 years | 25 years to life |

Viewed objectively, these prison terms are not draconian but sensible, if members of the public are to be protected from a legacy of violence they did not want or seek. In contrast, all prisoners are volunteers, and all that is required of them to avoid spending more and more time behind bars is to be law abiding. Not, perhaps, too much to ask.

This proposed 2-strike system would be aimed at those who are sane. But how should we deal with those diagnosed as mentally ill? Whatever provision we make for them we should not lose sight of the fact that their state of mind makes no difference to the impact their violence makes on the lives of the victims and their families. Between 2004 and 2014, 694 people were killed by those who were mentally ill, an average of 63 per year. In 2013, London Mental Health NHS Trusts announced that in the capital, 96 people had been killed by mentally ill patients over an eight-year period (2005–2012).[574] [575] [576] [577]

Mentally ill patients who have killed are subject, at least on paper, to strict follow up conditions if, after a period in secure hospital conditions, they are released into the community. But no system of community care and supervision is fool proof, and examples of further violence and killing by such patients are rarely out of the press for long. In 2006, a psychiatrically ill woman, Nicola Edgington, then 25, stabbed her mother to death in their home, and was detained indefinitely under the Mental Health Act. She was released in 2009, to be monitored in the community by a doctor, nurse and social worker. But in 2012 she attacked a stranger, 58-year-old grandmother, Sally Hodkin, in the street, and killed her by cutting her throat with a butcher's knife.[578]

The supervision arrangements for patients convicted initially for serious violence, but not homicide, are, for a variety of reasons, often far less satisfactory and sometimes almost non-existent, leading to tragic consequences in many cases. The size of this threat can be judged by the results of research by the Department of Health in 2006 which found, from a review of 25 killings committed by severely ill psychiatric patients under the care in the community, that in every case the killer was known to have a history of violence, but the signs of risk were not acted upon by the professionals in charge.[579]

For example, in 2013, a schizophrenic, Ghodratollah Barani, was turned away from hospital twice because doctors thought he was faking his illness to support his asylum claim.[580] A little later, after repeatedly visiting Buckingham Palace and demanding to see the Queen, he strangled a rough sleeper; he said his voices told him to do it, so he could become king. Once at court he was assessed as mentally ill and detained indefinitely, but if the previous medical assessments were correct, he was sane and should have been charged with murder.

It was recently reported that medical staff, police and the prison service had, over a 12-year period, missed a string of chances to refer immigrant Philip Simelane for treatment. He finally stabbed a young girl to death while on a bus.[581] Psychiatrists had told a court that mentally ill Anthony Thompson was such a danger to the public that he should be locked up. But he was released because no secure hospital place could be found. Within hours, Thompson, whose 43 convictions included offences of violence, went on to beat and rape a pregnant woman.[582]

But these failings of diagnosis, oversight and community care, throw up the crucial question – what to do with mentally ill patients who have killed or who have exhibited high levels of dangerousness to others, who are, after a period of incarceration, stabilised by drug treatment? Many in the medical and legal world argue that it would be an injustice to keep them locked up once they are deemed to be 'cured'. But no schizophrenic can be said to be cured, because no medical source can say for certain that there will be no relapse. The best that can be said is that some categories of mental illness are 'less likely' than others to return. There are no certainties. The risk to the public is heightened by the fact that even close supervision of such patients in the community can never guarantee they will always take their medication, the absence of which may well trigger the onset once again of their dangerous symptoms. In 2015, mentally ill Femi Nandap, 23, stabbed Dr. Ensink, a 41-year-old biologist, to death. Six days earlier, Nandap had stopped taking the medication that controlled his psychosis.[583]

Logically, if the public is to be given maximum protection, this amounts to an argument for keeping mentally ill patients, known to be dangerous, permanently incarcerated. But whether the public would support such a policy, or are prepared to live with a system that involves some risk to them, needs to be tested. In whose favour the balance of justice should be tilted, as in the right of the stabilised patient to freedom, or the right of the public to be protected, should be based on a system known to have public support. It is they who must live with the consequences of such decisions. The legal and medical elite might well jibe at such 'populist' arrangements, but well placed and highly educated though some of them are, they do not have a monopoly on common sense or wisdom, and they do not form the majority. In any case, the decision they would have to accept is not about technical medical or legal matters, but what level of risk the public are prepared to accept from violent, mentally ill offenders.

Fixed mandatory sentences for those who are sane and convicted of murder would be more just than the indefinite term they now face, because both killer and the victim's family would know exactly how long the prison sentence would be. As matters stand victim's families can have no such certainty or peace of mind.

Fixed mandatory prison terms would avoid the postcode lottery system which operates in our courts. For example, an analysis by Philip Davies MP, revealed that out of 72 crown courts only 15 routinely locked up four out of five sex offenders. Only

37% of sex offenders are jailed in Salisbury, Wiltshire, compared to 94% in Aylesbury, Buckinghamshire. One court gave 11 years for a violent mugging, while another set 11 years as the minimum tariff for a murder.[584]

It would be made clear that prisons should be regarded as places of punishment for what offenders had done, not as rehabilitation or therapy centres. Judges would be re-educated to see that violent criminals cannot be cured of their violence, as it is not a symptom of an illness, but that they (or most of them) can be dissuaded from further violent assaults by severe sentences of imprisonment. In 2012, three men attacked another in his home with such vehemence that he almost died. During a prolonged assault, 47-year-old Andre Morris, suffered fractures to his skull, upper spine, eye sockets and cheekbones. He was then robbed of his wallet, and dragged outside of his home in Darlington, County Durham, to make it look as if he had been attacked by others in the street.[585] But instead of ensuring the length of the sentence matched the dreadful crime, the judge stated that the ringleader, 23-year-old Sean O'Brien, would be let out of prison when he was declared 'safe'.

But it is beyond the skill of any professional to know for certain that a prisoner is 'cured or rehabilitated, or safe'. Such changes can easily be faked. But even if we had the means to know he had changed for the better, and was truly remorseful, this is the wrong principle to trigger his release. In 1961, 14-year-old Graham Young killed two people by poisoning and he narrowly failed to kill two members of his own family. Young grew up in Neasden, in the words of his sister "in a prim little house with a neat little garden", in an area of London that could not have been more ordinary. So ordinary, in fact, that satirists of the BBC and *Private Eye* made fun of it as a symbol of drab urban conformity. Yet in this most unremarkable place, Graham Young developed an obsessive and, in time, expert interest in poisons, and became one of the most callous killers of the 20th century. He became, in the words of his sister, "a man so dangerous and so far beyond the reach of normal human instinct that he tried to poison even his own father and me."

There was no history of malice between him and his family. Young simply enjoyed watching the results of his experiments. Following his conviction when he was 14 years old, he was sent to Broadmoor Prison Hospital, where he poisoned the tea prepared for 70 people. He spoke openly to his fellow inmates of his ambition to use his detailed knowledge to become a notorious multiple killer. The nursing staff were aware of these conversations and noted them in their ward records, along with other indicators of Young's continuing fascination with these dangerous substances.

He eventually told other inmates that, in a bid to get himself released, he was going to pretend to his psychiatrist that he was losing interest in poisons, and that he had realised the folly of his ways. Over several months, during his regular sessions with him, he persuaded his medical supervisor, Dr Udwin that he had changed. South-African born Dr Udwin, the senior psychiatrist who had been trying to help Young for several years, was completely taken in by this performance, and he noted 'profound changes' that had taken place in Young's condition. In 1971, clearly flattered by what he saw as the results of his skilled psychiatric intervention, the psychiatrist recommended Young's release to the Home Office, who agreed, even though they knew that he had made similar but mistaken recommendations in the past. He did not consult the hospital nursing staff, whose experience and records would have given him a different view of Young. Following the psychiatrist's declaration that he was 'safe' and 'cured' of his obsession, Young, now 21 years old, was freed. He immediately set about his deadly business once more, and poisoned to death at least two other people. Young was re-committed to Broadmoor for life, and died in his fifties while still in custody.[586]

The sentencing of the murderers of Gunner Lee Rigby in Woolwich in 2014, showed the extent to which judges now view prisons as places of therapy and rehabilitation. Lee Rigby was hacked to death on the streets of south-east London by two Muslim extremists. One of them tried to decapitate the soldier as he lay dying on the pavement. The younger of the two, 22-year-old Michael Adebowale was given a life sentence with a minimum tariff of 22 years. Thus, the judge acted on the premise that one day a panel of officials might judge that Adebowale, having been subjected to various psychological programmes provided in prison, would be cured and safe enough to let out. The judge excused this lesser sentence because, he said, Adebowale had played a more minor role in the attack than did 29-year-old Michael Adebolajo. The judge appeared to think that Adebowale's repeated stabbing of the victim's torso with the obvious intent of killing him, was not quite so bad as Adebolajo's hacking at the neck of the victim, a difference Lee Rigby's family would no doubt struggle to understand. Adebolajo, on the other hand, was sentenced to a whole life term of imprisonment. This was because the judge regarded his role as the major one and additionally, he thought Adebelajo was 'beyond rehabilitation'.

Even aside from the question about how the judge could possibly know this, it was an extraordinary pronouncement. Whether his own decision or prompted by psychologists' reports, for this to be included as a reason for deciding on a whole life term was manifestly unjust, first, because it meant that Adebowale, convicted of the same crime, received a lesser sentence, and secondly, the killers did not get arrested because one of them was in need of rehabilitation and the other beyond it, but because both of them had committed a foul and cold blooded murder on a public street in the full light of day.[587] No doubt the majority of the public would have agreed with whole life terms for both killers because of what they had done and to show their complete rejection of their vile behaviour. Neither of them was insane, and both knew what they were doing. If, at some point in the future, these killers did genuinely regret their crime, the public would likewise understand why they, nevertheless, should stay in jail for the duration of their sentence – even if it were for the rest of their lives.

If my proposals were accepted, it would not be the first time a 2-strike system became law in Britain. But its re-introduction would require our MPs to reassert the influence of parliament, and to understand how, over the last 19 years, authority over these matters has slipped from them to our unelected liberal judiciary.

In 1997, Michael Howard, the then Home Secretary, introduced automatic life sentences for criminals convicted a second time of attempted murder, rape, and other dangerous and life threatening crimes.[588] The legislation was passed against a torrent of opposition, from the liberal pro-criminal lobby both inside and out of government, and by the judges who, behaving like trades unionists, resented their loss of influence over the sentencing of these offences. The system that the liberal elite fought tooth and nail to preserve had allowed, for example, Roy Whiting, a highly dangerous sexual predator, to be sentenced in 1995 to four years imprisonment for abducting a small child,[589] and released after only two and a half years. He went on to abduct and murder six-year-old Sarah Payne. Howard's 2-strike bill was only passed onto the statute book because of a clause that enabled judges to fix the minimum term for the life sentence to be served and to avoid it all together in 'exceptional' circumstances.

These new provisions did not last long. A new government introduced the 2002 Powers of Criminal Courts (Sentencing) Act that did away with the 1997 legislation. It replaced automatic life sentences with 'longer than proportionate sentences'. This could mean whatever the judges argued it to be and so the effect was to give back to the judiciary much of the discretion they had lost.

In 2003, under the pretence of providing the public with more protection, the government passed legislation which allowed the courts to hand down an 'indeterminate sentence for public protection', (IPPs) for those convicted of dangerous violent and sex crimes, and who were judged to pose a risk of further harm.[590] This meant that, as with life sentences for murder, these offenders were to stay in prison indefinitely, once their tariff had been served, until they were thought 'safe enough' to let out. To commit prisoners, no matter what they have done, to such prolonged periods of uncertainty, could be judged cruel and contrary to justice, but the government hoped the public would be impressed by what they presented as an unusually tough measure. But once again, all was not what it seemed. As with automatic life sentences, the judges were left to decide on the minimum tariff that should be served before parole could be applied for. When figures were later published, which showed that over 70% of IPPs were for less than four years, and nearly a quarter less than two years, it became clear that the judges had turned the so-called protection element upside down, and these sentences had become no more than paper tigers.[591]

But from the start, there was a case to say that IPPs were wrong in principle because justice requires that a criminal should know from the outset the length of the prison sentence he must serve for the crime committed or, in the case of a whole life term, be informed he will die in prison. The practice of releasing prisoners from indeterminate sentences because it is believed they are reformed or cured is also a violation of justice (and common sense) because, as pointed out previously, the prisoner's true state of mind can never be known. It is also wrong to leave the question of their release to an arbitrary decision of a parole panel who can only guess about a prisoner's future behaviour if given his freedom.

Locking up repeat violent offenders early in their criminal career should not be regarded as shameful or repressive, but the sign of a community that has the confidence to know when to reject wrong-doing. There is nothing wrong per se with dangerous criminals spending most or perhaps all their lives behind bars, provided that they are convicted after a fair trial, that has allowed them to present the most rigorous defence possible. Equally, we should suffer no inhibitions about running a prison system without parole. There is no good reason to parole *any* offender. It is no accident that the country with probably the best crime control record in the world – Singapore – has achieved this enviable position without it.

The idea that prisoners need parole because otherwise they would find imprisonment impossible to bear, or would cause trouble without it, is an invention. It is also an implied blackmail which we must resist. Parole should not be seen as a reward for good behaviour, but a reward for bad behaviour, and therefore abolished. The abolition of parole would bring significant financial savings, and free prison staff from the endless demand for prisoner assessments and other paperwork. For all prisoners, those serving sentences for strike offences and others for less serious crimes, the reward for good behaviour would be the certain knowledge that they would serve no more than the sentence they were originally given. Further violence, rule breaking and rioting would result in time added on to their sentence, and it would be up to them whether they were freed on their first release date.

Parole is a cruel absurdity. It is cruel because every parole review ignites for the victims and or their families the horrors associated with their loss at the hands of the killer, rapist or other attacker, and the possibility that he may be freed. Parole is an absurdity because the parole board members have, as repeatedly stressed, no special skills that enable them to know when a violent prisoner is 'safe enough to let out'. They must guess and there is no reason to think that their guesses are better than those of anyone else. They are often wrong with disastrous results, and it is on these mistakes that they must be judged, not on the number of parole applications they turn down, or the number of prisoners they release who do not come to notice.

In 2006, they released 28-year-old Yousef Bouhaddaou early from a five-and-a-half-year prison sentence, given for burglary and aggravated vehicle taking. He was an established criminal with at least 19 previous convictions. Yet the probation service had declared him as being low to medium risk of re-offending. But the Board had no reason to think that probation officers could assess, with any certainty, the risk level presented by a prisoner, and therefore, how he would behave in the future. Five weeks after his release, Bouhaddaou underlined this when he broke into the home of the Symmonds family, in Chiswick, West London. He stabbed 45-year-old Robert Symmonds to death with a kitchen knife, while his two young children slept upstairs. He died in his wife's arms. His distraught family called for the authorities to consider returning the death penalty, as the only means to stop dangerous career criminals with any certainty.[592]

Parole serves no purpose other than as a device to free up prison space. This objective became clear when between 1991 and 2008, for most prisoners, all pretence at selecting only those most suitable for early release to ensure the safety of the public, was abandoned. From 1991 all prisoners serving less than four years were released automatically at the halfway stage of their sentence.[593] Then in 2008 the government abolished parole reviews for all prisoners serving determinate (fixed) sentences (except for certain specified violent and sexual offences), and ruled that they should all be released automatically at the halfway point of their prison term.[594] [595] The reason for this was that a backlog of parole assessments had begun to appear, due, among other things, to large numbers of prisoners arriving in prison with relatively short tariffs, particularly those sentenced to 'indeterminate sentences for public protection'.

Prisoners knew they had to complete pre-release/rehabilitation courses before they could be considered for parole, and the system could not keep up with the number of prisoners demanding what they quickly perceived was the key to the prison door. Several of them with especially short minimum terms had served their tariffs before a course had been organised for them, and sued the government for delaying their chances of making an application to the parole board. (Once freed how long will it be before they seize the chance to sue them again because the programme failed to stop them committing crime?) To rid themselves of this embarrassment, and at the same time free themselves of a heavy administrative burden, and free up large numbers of prison places, the civil servants simply crossed out 'parole assessments' from the rule book, with one, efficient stroke of their pen, for all prisoners except those serving life and those sentenced to indeterminate sentences for public protection (IPPs).

Releasing prisoners after they have only served half of their sentence means that they can return to their criminal business sooner, for which the public pays a high price. Even before this change was introduced, thousands of prisoners released on licence between 1999 and 2014, had to be recalled, even though they were being supervised.[596]

Some investigators have found reconviction rates for parolees were less than predicted, though such differences were small.[597] But such results are theoretical, and of no use to the public whose concern is the actual number of offences committed against them by released prisoners. In any case, researchers have failed to demonstrate that differences between actual and predicted reconviction rates are due to parole supervision per se, and have admitted that other factors may be at work.[598] However, whatever the government really believed about this, they always maintained that the assessment of prisoners for parole was essential for public safety. Yet, when the moment came, they were prepared to discard it for administrative convenience.

Four years ago, the parole board admitted that there was no accurate data on how many of the most serious criminals go on, after release, to commit further serious offences.[599] Justice officials immediately promised to review their statistics. But whatever figures they publish, they can have no idea how many further crimes these criminals have committed, but only those for which they have been caught and convicted. A 2016 Government report indicated that the number of IPP prisoners recalled to prison due to further criminal charges was increasing and, overall, the numbers of recalled IPP prisoners was high.[600] This suggests a willingness to release more who are high risk. But why? The numbers of lifer prisoners released, or moved to open prison conditions, or allowed to go forward in the parole application process to an oral review, when expressed as a percentage of all those reviewed for parole, have seen an uninterrupted rise over the last seven years. Similar trends apply to those who have been paroled and returned to prison due to further offending or breach of their rules. In 2009, 51% of recalled lifer parolees were paroled again. In 2015 it was 62%, while for IPP prisoners the increase went from 33% to 60% for the same period.[601] [602] Over this seven-year period we would have expected to see some variations in the results, but such consistency, in the same direction, invites speculation over whose mission the parole board members are following.

One such prisoner the parole board were determined to release, was 49-year-old Alan Wilmot, a highly dangerous man serving a life sentence, which he was given in 1987, aged 21, for robbing and raping four women in West London. To get close to his victims, he posed as a cameraman working on *Eastenders*, and over a period of five months, scouring the streets of Paddington for targets, he raped three prostitutes and a pregnant woman. She had accepted his offer of a lift to Paddington station but instead Wilmot drove her to a lonely spot where he beat her, raped her, and robbed her of money and jewellery. His victim was so traumatised that she could not go ahead with her pregnancy and had an abortion.

On the recommendation of the parole board Wilmot was, in 2004, transferred to HMP Leyhill, an open prison for lifers being prepared for release. Within a year, the authorities were forced to move him back to more secure conditions because of his 'inappropriate behaviour'. But there was to be no mission creep for the parole board officials and despite being overruled by the government on several occasions, they made repeated attempts to get him returned to a less restricted environment. Such interventions by the Secretary of State are rare, with less than 1% of the parole board's recommendations being turned down in the last five years,[603] making it clear Wilmot was thought to be highly dangerous.

But their self-appointed mission to save Wilmot from further years of incarceration (what a waste that would be!), freed the Board from worrying about such matters. In the face of warnings from prison officers and a prison psychologist that Wilmot presented an 'unmanageable risk' and should stay in a secure jail, and despite knowing he had abused an earlier such transfer to make liaisons with vulnerable women, they again recommended he be moved to less secure conditions.

The government eventually gave in to them, and in 2015, Wilmot was moved from HMP North Sea Camp in Norfolk, into open prison conditions once more.[604]

It was not long before he was granted a series of day-releases, and during one of these he raped a 27-year-old woman at knife point in her home, in front of her close friend, whom he had tied up to make her watch her friend's ordeal. It emerged he had found his victim's contact details in 2013 in an online advert she had placed to sell a dog. Wilmot exchanged scores of text messages with his victim-to-be while posing as his handsome fireman nephew Richard, known as Rico. Wilmot promised her a new life with him. She in turn found a photo of the real Rico on Facebook, and was immediately attracted to him. Finally, in September 2013, the victim, in the company of her friend, agreed to spend the day with Wilmot during one of his three-monthly day-releases. Once in the 27-year-old's flat he tied up both women, threatened to kill them if they screamed and carried out the rape attack. Yet this is the man that the parole board put in overtime for – and would not rest until he was put on the moving stairway to freedom.

Their confident championing of Wilmot is not an isolated case. In 2003, they took Mark Shirley under their wing, and decided he had spent enough time in jail. In 1987 he was convicted of the murder of a 67-year-old woman in her flat in Cardiff, and the judge who sentenced him described him as a 'highly dangerous and evil man'. But, as previously noted, the more dangerous the prisoner the more missionary-like and zealous can the board sometimes be in its efforts to save him from further time in jail. They released him in

2003 after he had served 16 years of a life sentence. He was then twice recalled on licence, but released yet again in 2004.

Whatever rationalisations the parole board had managed to cook up in their own minds to justify giving Shirley his freedom, despite his attempts to show them he could not be trusted, the threat of recall meant nothing to him. In 2005 he brutally raped another woman, subjecting her to a violent and humiliating ordeal that lasted several hours. She was so terrified she did not tell the police until 2012. In 2009 Shirley struck again and violently raped a third woman (or at least the third one known about). For this crime, he received six life sentences, which were all concurrent, and given a minimum tariff of only nine years. The victim was appalled at what she described as a sham sentence, but the lawyers were triumphant. The CPS told her that the nine-year minimum would not be judged as unduly lenient.

Finally, in 2012 he was sentenced for the earlier rape, and given several more life sentences (again all concurrent) and a minimum tariff of 16 years – once more concurrent with the nine-year tariff.[605] Although the judge expressed the view he should stay in prison for ever, he left the prison door ajar, because the effect of the multiple concurrent life sentences and a 16-year tariff meant that the prison gates have still not yet finally and permanently closed on this violent and dangerous man. In 2028, when Shirley will be able to apply for parole – yet again – his rape victims will no doubt suffer much anxiety over fears he may be released, and it remains a dreadful truth that the record of our parole board leaves the victims and the public no room for comfort on that score.

British courts frequently minimise the impact of multiple sentences by making them concurrent, as happened with Shirley. Consecutive sentences are rare. The US courts, whose crime reduction record is far better than ours, show no similar inhibitions. In 2006, for example, a court in the State of Georgia gave seven consecutive life sentences plus 265 years to each of two violent criminals who had committed a string of armed robberies. In Tucson, Arizona, a 24-year-old violent criminal was given seven consecutive life sentences with no parole, for a mass shooting that left six people dead. One woman survived despite being shot in the head.

In California in 1973, twenty-five consecutive life sentences were handed down to a Mexican American, Juan Corona. He had been convicted of murdering twenty-five migrant farm workers.[606] Who can say that his sentence was unjust?

The 2005 British Parole Board Report showed a photograph of the board members smiling complacently into the camera. There is in this picture no evidence of diminution of confidence – no lessening of self-belief, and the text of the report drips self-satisfaction. Yet only a few months before they had released probably one of the most dangerous men in the prison system – Damion Hanson, who, as described in a previous chapter, went on to murder John Monckton and maim his wife in their own home. The absurd nature of the parole proceedings that released Hanson can be seen from the fact that the judge who tried him for these crimes, described him as a 'very, very dangerous man', only a short while after the parole board decided he was 'an acceptable risk' for release.

The parole board members later said they went through much soul-searching after this tragedy, but there was no need for such deep introspection. It was obvious what had happened – they had guessed wrongly and made a terrible mistake. It wasn't the first, as hundreds of people have been killed by violent criminals released in similar circumstances, and it won't be the last while the present Punch and Judy like parole system continues.

Had a 2-strike system been in place Hanson would not have been at liberty to attack the Monckton family and John Monckton would be alive today. Hanson was 15 years old when he was convicted of grievous bodily harm and wounding. The following table shows the sentences he received and the effect of the long prison sentence that he would have been given under the proposed sentencing code suggested here.[607] This is on the assumption that parliament would decide that all first strikers, because of the danger they present, would be dealt with in the same way, irrespective of their age. Hanson had a previous conviction for violence when he was convicted of grievous bodily harm in 1996 and so would qualify for the more severe first-strike sentence of 17 years without parole. He would then not have been released until 2013, when he was 32 years old. At this point it would have been made clear to him, that if he was convicted of another strike offence identified on the list legislated for by parliament, he would go to prison for the rest of his life. The probation service and other helping agencies would be galvanised to help him settle into the community, but whether he gave up his criminal life style or continued to be violent would be up to him.

| Date | Offence | Actual sentence | Actual time served in jail | Effect of sentence under new code | Offences prevented |
|---|---|---|---|---|---|
| 1993 | Indecent assault | Supervision 6 months | none | n/a | |
| 1995 | Assault ABH | Attendance centre | none | n/a | |
| 1996 | GBH Wounding | 18 months prison | 11 months | 17 years imprisonment | |
| 1996 | Burglary | conditional discharge | none | in prison | offence prevented |
| 1997 | Att. burglary | 4 months | 3 months | in prison | offence prevented |
| 1998 | Att. murder+ robbery | 12 years (+ 8 conc') | 6 years | in prison | offence prevented |
| 2005 | Murder & att. murder | Life imp. min 36 years | | in prison | offence prevented |

A revamped two-strike sentencing law with no parole would be clear-cut in its effect and so put violent men such as Shirley and Hanson beyond the reach of anyone again. The case for stopping killers and other violent criminals from committing further violent crime is so obvious that the real question is why should our ruling elite be so against it?

We need have no inhibitions about imposing such a system. Two- and -three-strike sentencing policies have been enacted in various states in the US, (with slight variations), and they have seen significant and consistent reductions in all violent crime categories, except for four states which have only seen a reduction in some, but reductions nevertheless. In 1994, the US rate per 100,000 of the population for violent crime was 713.6. In 2015, it was 383. For murder the figures for these years are 9.0 and 4.9. For rape, they are 39.3 and 28.1 and for robbery 237.7 and 101.9.[608]

The ten states with the toughest 3-strike laws are those with the steepest declines in violence, murder, rape, robbery and aggravated assault. For example, South Carolina has almost halved its violent crime rate for these categories. It has an uncompromising 2-strike law with no parole. In contrast, the ten states with the most lenient 2- and 3-strike laws show more moderate declines in their violent crime rates (but declines nevertheless).[609] [610] [611] [612] [613] The evidence from California shows that their three-strike system resulted in a dramatic fifty per cent drop in crime. In contrast, a study of French inmates highlighted what happened when a group of criminals were rewarded. It found that the offenders who benefited most from a prison pardon (given in honour of Bastille Day) were later found to have the highest recidivism rates.[614]

We must not be put off by scaremongering from those who would argue the introduction of a 2-strike sentencing policy would cause a steep rise in prison numbers in Britain and therefore a vast increase in prison costs. There were similar fears expressed by civil servants in California, who predicted their prison population would double between 1994 (when their 3-strike legislation was enacted) and 1998, from 125,000 to 250,000, and would likely reach 350,000 by 2004. But these predictions were proved wrong. They were based on the belief that large numbers of prisoners would be given second-strike sentences for relatively minor crimes. But this did not happen, because the courts used the discretion open to them to avoid this. At the same time the judges did not hesitate to apply third-strike sentencing (25 years to life) to violent criminals who represented a clear danger to the public. Interestingly, of the 160,000 offenders incarcerated in 2002–2003, 20% were 2-strikers and only 5% were 3-strikers. Given the court's willingness to use the 3-strike offence where appropriate, this indicates that many violent criminals, faced with the threat of losing most, or all their liberty, threw in the towel after their second-strike sentence.[615]

In addition, the falling crime rate considerably lessened the demand for prison places, and between 1994 and 2004, the state prison population only increased by 35,000, (due, it is believed, to the six million growth in the general population), not by the 225,000 predicted. Further, incarceration costs in California have been offset by significant cost savings generated by the lower crime rates.[616] Nevertheless, critics have pointed to the high costs of their justice system compared to other states. But this is due to the high wages and standard of working conditions negotiated by its strong labour unions. The justice bill would be even higher if it were not for the millions of dollars saved by their 3-strike sentencing law.

The Californian research pinpoints what is well known about human nature and that is we all, criminals included, put off necessary change to the last moment. It has been said that during the French revolution the victims being taken to the guillotine for execution showed no fear until they reached the guillotine itself. They demonstrated the formidable capacity humans have for putting off the moment when they had to embrace reality. Until that moment came, there was always another street, or landmark to be passed which could occupy their thoughts.[617] Had California run a 5-strike system they would have found four times as many 4-strikers, as 5-strikers in their jails.

There is no reason to think that the majority of violent criminals in this country would respond differently, and that we would not reap similar social and financial benefits.

While those with the highest propensity for violence, at the far end of the violence spectrum, will commit violent crimes no matter how severe the punishment, a 2-strike law, if introduced in Britain, would ensure they would not be free to commit further crime beyond their second-strike conviction. The belief that many others would desist sooner, is supported by the US experience, quoted above, and the results of the New Zealand 3-strike law introduced in 2010. After five years, there were 5,400 first strikers in New Zealand's jails and only 76 second strikers.[618] [619] In addition, Singapore has maintained one of the best crime control records known by handing out increasingly long sentences to criminals after their third conviction, all served without parole.

Some critics might argue that a similar ratio of first and second strikers may have existed before New Zealand's 3-strike law was enacted. This, I suggest is unlikely, but even if this was demonstrated, it would be no argument against the 3-strike provision, whose benefit is that it identifies those very dangerous criminals who will not stop whatever threat is held over them. What their 3-strike law does which the old system did not is to make it certain that those convicted of a third strike offence will not get a further opportunity to do so again. Thus, all concerned can know that such prison terms have been accurately targeted, and therefore there is no need for doubt or reticence about the rightness of such sentences, or for there to be any fears of injustice.

As with California, contrary to the predictions from the 'experts', New Zealand's prisons are not overflowing – their prison muster is about the same as it was five years ago. There have been no shoot outs with desperate second strikers anxious to avoid a third, and no poor innocents have been locked up for petty theft.

Australia is now considering introducing its own version of a 3-strike law.

In 2013 the European Court of Human Rights (ECHR) ruled that whole life terms without the possibility for review or parole may well be contrary to the concept of 'human rights'. It indicated that Britain should review such sentences every 25 years. As far as can be judged, MPs are resistant to this idea and generally favour whole life terms for the worst murderers, whereas some members of the House of Lords appear to support the ECHR ruling. At the time of writing the British government has not made clear its official response to the ECHR, but a number of ministers have indicated that they do not agree that such sentences conflict with human rights law.[620]

Should there be no agreement on this matter, the proposals for whole life terms as part of a British 2-strike system would require Britain to separate itself from the ECHR in whatever way it can. Many would argue we should do this anyway. What is significant is that many of the European judges who determined that whole life terms violate human rights, even for the most dangerous and malign of killers, are from countries whose experience during the Second World War brought them much closer than Britain to the deeply malign violence practised by the Nazis. Yet, despite what their relatively recent history has taught them about the effects of such violence on individuals, families and indeed on whole nations, they are still not prepared to draw a final line and declare some violent murderers to be so bad that they are beyond the pale, and deserving of an unconditional whole life term in prison. If, for them, there are no limits to the brutality that they can tolerate, does this not make them brutes also?

The question of how long we should keep violent offenders locked up has dogged the thinking of penal reformers and others for many years. It was believed by many that following abolition, a life sentence would mean a whole life term, but in fact no firm ruling was made. Some MPs argued it would be inhumane to keep a man in prison for more than twenty years, as longer terms would be cruel and risk driving him to psychological collapse. But there are examples on record that suggest that offenders can survive very long periods of incarceration. In Britain triple police killer Harry Roberts, was released in 2014 after serving 48 years in prison.[621] In the USA in 1899, 22-year-old Richard Honeck and an accomplice entered a man's room armed with knives, guns and other weapons, and stabbed him to death. On remand in prison, following his arrest, Honek also stabbed a prison warden. He served 64 years in prison without further trouble, and was released in 1963, aged 84. He then lived successfully and quietly with his sister in Oregon, until his death in 1976, aged 97 years.[622]

The new sentencing code would mean that as far as dangerous and repeat violent criminals were concerned, the prisons would be reorganised around keeping them in, not, as is the case now, for the majority, getting them out. The daily routines in prison would be built on the expectation that many of the inmates would be prisoners for all or most of their active lives. Although a requirement to review whole life terms (if it is introduced) does not guarantee a whole life prisoner will be released, its presence would have a powerfully disruptive effect on inmates and the culture of the prison. It was Henry Romilly, the 19th century penal reformer, who put this point with great succinctness.[623] To those who argued that a whole life term was too harsh and leaves the prisoner with no hope, which in turn would make him more dangerous and attack his gaolers, he said this:

"Any violence from the inmate would be suppressed by the staff. If the prisoner continued to be violent he would be subject to disciplinary measures and his lot would be worse than what it was before. The gaolers would have no choice. No one could say they were being cruel in the application of legally sanctioned disciplinary measures – because the prisoner's remedy is in his own hands. If the prisoner becomes violent, who will be disadvantaged? Only the prisoner.

The answer is that the management of the prisons must not be put in the hands of weak and incompetent gaolers. In practice the prisoner has the strongest possible motive and interest in being on peaceable terms with the prison staff. Otherwise his lack of co-operation would mean that his life in gaol would be far less comfortable and happy than it could have been.

It is not the case that the prisoner with a whole life term 'has no hope'. The only hope that is extinguished is the hope of release. Given no other options, it is part of human nature to adapt to new surroundings, and to find new interests, solace and occupation in the new routine. This frame of mind is only possible when the prisoner is absolutely convinced there is no hope of release. Where this hope remains, it causes distress, restlessness, irritability, and makes the prisoner difficult to manage.

To begin with, the man is shocked by the sentence, depressed, and angry, but these are generally temporary conditions, and can be guarded against by the prison with proper precautions. Eventually the prisoner will realise it is in his interests to establish a new routine and find pleasure and satisfactions that he never probably dreamed of before his whole life sentence.

What chiefly unsettles a man's mind in prison is the hope of getting back to the pleasures and interests from which he has been suddenly cut off. When he knows for certain he cannot get them back he learns to accept his new position."

Henry Romilly knew what he was talking about. In 1967, when the then Home Secretary, Roy Jenkins, a prince of penological liberalism, introduced parole, I was deputed to interview a lifer prisoner (as were others) as part of the then new parole review process. After seeing the prisoner, I also spoke with the principle prison officer responsible for the inmate. He was very angry.

He told me that such visits caused him and his fellow officers considerable trouble, because they awakened in the prisoner his hopes and aspirations connected with the outside world. I do not know whether this officer had ever read Romilly's 19th century treatise on the subject, but he could have written a similar one just as powerfully and with even more authority. He listed, almost word for word, the problems Romilly had described when hope of release is rekindled for these prisoners. I was told I would leave the prison with an inmate once more in an agitated and distressed frame of mind, that meant trouble for the prisoner and the prison staff, made worse if parole was refused, which at that early stage of the prisoner's sentence, it was likely to be. The principle officer had seen it all before because I was not the first to arrive at his prison on such an errand. He knew what was coming. I left the prison ill at ease at the part I had played in this process.

In 2012, indeterminate sentences (IPPs) were scrapped. David Blunkett said the reason this provision had not worked was because the government had "not been sufficiently clear in setting the sentencing criteria for judges."[624] But they had. Although, as explained in an earlier chapter, the overall prison population had not increased as much as they had feared, following the introduction of IPPs in 2003, the government were caught off guard by the rise in numbers of this category of prisoner. They had estimated that they would add no more than 900 to the prison roll at any one time, but by 2012 with a different government, there were 6,000, most or all of whom must, at some time, be assessed for release. This was an administrative burden they wanted to be rid of, which, as indicated earlier, was causing them embarrassment. Their answer was to pass the Criminal Justice and Courts Act 2015, Section 236A of which created a new type of determinate sentence, the 'Special Custodial Sentence for Certain Offenders of Particular Concern' for the most serious violent and sexual offenders.[625] [626] Because this left the length of these prison terms largely to the judges, the government no doubt anticipated (hoped?) they would not be too long, and their fixed term removed the queue-forming associated with the indeterminate sentences (IPPs). Indeterminate sentences were unjust and for this reason needed to be scrapped, but what replaced them was driven by administrative convenience and not concerns for public safety.

Many of the MPs who passed this law were soon lining up to express their horror over the killings in Syria. But the grief of those whose friends and relatives have been killed by violent criminals allowed to roam free on the streets of Britain, is no less dreadful than that experienced by Syrians whose family and friends have been killed by barrel bombs. It is true that casualties of the Syrian war pose a far bigger problem, but does this mean that homicide, rape and maiming, is acceptable if it is measured in hundreds every year as opposed to thousands?

Is it not time that the concern and determination expressed by our ruling elite to find a way to end the killing in Syria and other places in the world, over which they have no control, should also be focused on the killing, raping and maiming in their own back yard, which they can and should do something about?

Towards the end of 2017 two cases involving the sentencing of highly dangerous men captured the headlines. The extraordinarily privileged treatment that both of these serial criminals received starkly revealed the cold indifference shown towards the public that is the hall mark of our justice system. The comment they provoked was focused on trivia, and in particular, parliament generally failed to seize upon the real problems they represented.

The first involved a serial killer called Theodore Johnson. He revealed to the world how dangerous he was in a spectacular manner. In 1981 he threw his wife off a ninth-floor balcony in Wolverhampton. He was allowed to plead guilty to manslaughter, which means that the court accepted his story that he did not mean to kill her. But wouldn't it be obvious even to a small child, that the drop from such a great height would be fatal? Yet the justice system closed ranks around him to protect him from a murder conviction, and in 1981, he was sentenced to just three years in jail. In 1992 he killed again, by strangling his girl friend. This time he was allowed to plead diminished responsibility because of 'depression', a condition that many at the time, and since, felt was tactical rather than real

He was detained in a psychiatric hospital and after two years he was released on condition that he told the authorities if he made relationships with women. He failed to do so and kept his contact with a new girl friend, Angela Best, a secret. Twenty-two year later, in 2016, he battered her to death with a claw hammer, after she discovered his violent, criminal past, and indicated she wanted to leave him. She was 51 years old. A few days before, he had been seen by a psychiatrist, who declared he was not depressed. (The public might ask even if he was – so what? What possible relevance could this have to his murderous behaviour? Depression is one of the most common problems known to exist in our society – are we to believe that all sufferers are potential killers?). The justice system had twice previously protected Johnson from his just desserts, but after his third killing, finally accepted it could shield this 64-year-old man no more, and in early 2018 he was convicted of murder. He was sentenced to life imprisonment with a minimum tariff of 26 years. Although he will be 90 years old before he can apply for parole, he should, I would argue, have been sentenced to a whole life term, as a symbol of society's total rejection of his murderous behaviour.

The second case concerned a serial rapist, John Worboys, who had, as in the case of Johnson, benefited from a spectacularly privileged sentence. He was convicted of several rapes and it became known that he committed many of these crimes in his taxi, sometimes drugging the victims first. The level of malignancy displayed in these crimes should have made it clear that Warboys was deserving of a whole life sentence. Yet he was given an indeterminate sentence with a minimum tariff of 10 years.

When that point was reached, the parole board announced that it was going to release him. There followed several days of media and parliamentary comment principally over the anxieties caused to some of his victims, who had not been informed of the board's decision. It was as if those concerned believed that had the women been informed at the appropriate time, this would have brought them peace of mind. But is it not obvious that even, had his victims been told of his pending release, this would not have quelled their anxieties – why should it?

The naive, not to say ridiculous nature of this debate was then made worse by concerns over whether Worboys was 'safe enough' to let out. The question was asked – had he received proper 'treatment'? i.e. attended a suitable sex offender programme while he was in prison? I listened while a number of officials, BBC interviewers, and even Victim Support workers, raised their concerns about this. Once again, it was as if they thought it would be all right to release him once it was known he had attended one of these programmes. Is it the case that they are so naive that they believe these programmes actually work? The fact of their failure is well established. To emphasise this, on 5 of January 2018 a researcher, quoting a 2017 government report, told the interviewer on the 1pm News on BBC Radio 4, that the "evidence makes it clear that sex offender programmes not only do not work, but in many cases the offending of those who attend them becomes worse." The interviewer made it known how surprised he was. No member of parliament intervened to ask the question – why it was then, that the prison service and the probation service were still running them? Should the public see the avoidance of such an obvious line of enquiry as indicating that many MPs are ignorant of these facts, or that they do not understand their implications?

Over the next few days the focus switched to whether the parole board chairman should be made to explain the reasons for releasing Worboys. Parliament, it was decided, should intervene, and call for the board to make their reasons known. But what difference will this make? He will still be released. *That* is the problem.

Focussing on irrelevancies only serve to detract the public's attention from the real problem facing them and victims alike which is that the parole board should be abolished. Worboys (and all other criminals) should receive a sentence, the objective of which is not to 'make them better' or get them to apologise and show remorse (all of which can be and are fabricated by prisoners wanting to get out of prison), but to punish them for what they have done. The subject of their fitness for early release should not arise.

Even if the sex offender programmes were successful in a 100% of cases, or the parole board, psychologists, and probation staff had other means to know for certain (which they do not) that Worboys (or other offenders) was genuinely reformed and would never commit another offence, this should not trigger his release. He should stay in prison for the duration of his sentence, which a well ordered justice system would have ensured was for the rest of his life.

# Epilogue

In early January 2017, three policemen in Northumbria went looking for a man who had violently assaulted his partner, causing her severe injuries. They first went to his address but he was not there. They then drove around the neighbourhood and spotted him walking along the pavement. It was dark, so when they pulled up alongside him he was caught in the glare of their headlights. The three police officers jumped from their car and surrounded him. But instead of placing him under arrest and handcuffing him while reading him his rights, they engaged him in conversation about what he had done, and pleaded with him to take part in a domestic violence programme, which they said would help him manage his anger.

# Selected Bibliography

Bailey, B., *Hangmen of England, A History of Execution from Jack Ketch to Albert pierrepoint*, W H Allen, 1989

Berry-Dee, C., *Talking with Serial Killers*, John Blake, 2003

Booth Davies, J., *The Myth of Addiction*, Harwood Academic Publishers, 1992

Briggs, M., Jordan, P., *Economic History Of England*, University Tutorial Press Ltd, 1954

Browning, C. R., *Ordinary Men, Reserve Police Battalion 101 And The Final Solution In Poland*, Penguin Books, 1992

Christoph, J. B., *Capital Punishment And British Politics*, George Allen & Unwin Ltd, 1962

Cohen, A. K., *Deviance and Control*, Prentice-Hall, 1966

Copperfield, D., *Wasting Police Time*, Monday Books, 2006

Dalrymple, T., *Admirable Evasions, How Psychology Undermines Morality*, Encounter Books, 2015

Dalrymple, T., *Mr Clarke's Modest Proposal: Supportive Evidence from Yeovil*, The Social Affairs Unit, 2011

Dalrymple, T., *Not With A Bang But A Whimper, The Politics & Culture of Decline*, Monday Books, 2009

Dalrymple, T., *Spoilt Rotten! The Toxic Cult of Sentimentality*, Gibson Square, 2010

Davies, J. G., *Small Corroding Words, The Slighting of Great Britain by the EHRC*, Civitas, 2011

Davies, M., *Probationers in their Social Environment, A Home Office Research Unit Report*, HMSO 1969

Dennis, N., and Erdos, G., *Culture and Crimes, Policing in Four Nations,* Civitas, 2005

Elkin, W. A., The English Penal System, Pelican Books, 1957

Emsley, C., *Crime and Society in England 1750-1900*, Longman, 1987

Fraser, D., *A Land Fit for Criminals, An Insider's View of Crime, Punishment and Justice in the UK,* Book Guild, 2006

Fyvel, T. R., *The Insecure Offenders*, Chatto and Windus, 1961

Gadget, I., *Perverting the Course of Justice*, Monday Books, 2008

Garrett, D., *A Life For A Life, A Case For Capital Punishment*, Hazard Press, 1999

Gaute, J. H. H., & Odell, R., *The Murderers' Who's Who*, Pan Books 1979

Gibson, E., *Homicide in England and Wales 1967–1971, A Home Office Statistical Report*, HMSO, 1975

Green, D., et al., *Crime and Civil Society*, Civitas, 2005

Greenwood, C., *Firearms Control, A Study of Armed Crime and Firearms Control in England and Wales,* Routledge & Kegan Paul, 1972

Grierson, E., *Confessions of a Country Magistrate*, Victor Gollancz, 1972

Hitchins, P., *A Brief History of Crime, The Decline of Order, Justice and Liberty in England*, Atlantic Books, 2003

Home Office, *Police and Criminal Evidence Act 1984, Codes of Practice*, HMSO, 1995

Hughes, M., *Judgement Impaired: Law, Disorder and Injustice to Victims in 21st century Britain,* Hands-Cuffe Publications Ltd, 2005

Jones, F., *Murderous Women*, Headline, 1991

Jones, H., *Crime and the Penal System*, University Tutorial Press Ltd, 1962

Jones, H., *Crime in a Changing Society*, Pelican Books, 1965

Jones, H., *Reluctant Rebels*, Tavistock Publications, 1960

Lawrence, B., *They Call It Justice,* The Book Guild Ltd, 1999

Mays, J. B., *Crime and the Social Structure*, Faber and Faber Ltd, 1963

Mays, J. B., *Growing Up In The City*, University Press of Liverpool, 1954

Mays, J. B., *The Young Pretenders,* Michael Joseph, 1965    200

McGuire, J., *What Works: Reducing Reoffending, Guidelines from Research and Practice*, Wiley, 1995

Miller, D., *The Age Between, Adolescents in a disturbed society*, 1969

Murray, C., *Does Prison Work?* The IEA Health and Welfare Unit, in association with *The Sunday Times,* 1997

Murray, C., *Simple Justice*, Civitas, 2005    199

Newbold, G., *The Problem of Prisons, Corrections Reforms in New Zealand,* Dunmore Publishing Ltd, 2007

Oborne, P., *The Rise of Political Lying*, Simon & Schuster, 2005

Oborne, P., *The Triumph Of The Political Class*, Simon & Schuster, 2007

'Penal Practice in a Changing Society'. *White Paper on Penal Reform* C. (58) 251, 1958, Home Office

Pollard, S., *Ten Days that Changed the Nation, The Making of Modern Britain*, Simon & Schuster, 2009

Prison Reform Trust, *Male Prisoners and Young Offenders*, 1999

Rees, S., *The Floating Brothel*, Headline Book Publishing, 2001

Romilly, H., *The Punishment of Death*, John Murray, 1886

Saunders, P., *Social Mobility Myths*, Civitas, 2010

Saunders, P., *The Rise of the Equality Industry*, Civitas, 2011

Sergeant, H., *The Public and The Police*, Civitas, 2008

Sharpe, J. A., *Crime in Early Modern England*, longman, 1984

Snowdon, C., *The Spirit Level Delusion*, Little Dice, 2010

Spierenburg, P., *A History of Murder, Personal Violence in Europe from the Middle Ages to the Present,* Polity, 2008

Sugden, K., (Ed), Arkell, C., et al., Criminal Islington, *The Story of Crime and Punishment in a Victorian Suburb,* Islington Archaeology and History Society, 1989

Taylor, I., et al., *The New Criminology: for a social theory of deviance,* Routledge & KeganPaul, 1973

Tolmie, J., (Ed), Brookbanks, W., et al., *Criminal Justice in New Zealand,* LexisNexis Ltd, Wellington, 2007

Wasik, M., and Taylor., R. D., *Blackstone's Guide to the Criminal Justice Act 1991,* Blackstone Press Ltd, 1991

West, D. J., *Murder Followed By Suicide,* Harvard University Press, 1966

Wolfgang, M. E., Savitz, L., Johnston, N., (Eds) *The Sociology of Crime and Delinquency,* John Wiley & Sons, 1962

# Notes

Questions prepared for my interview with Lord Birt:

Why do you think Tony Blair asked you to carry out this investigation? Did he explain its purpose?

How long did it take?

What was the source of your information? Was it easy to find?

What was your reaction to what you found concerning the number of crimes committed in this country each year?

Did you discuss the report with anyone during its compilation? Did you give Tony Blair interim reports?

What was Tony Blair's reaction when you made known to him the report's findings? Did you suspect he was going to hide it from the public?

How did the Home Office officials who helped you compile it, react to what you and they had discovered concerning the number of crimes committed in Britain? How many Home Office officials were involved?

Could you comment on why you have never discussed the report with anyone since you completed it?

Was the assumption from the outset that the report would never be made public?

If you did not know at the time, did you later discover that Tony Blair had hidden the report?

Were you requested or instructed by Tony Blair or anyone else, not to speak about the report? If this was the case, can you say why this embargo was placed on you?

# Endnotes

## References

### Chapter 1

1   A Field Evaluation of the VIPER system. A New Technique for eliciting
    eyewitness identification. Memon et al., Dept. of Psychology, Royal
    Holloway College, University of London
    http://www.pc.rhul.ac.uk/sites/rheg/papers/memonpclin%20press.pdf
2   Valentine T., Heaton P., (1999) An evaluation of fairness of police line-
    ups and video identifications. Applied Cognitive Psychology 13, S59-S72
    (quoted in 1 Memon et al., above).
3   *They Call It Justice*. Brian Lawrence, The Book Guild, (2002)
4   GOV.UK Ministry of Justice: press Release 13 August 2015. Average
    sentence for sex offences in England and Wales is 5 years.
    https://www.gov.uk/government/news/sex-offender-sentences-hit-record-
    levels
5   'I'm invisible to men – except when I go jogging.' The *Daily Telegraph* 14
    January 2017

### Chapter 2

6 European Sourcebook of Crime and Criminal Justice Statistics 2014, 5th Edition
http://www.heuni.fi/material./attachments/heuni/reports/qrMWoCVTF/
HEUNI_report_80_European_Sourcebook.pdf

7 'London worse for crime than New York.' The *Daily Telegraph*, 21 October 2017

8 European Sourcebook of Crime and Criminal Justice Statistics, published 2014.

9 Eurostats: Crime and Criminal Justice Statistics / Main Statistical Findings / Crime and Criminal Justice Tables / article tables (assaults table 02: prison population table 20)

10 *The Dark Figure of British Crime*, City New York Journal, Spring 2009, Claire Berlinski

11 Data.gov A Summary of Recorded Crime Data 1898–2001
https://Data.gov.uk/dataset/recorded-crime-data-1898-2001-02/resource/
b5b1c3fe-338e-472e-b844-75108c57436c

12 HO Stats Bulletin Crime in England and Wales 2010/11 HOSB: 10/11
http://www.cjp.org.uk/publications/government/crime-in-england-and-
Wales-2010-11-14-07-2011/

13 Home Office Statistical Bulletin Crimes detected in England and Wales 2012/13 HOSB: 02/13
https://www.gov.uk/government/uploads/system/uploads/attachment_data/
file/224037/hosb0213.pdf

14 Office for National Statistics Crime in England and Wales: Year ending March 2015
https://www.ons.gov.uk/peoplepopulationandcommunity/crimeandjustice/
bulletins/crimeinenglandandWales/2015-07-16

15 'Robbed of £17,500, and the bank got me back 10p.' The *Daily Telegraph*, 23 July 2016
http://www.telegraph.co.uk/personal.-banking/current-accounts/i-was-
robbed-of-17500--the-bank-refunded-me-10p/

16 Data.gov A Summary of Recorded Crime Data 1898–2001
https://Data.gov.uk/dataset/recorded-crime-data-1898-2001-02/resource/
b5b1c3fe-338e-472e-b844-75108c57436c

17 Dennis, N., Erdos, G., (2005) Cultures and Crimes, Policing in Four Nations, Civitas

18 CIVITAS: Forces of law and order have lost control, Media Release, 7 April 2003 and: Normans Dennis and George Erdos, 'Cultures and Crimes, Policing in Four Nations, Civitas (2005), p. xxiii

19 'Number of victims of street fights soars.' The *Daily Telegraph*, 4 May 2009

20 Data relating to the number of attacks on National Health staff from 403 Health bodies across Britain found in: NHS Protect-Physical. Assaults Against Staff 2010/11.
http://www.nhsbsa.nhs.uk/documents/securityManagement/2010-11_NHS_Violence_Against_Staff_Final_01-11-20.pdf

21 The Journal of Forensic Psychiatry, 'Harassment and Stalking of Members of the United Kingdom Parliament: associations and consequences.' David V James et al., 19 January, 2016.
http://www.tandfonline.com/doi full/10.1080/14789949.2015.1124909# abstract
See also: 'MPs scared to leave home due to angry voters.' The *Times* 25 January 2016
See also: 'Labour MP Jo Cox dies after being shot and stabbed as husband urges people to 'fight against the hate that killed her.' The *Daily Telegraph*, 17 June 2016

22 Progressively Worse, The Burden of bad ideas in British schools. Robert Peal, Civitas (2014).
See also: 'The worst behaved pupils in the world.' *Daily Mail*, 24 April 2014

23 'Police called to 10,000 violent attacks in schools in just one year, *Daily Mail*, 23 December 2008

24 '188,000 pupil exclusions an improvement.' The *Daily Telegraph*, 31 July 2009

25 'Teachers need shin pads for violent pupils.' The *Daily Telegraph*, 5 August 2011

26 'Six school staff are attacked by pupils every week.' The *Daily Telegraph*, 13 November 2010

27 'Class Violence.' The *Daily Telegraph*, 8 July 2009

28 'One teacher a week is seriously assaulted.' The *Daily Telegraph*, 20 November 2010

29 'Teacher sues for stress brought on by nightmare pupils.' The *Daily Telegraph*, 16 October 2009

30 'Children have all the power now. Teachers are terrified.' The *Daily Telegraph*, 24 October, 2009

31 'Released by his parents, haunting last picture of a bullied boy aged 12.' *Daily Mail*, 27 August 2014

32 'Bullied schoolboy 13, wins payout over violent attack in classroom.' The *Daily Telegraph*, 17 September 2011

33 1950 crime figures in: Data.gov A Summary of Recorded Crime Data 1898-2002

https://Data.gov.uk/dataset/recorded-crime-data-1898-2001-02/resource/b5b1c3fe-338e-472e-b844-75108c57436c

2013/14 figures (latest found) for arson: Office for National Statistics, Crime in England and Wales, Year ending December 2014:

http://www.ons.gov.uk/peoplepopulationandcommunity/crimeandjustice/bulletins/crimeinenglandandWales/2015-04-23#

Criminal-damage

For robbery: Home Office Statistical Bulletin: Crime Outcomes in England and Wales 2013/14, HOSB 01/14

https://www.gov.uk/government/uploads/system/uploads/attachment_data/file/331597/hosb0114.pdf.pdf

For serious wounding: Home Office Statistical Bulletin Crime Detected in England and Wales 2012/13 HOSB:02/13

https://www.gov.uk/government/uploads/system/uploads/attachment_data/file/224037/hosb0213.pd

34 'David Cameron marks British 1919 Amritsar massacre.' *BBC News*, 20 February 2013

35 *BBC News*, March 2011: 'Government outrage at the killing of Libyans.' Also: *BBC Radio 4 News*, 12 April 2011, Interview with the Foreign Secretary

36 *Population 1942-1980: British Historica*, Statistics by B.R. Mitchell (Page 14)

https://books.google.co.uk/books?id =Oyg9AAAAIAAJ&pg= PA1&source= gbs_toc_r&cad=3#v=onepage&q&f=false

1980-2008 Annual Abstract of Statistics, No. 146, 2010 Edition
http://www.ons.gov.uk/ons/rel/ctu/Annual-abstract-of-statistics/no-146--
2010-edition/index.html

2009-2011 Office for National Statistics, Population Estimates for
England and Wales, Mid-2002 to Mid-2010 http://www.ons.gov.uk/ons/
dcp171778_288817.pdf

2012 Office for National Statistics Population Estimates for England and
Wales 2012 http://www.ons.gov.uk/ons/rel/pop-estimate/population-
estimates-for-england-and-Wales/mid-2012/index.html

2013 Office for National Statistics Annual Mid-Year Population Estimates,
http://www.ons.gov.uk/ons/dcp171778_367167.pdf

2014 Office for National Statistics Annual Mid-Year Population Estimates,
http://www.ons.gov.uk/ons/dcp171778_406922.pdf

2015 Population Estimates for UK, England and Wales, Scotland and
Northern Ireland: https://www.ons.gov.uk/peoplepopulationandcommunity/
populationandmigration/populationestimates/bulletins/
Annualmidyearpopulationestimates/latest

37   Data.gov A Summary of Recorded Crime Data 1898-2001
https://Data.gov.uk/dataset/recorded-crime-data-1898-2001-02/resource/
b5b1c3fe-338e-472e-b844-75108c57436c

38   For Violence Against the Person crime numbers from 2001/02 to 2008/09:
Home Office Statistical Bulletin Crime in England and Wales 2010/11
HOSB 10/11
http://www.cjp.org.uk/publications/government/crime-in-england-and-
Wales-2010-11-14-07-2011/

39   Violence Against the Person 2009/10–2013/14
HO Statistical Bulletin Crime Outcomes in England and Wales 2013/14
HOSB 01/14
https://www.gov.uk/government/uploads/system/uploads/attachment_data/
file/331597/hosb0114.pdf.pdf

40   Home Office Crime Outcomes in England and Wales 2014/15, Statistical
Bulletin https://www.gov.uk/government/uploads/system/uploads/
attachment data/file445753/hosb0115.pdf

41   'Officer knifed by thief in bookmakers.' The *Daily Telegraph*, 20 May 2010

42  'Boy, 15, stabbed to death over Facebook insult.' The *Daily Telegraph*, 13 May 2010

43  'Gang may have filmed killing on mobile phone.' The *Daily Telegraph*, 28 May 2008

44  'TV actress blinded in glass attack.' *Daily Express*, 13 April 2011, see also 'Clubber sobs as she is jailed for blinding Hollyoaks actress with wine glass.' *Manchester Evening News*, 9 April 2011

45  See for example: '40 years for hitman.' The *Daily Telegraph*, 9 February 2013

46  'Soldier attacked.' The *Daily Telegraph*, 13 May 2010

47  'Honour killing claims a victim every month.' The *Daily Telegraph*, 18 December 2009

48  'Met accuses honour crimes whistleblower of misconduct.' The *Daily Telegraph*, 14 January 2017

49  'Police blast 5 people with Tazers every day.' *Daily Mail*, 16 October 2014

50  'Women killed by partners or former partners.' *Women's Hour*, BBC Radio 4, 2013

51  'Women killed by partners or former partners.' *Women's Hour*, BBC Radio 4, 2013

52  'Another day in Britain. 18 more rapes reported. So why are convictions so low?' The *Independent*, 16 June 1998

53  'It is a national disgrace that in 2009 rape almost always goes unpunished.' The *Guardian*, 15 April 2009

54  Statistical Bulletin12/10, Crime in England and Wales 2009/10: Findings from the British Crime Survey and police recorded crime https://www.gov.uk/government/uploads/system/uploads/attachment_data/file/116347/hosb1210.pdf

55  Government Equalities Office: Home Office, The Stern Review, An Independent Review into the Handling of Rape Complaints in England and Wales http://webarchive.nationalarchives.gov.uk/20110608160754/http:/www.Equalities.gov.uk/pdf/stern_review_acc_finalpdf

56  26 February 2013, BBC Radio News 1PM, Rape case not investigated.

57  'Rapes now at their highest ever level, ONS figures reveal.' The *Daily Telegraph*, 16 October 2014.

http://www.telegraph.co.uk/news/uknews/crime/11165613/Rapes-now-at-their-highest-ever-level-ONS-figures-reveal.html

58 Ministry of Justice crime statistics quoted in 'Conviction rates for sex crimes plunge.' *Daily Mail*, 11 December 2014

59 'Police reopen 68 rape inquiries they admit were wrongly dismissed.' *Daily Mail*, 7 October 2014

60 Violent Crimes per 1000 of the population from various towns in Britain found on: http://www.findaproperty.com/crime facts

61 'Licensees help in crime crackdown.' *Tavistock Times Gazette*, 4 February 2016

62 http://www.tavistocktoday.co.uk articlecfm?id=411874&headline =Licensees%20help %20in%20crime%20crackdown%20in%20 Tavistock&sectionIs=news&searchyear=2016

'Women's violent crimes increasing.' The *Independent,* 25 August 1995, and:

63 'Girls get violent.' The *Independent*, 1 May 1996 http://www.independent.co.uk/news/uk/girls-get-violent-1345290.html

64 Home Office, British Crime Survey 2009: Figures quoted in The *Daily Telegraph*, 27 May 2009, 'Thugettes are outnumbered.' http://www.telegraph.co.uk/comment/personal.-view/5389474/Ruth-Padel-poetry-has-always-been-a-rotten-business.html

65 Figures released by the Ministry of Justice and reported on in The *Times*, 31 July 2008, 'Violence takes over as crime women most often commit.' http://www.thetimes.co.uk/tto/news/uk/crime/article1874784.ece

66 Ministry of Justice: Statistics on Women in the Criminal Justice System, published 2010 https://www.gov.uk/government/uploads/system/uploads/attachment_data/file/217824/statistics-women-cjs-2010.pdf

67 'Girls get violent.' The *Independent*, 1 May 1996 http://www.independent.co.uk/news/uk/girls-get-violent-1345290.html

68 Prison Population Statistics, House of Commons Library Paper, No. SN/SG/4334, 29 July 2013 http://researchbriefings.files.parliament.uk/documents/SN04334/SN04334.pdf

69 Ministry of Justice, Statistics on Women and the Criminal Justice System, 2013

https://www.gov.uk/government/uploads/system/uploads/attachment_data/file/380090/women-cjs-2013.pdf

70  Ministry of Justice, National Statistics. Statistics on Women and the Criminal Justice System 2013
https://www.gov.uk/government/uploads/system/uploads/attachment_data/file/380090 /women-cjs-2013.pdf

71  'Woman beat pensioner to death for cash from sale of his house.' The *Daily Telegraph*, 5 August 2011
http://www.telegraph.co.uk/news/uknews/crime/8048958/Woman-arrested-over-murder-of-missing-Surrey-pensioner.html

72  'Savage Clockwork Orange girls kick gay man to death.' *Daily Express*, 20 April 2010
http://www.express.co.uk/news/uk/170268/Savage-Clockwork-Orange-girls-kick-gay-man-to-death

73  An Estimate of Youth Crime in England and Wales 2009/10: Home Office Research Report 64, published 2012
https://www.gov.uk/government/uploads/system/uploads/attachment_data/file/167982/horr64.pdf

74  *Mail Online,* 26 May 2012, 'Under 18s commit a quarter of all crime.'
http://www.dailymail.co.uk/news/article-2150187/Under-18s-commit-quarter-crimes-Young-offenders-responsible-million-crimes-just-year.html

75  '"I only stopped because my arms were aching," says torture boy.' *Daily Express*, 22 January 2010
http://www.dailymail.co.uk/news/article-1244984/I-stopped-arms-aching-Horrific-confession-11-year-old-sadist-tortured-young-boys.html

76  'Boys, 10, searched for site to rape girl, 8, court told.' The *Daily Telegraph*, 13 May, 2010
http://metro.co.uk/2010/05/13/girl-8-was-raped-by-two-10-year-old-boys-304202/

77  'Boy, 6, threatens to chop his teacher's head off with knife he brought into school.' *The Argus*, 17 July 2015 http://www.theargus.co.uk/news/13439833.Boy__6__threatened_to__chop_his_teacher___s_head_off__with_knife_he_brought_into_school/

78   'Gangs are getting younger and more violent, warns Met chief.' The
     *Guardian*, 20 December 2008
     https://www.theguardian.com/uk/2008/dec/20/gangs-younger-violent

79   'Children taught how to save their stabbed friends lives.' *Daily Express*, 6
     February 2009
     http://www.express.co.uk/news/uk/83663/Children-taught-how-to-save-
     their-stabbed-friends
     see also: '13-year old convicted of murder.' The *Guardian*, 17 April 2015
     https://www.theguardian.com/uk-news/2015/apr/17/boy-13-jailed-11-years-
     killing-woman-stamping-on-face

80   'Children aged 11 lost to a life of crime.' The *Daily Telegraph*, 21 October
     2010

81   'Gang hunted down 15-year-old boy to stab to stab to death, in rush-hour
     London station.' The *Daily Telegraph*, 26 January, 2011
     http://www.telegraph.co.uk/news/uknews/crime/8281558/Gang-hunted-
     down-15-year-old-boy-to-stab-to-death-in-rush-hour-London-station.html

82   'Girl arrested with knife had hit-list of classmates and teachers.' The *Daily
     Telegraph*, 26 March, 2010

83   'Supervision order for girl in razor attack at school.' The *Daily Telegraph*, 1
     July 2006
     http://www.telegraph.co.uk/news/uknews/1522784/Supervision-order-for-
     girl-in-razor-attack-at-school.html

84   'PE Teacher shot by school boy for making him play rugby.' *Thaindian
     News*, 6 November 2010
     http://www.thaindian.com/newsportal./odd-news/pe-teacher-shot-by-
     school-boy-for-making-him-play-rugby_100455680.html

85   Ministry of Justice, 2013 Compendium of reoffending statistics and analysis
     https://www.gov.uk/government/uploads/system/uploads/attachment_data/
     file/278133/compendium-reoffending-stats-2013.pdf

86   Ministry of Justice Criminal Justice Statistics, Quarterly Update to June 2012
     https://www.gov.uk/government/uploads/system/uploads/attachment_data/
     file/217632/Criminal-justice-stats-june-2012.pdf

87   Offender Management Statistics Quarterly, July to September 2015
     Front page of web site:

https://www.gov.uk/government/statistics/offender-management-statistics-
quarterly-july-to-september-2015
data on:
https://www.gov.uk/government/uploads/system/uploads/attachment_data/
file/495321/offender-management-statistics-quarterly-bulletin-jul-sep-2015.pdf

88  Offender Management Statistics Bulletin, England and Wales, Quarterly
January to March 2016
https://www.gov.uk/government/uploads/system/uploads/attachment_data/
file/541499/offender-management-statistics-quarterly-bulletin-jan2-
mar-2016.pdf

89  Ministry of Justice, Proven Reoffending Statistics, Quarterly Bulletin, July
2013 to June 2014
https://www.gov.uk/government/uploads/system/uploads/attachment_data/
file/519643/proven-reoffending-2014Q2.pdf

90  The Hertfordshire Constabulary C2 Programme
https://www.herts.police.uk/hertfordshire_constabulary/about_us/c2_
programme.aspx

91  The Halliday Report, Making Punishments Work, published by the Home
Office, July 2001. Quoted in 'Number of Offences Committed by Offenders
in a Year Self-Report 140 Offences per year', published by CIVITAS, 2010,
on http://www.civitas.org.uk/data/1993Prisons.php
NB: The Civitas paper quotes Appendix 6, page 130, of the Halliday Report
as the source. However, the current version (2016) of the Halliday Report
on the website, does not include the Appendices.

92  'I bet I'll offend again.' The Times, 16 November 1998:

93  'I get such a buzz from stealing.' Daily Mail, 10 December 1993 and:
Judgement Impaired by Michael Hughes, published by Hande-Cuffe
Publications Ltd, 2005

94  Ministry of Justice, Proven Reoffending Statistics Quarterly Bulletin, April
2009–March 2010, England and Wales
https://www.gov.uk/government/uploads/system/uploads/attachment_data/
file/218470/proven-reoffending-apr09-mar10.pdf

95  Ministry of Justice, Proven Reoffending Statistics, Quarterly Bulletin, July
2013 to June 2014

https://www.gov.uk/government/uploads/system/uploads/attachment_data/
file/519643/proven-reoffending-2014Q2.pdf

96  Ministry of Justice, 2013 Compendium of reoffending statistics and analysis
    https://www.gov.uk/government/uploads/system/uploads/attachment_data/
    file/278133/compendium-reoffending-stats-2013.pdf

97  Adult reconvictions: results from the 2009 cohort, England and Wales,
    Ministry of Justice Statistics Bulletin, published March 2011
    http://webarchive.nationalarchives.gov.uk/20120104233117/
    http:/www.justice.gov.uk/downloads/publications/statistics-and-data/
    mojstats/adult-reoffending-statistics-09.pdf

98  Ministry of Justice Compendium of Reoffending Statistics and analysis,
    published 4 November 2010
    https://www.gov.uk/government/uploads/system/uploads/attachment_data/
    file/199224/compendium-of-reoffending-statistics-and-analysis.pdf
    and:
    Maguire, M, The Construction of Crime Statistics, 2012, found on http://
    fds.oup.com/www.oup.com/pdf/13/9780199590278_prelim.pdf

99  Life Sentence for jeweller killer, BBC Online News Channel, 5 May 2005:
    http://news.bbc.co.uk/1/hi/england/nottinghamshire/4354467.stm
    and:
    https://www.theguardian.com/uk/2005/mar/22/ukcrime.ukguns1
    and:
    http://www.nottinghampost.com/Marian-Bates-death-arrested-hunt-James-
    Brodie-s/story-18077909-detail/story.html
    See also:
    HM Inspectorate of Probation Enquiry into the supervision of Peter
    Williams by Nottingham City Youth Offending Team, 2005
    http://www.justiceinspectorates.gov.uk/probation/wp-content/uploads/
    sites/5/2014/03/peterwilliamsenquiry-rps.pdf

100 Maguire, M, The Construction of Crime Statistics, 2012, found on
    http://s3.amazonaws.com/zanran_storage/www.oup.com/
    ContentPages/2551961264.pdf

101 'Police forces to cut more than 34,000 officers and staff.' The *Guardian*, 21
    July 2011

https://www.theguardian.com/uk/2011/jul/21/police-cut-30000-officers-staff

102 Data.gov A Summary of Recorded Crime Data 1898-2001
https://www.gov.uk/government/statistics/historical-crime-data

103 Police Numbers House of Commons Library Research paper 99/11. A Century of Change: Trends in UK Statistics since 1900

104 Home Office, National Statistics, Police workforce, England and Wales: 31 March 2015
https://www.gov.uk/government/publications/police-workforce-england-and-Wales-31-march-2015/police-workforce-england-and-Wales-31-march-2015

105 Office for National Statistics, Statistical Bulletin, Crime in England and Wales, Year ending June 2015
https://www.theguardian.com/uk/2011/jul/21/police-cut-30000-officers-staff

106 Crime Survey of England and Wales 2015
http://www.ons.gov.uk/ons/publications/re-reference-tables.html?edition=tcm%3A77-373428

107 European Sourcebook of Crime and Criminal Justice Statistics 2014, 5th Edition
http://www.heuni.fi/material./attachments/heuni/reports/qrMWoCVTF/HEUNI_report_80_European_Sourcebook.pdf

108 The Stephen Lawrence Enquiry: Report of and Inquiry by Sir William Macpherson of Cluny. February 1999, Cm 4262-I
https://www.gov.uk/government/uploads/system/uploads/attachment_data/file/277111/4262.pdf
and:
The Stephen Lawrence Independent Review: HC 1094, March 2014
https://www.gov.uk/government/uploads/system/uploads/attachment_data/file/287030/stephen_lawrence_review_summary.pdf

109 Davies, J. G., (2011), Small Corroding Words, The Slighting of Great Britain by the EHRC, published by Civitas:
and:
The Stephen Lawrence Enquiry. Report of and Inquiry by Sir William Macpherson of Cluny: February 1999, Cm 4262-I

https://www.gov.uk/government/uploads/system/uploads/attachment_data/file/277111/4262.pdf

110 Miller, J., (2000), Profiling Populations Available for Stops and Searches: London, Policing and Reducing Crime Unit, Research, Development and Statistics Directorate, Home Office
https://www.westmidlands-pcc.gov.uk/media/238047/prs131_profiling_populations_available_for_stops_and_searches.pdf

111 Fitzgerald, M., (1999), Final Report into Stop and Search, Metropolitan Police Quoted in: Waddington, P, A, J, et al., (2004), Stop and Search Research, In Proportion, British Journal of Criminology, 44, 889-914
https://www.ncjrs.gov/App/publications/abstract.aspx?ID=208312

112 Waddington, P. A. J., et al., (2004), Stop and Search Research, In Proportion, British Journal of Criminology, 44, 889-914
https://www.ncjrs.gov/App/publications/abstract.aspx?ID=208312

113 Home Office Statistical Bulletin 18/04, Arrests for Notifiable Offences and the Operation of Certain Powers under PACE, England and Wales, 2003/04.
http://webarchive.nationalarchives.gov.uk/20110218135832/http://rds.homeoffice.gov.uk/rds/pdfs04/hosb1804.pdf

114 *They Call It Justice*. Brian Lawrence, Book Guild (2002).

115 'CPS Director faces dissent from lawyers.' The *Independent*, 12 November 1993

116 'Evidence failed vital test.' The *Times*, 6 December 1993

117 'CPS goes on trial as convictions plunge by a third.' *Daily Mail*, 13 June 1997

118 The Public and the Police, Harriet Sergeant, Civitas, 2008

119 '"Now justice is a joke" says veteran bobby.' *Daily Express*, 11 February 2011
https://www.google.co.uk/?gws_veteran+bobby%2C+ Daily+Express+11+February+2011

120 Crown Prosecution Service: Annual Report and Accounts 2012/13
https://www.cps.gov.uk/publications/docs/Annual_report_2012_13.pdf

121 Crown Prosecution Service: Annual Report and Accounts 2014/15
https://www.cps.gov.uk/publications/docs/Annual_report_2014_15.pdf

122 Home Office Criminal Statistics England & Wales 2000, cm 5312

https://www.gov.uk/government/uploads/system/uploads/attachment_data/file/250902/crimestats.pdf

123 Home Office Statistical Bulletin: Crime Outcomes in England and Wales 2013/14, HOSB 01/14
https://www.gov.uk/government/uploads/system/uploads/attachment_data/file/331597/hosb0114.pdf.pdf

124 Dennis, N., Erdos, G., (2005) Cultures and Crimes, Policing in Four Nations, Civitas

125 Gorer, G., (1955) Exploring English Character, London: The Crescent Press: see also Davies, J., G., (2011) Small Corroding Words, The Slighting of Great Britain by the EHRC, Civitas

126 Davies, Gower Jon, Small Corroding Words, The Slighting of Great Britain by the EHRC, Civitas
see also: 'Police officer bitten in vicious mob attack… after asking girl to pick up a piece of litter.' *Daily Mail*, 18 July, 2008
http://www.dailymail.co.uk/news/article-1036250/Police-officer-bitten-vicious-mob-attack--asking-girl-pick-piece-litter.html

127 'Fifty officers a day on sick leave.' The *Daily Telegraph*, 22 February 2010

128 'Police public meeting that lacked a public.' The *Daily Telegraph*, 15 June 2011

129 'Police spend a £100,000 a day on spin doctors.' The *Daily Telegraph*, 16 April 2011
http://www.telegraph.co.uk/news/uknews/law-and-order/8454094/Police-spending-100000-a-day-on-press-officers.html

130 'Consultants paid £3,000 a day to help police.' The *Daily Telegraph*, 16 December 2009

131 'Public ride along with police patrols to bolster community confidence in officers.' The *Daily Telegraph*, 22 November 2014
http://www.telegraph.co.uk/news/uknews/law-and-order/11247437/Public-ride-along-with-police-patrols-to-boost-confidence-in-officers.html

132 'Police intervene in cheese rolling event.' The *Daily Telegraph*, 23 May 2013
http://www.telegraph.co.uk/news/newstopics/howaboutthat/10076336/Grandmother-wont-make-Double-Gloucester-for-cheese-rolling-event-after-heavy-handed-threats-from-police.html

133 'Cut all liaison jobs argues police watchdog.' The *Daily Telegraph*, 6 August 2010

134 'Police spend only 13% of their time investigating crime.' *Daily Express*, 18 March 2010
http://www.express.co.uk/news/uk/163608/Police-spend-only-13-of-their-time-investigating-crime

135 'Chief Constable to face misconduct panel.' The *Daily Telegraph*, 1 November 2014.
See also: 'Law Breaking view is 'strange' letters.' The *Bristol Post*, 25 June 2013

136 Dr. Rodger Patrick, (2014), *A Tangled Web: Why You Can't Believe Crime Statistics*, Civitas

137 'Birmingham schoolboy robbed at gunpoint – but police did not believe him.' *Sunday Mercury*, 15 July 2012
http://www.birminghammail.co.uk/news/local.-news/birmingham-schoolboy-robbed-at-gunpoint---231114

138 'We regularly fiddle the crime numbers, admit police.' The *Times*, 20 November 2013
http://www.thetimes.co.uk/tto/news/politics/article3926668.ece

139 Dr Rodger Patrick, (2014), *A Tangled Web: Why You Can't Believe Crime Statistics*, Civitas

140 'Street crime figures 'fiddled'.' The *Daily Telegraph*, 15 September 2002

141 '11 million crime left out of the figures.' *Daily Mail*, 2006

142 'Violent crimes are being ignored by the police, says report.' The *Independent*, 22 October 2009
http://www.independent.co.uk/news/uk/crime/violent-crimes-are-being-ignored-by-police-says-report-1807095.html

143 'Police encouraged to reclassify crimes to keep numbers down'.' The *Metro*, 4 April 2011
http://metro.co.uk/2011/04/04/police-encouraged-to-reclassify-crimes-to-keep-numbers-down-648467/

144 'Have the men in blue crossed the line?' The *Daily Telegraph*, 21 December 2012
http://www.telegraph.co.uk/news/uknews/law-and-order/9761022/Have-the-men-in-blue-crossed-the-line.html

145 Dr Rodger Patrick, (2014), *A Tangled Web: Why You Can't Believe Crime Statistics*, Civitas

146 'Police chief: You can't trust crime figures.' *Daily Mail*, 21 November 2013 www.dailymail.co.uk/news/article-2510952/You-trust-crime-figures-says-police-chief-Derbyshires-officer-breaks-ranks-say-staff-level-inadvertently-manipulate-figures.html

147 'Watchdog strips official status from police crime figures.' The *Daily Telegraph*, 15 January 2014 http://www.telegraph.co.uk/news/uknews/crime/10574424/Watchdog-strips-official-status-from-police-crime-figures.html

148 'Police failing to record one in five crimes.' *Daily Mail*, 1 May 2014 http://www.dailymail.co.uk/news/article-2617353/Police-failing-record-one-five-crimes-Official-report-says-740-000-victims-denied-justice.html

149 Information supplied by Dr Roger Patrick the researcher responsible for the original. revelations to the House of Commons All Party Committee in 2014, concerning the improper recording of crime figures by the police. Author of: A Tangled Web. Why You Can't Believe Crime Statistics, Civitas December 2014

150 'Watchdog says stats haven't been properly checked for FIVE YEARS.' *Daily Mail*, 22 January 2014 http://www.dailymail.co.uk/news/article-2543438/Get-ready-sharp-rise-crime-Statistics-not-audited-FIVE-years-police-continued-say-crime-falling.html

151 Dr Rodger Patrick, (2014), *A Tangled Web: Why You Can't Believe Crime Statistics*, Civitas

152 Smith, A. (2006), Crime Statistics: An Independent Review. Home Office London http://webarchive.nationalarchives.gov.uk/20110218135832/http:/rds.homeoffice.gov.uk/rds/pdfs06/crime-statistics-independent-review-06.pdf

153 UK Statistics Authority, (2010), Overcoming Barriers to trust in crime statistics: England and Wales https://www.statisticsauthority.gov.uk/archive/reports---correspondence/reports/overcoming-barriers-to-trust-in-crime-statistics--england-and-Wales.pdf

154 National Statisticians Review of Crime Statistics: England and Wales, June

2011, Her Majesty's Government, London

https://www.statisticsauthority.gov.uk/archive/national-statistician/ns-reports--reviews-and-guidance/national-statistician-s-reports/national-statistician-s-review-of-crime-statistics.pdf

155 'A million violent crimes a year cut out of official figures.' The *Daily Telegraph*, 9 June 2015

http://www.telegraph.co.uk/news/uknews/crime/11662764/Million-violent-crimes-a-year-cut-out-of-official-figures.html

156 *BBC News*, 23 October 2008, Professor Marion Fitzgerald, Criminologist at the University of Kent

http://news.bbc.co.uk/1/hi/uk/7685908.stm

157 'A million violent crimes a year cut out of official figures'. The *Daily Telegraph*, 9 June 2015

http://www.telegraph.co.uk/news/uknews/crime/11662764/Million-violent-crimes-a-year-cut-out-of-official-figures.html

158 The Economic and Social costs of crime, Home Office Research Study 217

http://webarchive.nationalarchives.gov.uk/20110218135832/rds.homeoffice.gov.uk/rds/pdfs/hors217.pdf

159 *Reducing Crime: A Review* by John Birt, 20 December 2000

160 'Blue sky thinker with the eye of an accountant.' The *Guardian*, 4 July 2005

## Chapter 3

161 'Penal Practice in a Changing Society.' White Paper on Penal Reform C. (58) 251, 1958, Home Office

http://www.butlertrust.org.uk/wp-content/uploads/2015/07/RAB-white-paper-1959.pdf

162 For example:

T.R. Fyvel, *The Insecure Offenders*, Penguin Books, 1963

H. Jones, *Crime in a Changing Society*, Penguin Books, 1965

D. Miller, *The Age Between*, Hutchinson, 1969

H. Wilson, *Delinquency and Child Neglect*, Allen and Unwin, 1962

D. J. West, *The Habitual. Prisoner*, Macmillan, 1963

T.C.N. Gibbens, *Psychiatric Studies of Borstal Lads*, Oxford University Press, 1963

R.A. Cloward & L.E. Ohlin, *Delinquency and Opportunity*, Routledge & Kegan Paul, 1961

J. B. Mays, *Crime and the Social Structure*, Faber and Faber, 1963

163 Ian Taylor et al., *The New Criminology, For a Social theory of deviance*, 197, Routledge & Kegan Paul

164 'Intimidation Causes 30,000 court cases a year to collapse.' The *Daily Telegraph*, 10 March 2002

165 'A day in the life of British justice: witnesses too scared to testify, and a violent man walks free.' The *Independent*, 8 March 2002

166 Lord Chancellors Department

167 '£25 million for prisoner' legal aid bill.' The *Daily Telegraph*, 7 July 2011

168 'Britain has largest legal aid budget in Europe, says report.' The *Daily Telegraph*, 9 October 2014 http://www.telegraph.co.uk/news/uknews/law-and-order/11149868/Britain-has-largest-legal-aid-budget-in-Europe-says-report.html

169 'Law Chief: too many people are locked up.' The *Independent*, 25 September 2009

170 Offender Management Caseload Statistics 2009, Ministry of Justice Bulletin
https://www.gov.uk/government/uploads/system/uploads/attachment_data/file/218065/omcs-2009-complete-210710a.pdf

171 Ministry of Justice Population in Custody monthly tables August 2010
https://www.gov.uk/government/uploads/system/uploads/attachment_data/file/218160/pop-in-custody-aug2010.pdf

172 GOV. UK Official Statistics Prison Population Figures 2011, Prison Bulletin, Monthly December 2011
https://www.gov.uk/government/statistics/prison-population-2011
and: GOV. UK Official Statistics Prison Population Figures 2012, Prison Bulletin, Monthly December 2012
https://www.gov.uk/government/statistics/prison-population-2012
and: GOV. UK Official Statistics Prison Population Figures 2013, Prison Bulletin, Monthly November 2013

https://www.gov.uk/government/statistics/prison-population-figures
and: GOV. UK Official Statistics Prison Population Figures 2014, Prison
Bulletin, Monthly December 2014
https://www.gov.uk/government/statistics/prison-population-figures-2014

173  1898-1939, National Population figures:
Abstract of British Historical Statistics, B. R Mitchell
https://books.google.co.uk/books?id=ce0AAAAIAAJ&pg=PA1&source=gbs_
toc_r&cad=3#v=onepage&q&f=fal.se98
and for 1942-1980:
British Historical Statistics, B.R. Mitchell https://books.google.co.uk/
books?id=Oyg9AAAAIAAJ&pg=PA1&source=gbs_toc_r&cad=3#v=onepage
&q&f=false
and for 1981-2008:
Office of National Statistics, Annual Abstract of Statistics no.146, 2010
edition
http://www.ons.gov.uk/ons/rel/ctu/Annual-abstract-of-statistics/no-146--
2010-edition/index.html
and for 2009-2011:
Office for National Statistics, Population Estimates for England and Wales,
Mid-2002 to Mid-2010
http://www.ons.gov.uk/ons/dcp171778_288817.pdf
and for 2012:
Office for National Statistics Population Estimates for England and Wales 2012
http://www.ons.gov.uk/ons/rel/pop-estimate/population-estimates-for-
england-and-Wales/mid-2012/index.html
and for 2013:
Office for National Statistics Annual Mid-Year Population Estimates, 2013
http://www.ons.gov.uk/ons/dcp171778_367167.pdf
and for 2014:
Office for National Statistics Annual Mid-Year Population Estimates, 2014
http://www.ons.gov.uk/ons/dcp171778_406922.pdf

174  Data.gov A Summary of Recorded Crime Data 1898-2001
https://Data.gov.uk/dataset/recorded-crime-data-1898-2001-02/resource/
b5b1c3fe-338e-472e-b844-75108c57436c

175 Home Office Statistical Bulletin 07/03, Crime in England and Wales http:// webarchive.nationalarchives.gov.uk/20110220105210/rds.homeoffice.gov. uk/rds/pdfs2/hosb703.pdf

176 Home Office Statistical Bulletin 11/09, Crime in England and Wales 2008/09 http://webarchive.nationalarchives.gov.uk/20110220105210/rds.homeoffice. gov.uk/rds/pdfs09/hosb1109vol1.pdf

177 Crime in England and Wales, 2010/11, Findings from the British Crime Survey and police recorded crime (2nd Edition) HOSB: 20/11 https://www.gov.uk/government/uploads/system/uploads/attachment_data/ file/116417/hosb1011.pdf

178 Office of National Statistics, Crime in England and Wales 2014 http://www.ons.gov.uk/ons/dcp171778_371127.pdf

179 Crime in England and Wales 2013 https://www.google.co.uk/search?q=recorded+crime+in+england+and+Wal es+2012&hl=en-GB&rlz=1T4DKUK_en-GBGB270GB270&oq=recorde d+crime+in+england+and+Wales+2012&gs_l=heirloom-serp.12… 40545. 44211.0.45973.9.9.0.0.0.0.296.1557.0j7j2.9.0… .0… 1ac.1.34.heirloom- serp..1.8.1433.5YhcacRtVmE

180 Prison population data 1900-2009: Offender Management Caseload Statistics 2009, Ministry of Justice Bulletin https://www.gov.uk/government/uploads/system/uploads/attachment_data/ file/218065/omcs-2009- complete-210710a.pdf

181 Prison population for 2010: Ministry of Justice Population in Custody monthly tables August 2010 https://www.gov.uk/government/uploads/system/uploads/attachment_data/ file/218160/pop-in- custody-aug2010.pdf

182 Prison population for 2011: GOV. UK Official Statistics Prison Population Figures 2011, Prison Bulletin, Monthly December 2011 https://www.gov.uk/government/statistics/prison-population-2011 and for 2012: GOV. UK Official Statistics Prison Population Figures 2012, Prison Bulletin, Monthly December 2012

https://www.gov.uk/government/statistics/prison-population-2012
and for 2013:

GOV. UK Official Statistics Prison Population Figures 2013, Prison Bulletin, Monthly November 2013
https://www.gov.uk/government/statistics/prison-population-figures
and for 2014:

GOV. UK Official Statistics Prison Population Figures 2014, Prison Bulletin, Monthly December 2014
https://www.gov.uk/government/statistics/prison-population-figures-2014

183 Offender Management Caseload Statistics, England and Wales, Quarterly Jan–March 2013 & 2015:

https://www.gov.uk/government/uploads/system/uploads/attachment_data/file/449528/offender-management-statistics-bulletin-jan-mar-2015.pdf

Also:

GOV.UK Prison Population figures 2015, Population Bulletin August 2015
https://www.gov.uk/government/statistics/prison-population-figures-2015

Also note:

Numbers for Indeterminate prisoner and lifers are 2013 figures.

The figure for licence recalls is an average figure. Offender Management Caseload Statistics for 2015 reports that between 1999 and 2014 there were 181,926 licence recalls to prison.

Foreign prisoners are included in this list as it is assumed that the majority are serving long sentences to be followed by deportation.

184 *BBC News*, World Prison Populations. 'England and Wales have the highest per capita prison population in the Western Europe – 143 per 100,000 of the population.'

http://news.bbc.co.uk/1/shared/spl/hi/uk/06/prisons/html/nn1page.stm

185 Prison Population 2016:

Council of Europe Annual Penal Statistics
http://wp.unil.ch/space/space-i/prison-stock-on-1st-january/prison-stock-on-01-jan-2015-2016/

186 List of European Countries by Population, 2015:

United Nations Department of Economic and Social Affairs
http://statisticstimes.com/population/european-countries-by-population.php

187 Eurostat Crimes Recorded by the Police, published 2014
http://ec.europa.eu/eurostat/statistics- explained/images/d/d7/Crimes_
recorded_by_the_police%2C_2002%E2%80%9312_YB14.png

188 Channel NewsAsia
http://www.channelnewsasia.com/news/singapore/singapore-s-crime-up-4-
in/2509028.html

189 Data.gov.sg. Government of Singapore, Ministry of Home Affairs, Singapore
Prison Service
https://Data.gov.sg/dataset/remand-population

190 Office for National Statistics, Crime in England and Wales 2014
http://www.ons.gov.uk/ons/dcp171778_371127.pdf

191 GOV.UK Prison Population Figures 2014/population Bulletin monthly
December 2014
https://www.gov.uk/government/statistics/prison-population-figures-2014

192 Data.gov. Overall Crime Cases and Crime rate. Singapore Government
https://Data.gov.sg/dataset/overall-crime-cases-crime-rate/
resource/56987172-00a3-4f0c-be4f-12f3e7ec4e1a?view_id=4e163b21-679e-
48e8-a9dd-38de1239f940

193 Population in Brief 2015 (Singapore)
http://population.sg/population-in-brief/files/population-in-brief-2015.pdf

194 Office for National Statistics, Statistical Bulletin, Crime in England and
Wales, Year ending June 2015
https://www.ons.gov.uk/peoplepopulationandcommunity/crimeandjustice/
bulletins/crimeinenglandandWales/2015-10-15

195 National Population figures for 2014 found in: Office for National Statistics
Annual Mid-Year Population Estimates, 2014
http://www.ons.gov.uk/ons/dcp171778_406922.pdf

196 'Air rage drunk bit man and screamed 'Nazi b****' at hostess.' *Daily Mail*,
18 July 2016
http://www.dailymail.co.uk/news/article-3695549/Drunk-passenger-
called-air-hostess-f-ing-red-haired-Nazi-b-h-sank-teeth-man-s-arm-leaving-
infected-bite-air-rage-row-flight-Britain-Dubai.html

197 'Attacker walks free while another is jailed.' *Bristol Evening Post*, 5 January,
2011

198 National Offender Management Service: Report on Accommodation and Support Service for Bail and Home Detention Curfew (HDC) 26 June 2015 https://www.google.co.uk/?gws_ rd=ssl#q=National+Offender+Management+Service:+Report+on+Accommodation+Support+Service+for+Bail+and+Home+Detention +Curfew+(HDC)+26+June+2015

199 'Raise your right hand if you want to go to prison.' The *Daily Telegraph*, 24 August 2016

200 'Judge lets repeat sex attacker choose his own sentence.' *Daily Mail*, 24 August 2016
http://www.dailymail.co.uk/news/article-3754603/Mute-paedophile-flashed-mother-bus-stop-allowed-CHOOSE-sentence-judge-raising-hand-pick-option.html

201 Criminal Justice Statistics Quarterly, September 2015, Overview Tables, Page Q1.3
https://www.gov.uk/government/statistics/Criminal-justice-system-statistics-quarterly-september-2015

202 Ministry of Justice Criminal Justice Statistics December 2015, England and Wales
https://www.gov.uk/government/uploads/system/uploads/attachment_data/file/524429/Criminal-justice-statistics-quarterly-update-_Annual_-2015.pdf

203 Criminal Justice Statistics Quarterly, September 2015, Overview Tables, Page Q1.3
https://www.gov.uk/government/statistics/Criminal-justice-system-statistics-quarterly-september-2015

204 Ministry of Justice, Criminal Justice Statistics 2015, England and Wales
https://www.gov.uk/government/uploads/system/uploads/attachment_data/file/524429/Criminal-justice-statistics-quarterly-update-_Annual_-2015.pdf

205 'Now police attackers will walk free.' *Daily Express*, 17 March 2011
http://www.express.co.uk/news/uk/235035/Now-police-attackers-will-walk-free

206 'Justice system chaos as fines debt hits £1.5 billion.' *Daily Express*, 25 January 2011

207 Home Office Statistical Bulletin,11/06, PRISON POPULATION
PROJECTIONS 2006 – 2013, England and Wales, July 2006
http://webarchive.nationalarchives.gov.uk/20110218135832/rds.homeoffice.
gov.uk/rds/pdfs06/hosb1106.pdf

208 Criminal Justice Statistics Quarterly Update to June 24th 2011,
Ministry of Justice, Statistics Bulletinhttps://www.google.co.uk/?gws_
riminal+Justice+Statistics+Quarterly+Update+to+June+2011+

209 Home Office, Criminal Statistics England and Wales 2001: Statistics relating
to Criminal Proceedings for the year 2001
https://www.gov.uk/government/uploads/system/uploads/attachment_data/
file/251043/5696.pdf

210 Criminal Justice Statistics Quarterly, September 2015, Overview Tables,
Page Q1.3
https://www.gov.uk/government/statistics/Criminal-justice-system-statistics-
quarterly-september-2015

211 'Killing a man? It's no big deal.' *Daily Mail*, 27 February 2014
http://www.huffingtonpost.co.uk/2014/03/20/lewis-gill-has-sentence-
reviewed-killing-andrew-young_n_5000058.html
also see:
*Mail Online*: 28 February 2014. 'Savage past of the one punch killer'.
http://www.dailymail.co.uk/news/article-2570570/Savage-past-one-punch-
killer-calls-Capone-gang-robbed-teenager-bus.html
and:
The *Huffington Post*, 20 March 2014, Lewis Gill, 'man who killed Andrew
Young with single punch, has sentenced reviewed.'
http://www.huffingtonpost.co.uk/2014/03/20/lewis-gill-has-sentence-
reviewed-killing-andrew-young_n_5000058.html

212 Criminal Justice and Immigration Act 2008

213 Ministry of Justice, Criminal Justice Statistics Quarterly: September 2012.
Offending Histories Tables: Table Q71
Shows an increase in the number of VAP crimes by offenders with 15 or
more previous convictions.
https://www.gov.uk/government/statistics/Criminal-justice-statistics--2

214 Criminal Justice Statistics Quarterly, September 2015, Overview Tables,

Page Q1.3

https://www.gov.uk/government/statistics/Criminal-justice-system-statistics-quarterly-september-2015

215 'Downward spiral. into violence and Murder.' *Yorkshire Post*, 18 April 2005
http://www.yorkshirepost.co.uk/news/downward-spiral.-into-violence-and-murder-1-2366469

216 'Jailed for taking on armed robber.' The *Sun*, 15 December 2009

217 Rehabilitation and Probation in England and Wales, 1876-1962, by Raymond Gard
http://www.bloomsbury.com/uk/rehabilitation-and-probation-in-england-and-Wales-1876-1962-9781472532602/

218 Home Office Probation Statistics England and Wales, 1996

219 GOV.UK Official Statistics Criminal Justice Statistics Quarterly, March 2014
https://www.gov.uk/government/statistics/Criminal-justice-statistics-quarterly-april-2013-to-march-2014

220 The Adult Criminal: Young Fabian Pamphlet 15, 1967.
http://digitallibrary.lse.ac.uk/objects/lse:web842lox

221 Offender Management Statistics Quarterly, July to September 2015
https://www.gov.uk/government/uploads/system/uploads/attachment_data/file/495321/offender-management-statistics-quarterly-bulletin-jul-sep-2015.pdf

222 Home Office Statistical Bulletin, Issue 34/86, Reconviction of those given Probation Orders, published 1986

223 Ministry of Justice Compendium of Reoffending Statistics and analysis, published 4 November 2010
https://www.gov.uk/government/uploads/system/uploads/attachment_data/file/199224/compendium- of-reoffending-statistics-and-analysis.pdf

224 HM Inspectorate of Probation, Strategies for Effective Offender Supervision, 1998

225 HM Prison Service Annual Report, 2007/08 (for a list of 'risk factors' said to be drivers of crime).
https://www.gov.uk/government/uploads/system/uploads/attachment_data/file/229159/0860.pdf

226 Construction of Management Technologies

http://epubs.surrey.ac.uk/410692/1/Karen%20Bullock%20-%20The%20
construction%20and%20interpretation%20of%20Risk.pdf

227 Ministry of Justice: Transforming Rehabilitation: A Summary of the
evidence in reducing reoffending 2013
https://www.gov.uk/government/uploads/system/uploads/attachment_data/
file/243718/evidence-reduce-reoffending.pdf

228 European Sourcebook of Crime and Criminal Justice Statistics 2014,
5th Edition http://www.heuni.fi/material./attachments/heuni/reports/
qrMWoCVTF/HEUNI_report_80_European_Sourcebook.pdf

229 'Ken Clarke: Ex-cons need a flat, job, and a girl friend.' *Daily Mail*, 31 May,
2016
http://www.pressreader.com/uk/daily-mail/20160531/281728383769582

230 'Ken Clark: Rising prison numbers not linked to falling crime.' The
*Guardian*, 14 July 2010
https://www.theguardian.com/politics/2010/jul/14/kenneth-clarke-prison-
falling-crime

231 Data.gov A Summary of Recorded Crime Data 1898-2001
https://Data.gov.uk/dataset/recorded-crime-data-1898-2001-02/resource/
b5b1c3fe-338e-472e-b844-75108c57436c

232 Office for National Statistics, Statistical Bulletin, Crime in England and
Wales, Year ending June 2015
https://www.ons.gov.uk/peoplepopulationandcommunity/crimeandjustice/
bulletins/crimeinenglandandWales/2015-10-15

233 'The Great Myth of Poverty and Crime.' *Daily Mail*, 2 January 1997

234 Home Office Statistical Findings, Issue 1/94, A Study of the Relationship
Between Unemployment and Crime, 1994 (In: Home Office Research
Study 218: Working their way out of offending: an evaluation of two
probation employment schemes
http://library.college.police.uk/docs/hors/hors218.pdf)

235 Fraser, D., (September 2011), *Crime, Poverty and Imprisonment*, CIVITAS:
Institute for the Study of Civil Society
http://www.civitas.org.uk/2011/09/28/crime-poverty-and-imprisonment/

236 Probationers in their Social Environment: Home Office Research Study no.
2 (1969), Martin Davies

237  *Crime in Early Modern England 1550-1750*. J.A. Sharpe, Longman 1986 (page 176)

238  Probationers in their Social Environment. Home Office Research Study no. 2. (1969), Martin Davies

239  'Cameron's £1billion help for problem families a flop.' *Daily Mail*, 9 August, 2016

http://www.dailymail.co.uk/news/article-3730503/Cameron-s-1b-help-problem-families-flop-Flagship-scheme-failed-cut-crime-benefit-dependency-despite-huge-bill.html

240  'Judge: Why I was right to name the teacher's teen killer.' *Daily Mail*, 6 November 2014

http://www.dailymail.co.uk/news/article-2822850/Why-right-teacher-s-teen-killer-Judge-tells-critics-shame-act-clear-deterrent.html

241  'Exposé of Bobby Cummines, a man once dubbed Britain's most dangerous criminal.' *Daily Express*, 10 September 2009

242  Emsley, C., (1991), Crime and Society in England 1750–1900, Longman

243  Ministry of Justice, Compendium of reoffending statistics and analysis, 2010

https://www.gov.uk/government/uploads/system/uploads/attachment_data/file/199224/compendium-of-reoffending-statistics-and-analysis.pdf

244  GOV.UK Ministry of Justice Proven reoffending statistics quarterly: October 2013 to September 2014 (then choose Proven Reoffending Tables: October 2012 to September 2014. Table C2a

https://www.gov.uk/government/statistics/proven-reoffending-statistics-october-2013-to-september-2014

245  Ministry of Justice, Safety in Custody Statistics England and Wales. Deaths in prison custody to March 2016. Assaults and Self-harm to December 2015

https://www.gov.uk/government/uploads/system/uploads/attachment_data/file/519425/safety-in-custody-march-2016.pdf

246  NHS Regional Poverty Studies, The growth of Health inEqualities in Britain. Chapter 1 (Table 1.2)

http://www.bristol.ac.uk/poverty/downloads/regionalpovertystudies/NHS-RAR_1.pdf

247  BBC Radio News item: statement by Justice Minister on education provision in British prisons, 16 July 2015

248 House of Commons Library SN/SG/4334 Characteristics of Prison Population
http://researchbriefings.files.parliament.uk/documents/SN04334/SN04334.pdf

249 'Estimated income of Criminals from Criminal sources' found in: Reducing Crime, A Review by John Birt, 20 December 2000

250 'My daughter was brutally beaten. So Social workers wanted her attacker to be sent to swim with dolphins. Such lunacy can harm us all.' *Daily Mail*, 18 August 1993

251 'Safari Boy', *Mail Online*, 16 July 2012
http://www.dailymail.co.uk/news/article-2172454/Safari-Boy-Mark-Hook-sent-month-holiday-steer-away-crime-clocks-113th-offence.html

252 'Safari Boy', *Mail Online*, 16 July 2012
http://www.dailymail.co.uk/news/article-2172454/Safari-Boy-Mark-Hook-sent-month-holiday-steer-away-crime-clocks-113th-offence.html

253 'Safari Boy', *Mail Online,* 16 July 2012
http://www.dailymail.co.uk/news/article-2172454/Safari-Boy-Mark-Hook-sent-month-holiday-steer-away-crime-clocks-113th-offence.html

254 'Safari Boy', *Mail Online*, 16 July 2012
http://www.dailymail.co.uk/news/article-2172454/Safari-Boy-Mark-Hook-sent-month-holiday-steer-away-crime-clocks-113th-offence.html

255 Dalrymple, T., (2006) *Romancing Opiates, Pharmacological. Lies and the Addiction Bureaucracy*, Encounter Book, New York

256 'Drug addict burglars can escape prison.' *Daily Express*, 13 May 2009
http://www.express.co.uk/news/uk/100687/Soft-justice-for-thieving-drug-addicts

257 'Burglars addicted to drugs or drink to escape prison sentences.' The *Daily Telegraph*, 12 May 2009
http://www.telegraph.co.uk/news/uknews/law-and-order/5313833/Burglars-addicted-to-drugs-or-drink-to-escape-prison-sentences.html

258 Theodore Dalrymple, *Rewarding Bad Behaviour*, New York City Journal, August 2006
http://www.city-Journalorg/html/rewarding-bad-behavior-12999.html

259 Response to question put-down by David Davies MP concerning Compensation Claims by prisoners following their withdrawal. from heroin in prison

260 Theodore Dalrymple, *Rewarding Bad Behaviour*, City Journal, New York August 2006.

http://www.city-Journalorg/html/rewarding-bad-behavior-12999.html

261 Home Office Research Findings 148, Drug Use and Offending: Summary Results from the First Year of the NEW-ADAM drug programme, 2001

https://www.researchgate.net/publication/280111214_Drug_Use_and_ Offending_Summary_Results_from_the_First_Year_of_the_NEW-ADAM_ Research_Programme

262 R. Matthews and J. Trickey, Drugs and Crime: A Study Amongst Young People in Leicester, University of Leicester, Centre for the Study of Public Order, in association with Middlesex University, 1996

https://www.ncjrs.gov/App/Publications/abstract.aspx?ID=166879

263 Drugs misuse and the Criminal justice system: a review of the literature. Michael Hough Professor of Social Policy, South Bank University

http://www.dldocs.stir.ac.uk/documents/houghdrugscrime.pdf

And:

'Jailing Addicts fails to make them quit drugs.' *The Independent*, 19 October 1999

http://www.independent.co.uk/news/uk/crime/jailing-addicts-fails-to-make-them-quit-drugs-739628.html

264 'Female serial killer was on probation when she killed men.' The *Daily Telegraph*, 19 March 2016

http://www.telegraph.co.uk/news/uknews/crime/12198100/Serial-killer-Joanne-Dennehy-was-under-probation-care-report-reveal.s.html

265 'Clever, sporty and a keen musician… then Joanna turned into a monster.' *Daily Mail*, 13 February, 2014

http://www.dailymail.co.uk/news/article-2557817/Guilty-Accomplices-spell-bloodthirsty-murderess-Joanna-Dennehy-went-twisted-10-day-killing-spree-fun.html

266 'Female serial killer was on probation when she killed men.' The *Daily Telegraph*, 19 March 2016

http://www.telegraph.co.uk/news/uknews/crime/12198100/Serial-killer-Joanne-Dennehy-was-under-probation-care-report-reveal.s.html

267 *The Myth of Addiction*, John Booth Davies, published by Harwood Academic, 1992ji

268  T*he Biology of Desire*, Professor Marc Lewis, published by Perseus, 2015
http://www.foyles.co.uk/Blog-Biology-of-Desire

269  Theodore Dalrymple, 'Treating' Drug Abuse: If you can bribe drug abusers to stay off drugs, doesn't that mean they can quit anytime? New York City Journal, August 2006
http://www.city-Journalorg/html/%E2%80%9Ctreating%E2%80%9D-drug-abuse-10192.html

270  Contingency Management treatments, Nancy M. Petry, The British Journal of Psychiatry, July 2006, 189 (2) 97-98;
http://bjp.rcpsych.org/content/189/2/97

271  Dalrymple, T., (2006) Romancing Opiates, Pharmacological. Lies and the Addiction Bureaucracy, Encounter Book, New York

272  'Killed by methadone.' The *Daily Telegraph*, 1 September 2009

273  The Drug Treatment Outcomes Research Study (DTORS): Research Design and Baseline Data. Michael Donmall et al., (2012)
http://benthamopen.com/contents/pdf/TOADDJ/TOADDJ-5-1.pdf

274  Home Office Research Study no.286, Evaluation of a drug testing in the Criminal justice system
http://optimityadvisors.com/sites/default/files/research-papers/evaluation-of-drug-testing.pdf

275  Home Office Research Findings no.120, Impact of Methadone Treatment on Drug Misuse and Crime, 2000
https://www.ncjrs.gov/App/Publications/abstract.aspx?ID=187821

276  Home Office Research Findings no.148, Drug Use and Offending: Summary Results from the First Year of the NEW-ADAM drug programme, 2001
https://www.researchgate.net/publication/280111214_Drug_Use_and_Offending_Summary_Results_from_the_First_Year_of_the_NEW-ADAM_Research_Programme

277  HO Bulletin 15/04 Offender Management Caseload Statistics 2003, published December 2004
http://webarchive.nationalarchives.gov.uk/20110220105210/rds.homeoffice.gov.uk/rds/pdfs04/hosb1504.pdf

278  Home Office Research Findings no.184: The Impact of Drug Treatment and Testing Orders on Offending: 2-year reconviction rates.

http://www.icpr.org.uk/media/5602/Dtto%20findings.pdf

279 Raynor, P. & Vanstone, M. (1994), STOP Programme for Offenders. Third Interim Evaluation Report, Glamorgan Probation Service.
and:
Raynor, P. & Vanstone, M. (1994), Probation Practice. Effectiveness and non-treatment paradigm. British Journal of Social Work, 24, 387-404

280 Home Office Research Development and Statistics Directorate, Research Finding no. 81: Motor Projects in England and Wales. An Evaluation by Darren Sugg (1998)

281 Home Office Probation Circular 35/1998: Effective Practice Initiative. A National Implementation Plan for the Effective Supervision of Offenders

282 'Meet the new director: Eithne Wallis shares her plans and aspirations.' The Probation Manager, July 2001

283 'Ex-New York cop sacked from Probation Service for putting public safety first.' Daily Mail, 5 June 2006 (Refers to Essex probation service giving anger diary to violent criminal who later assaulted his parents and the police.)
http://www.dailymail.co.uk/news/article-389092/Ex-New-York-cop-sacked-probation-service-putting-public-safety-first.html

284 New Choreography: The Strategic Framework for the National Probation Service, 2001-2002

285 Accredited Programmes, NAPO News, Issue 157, March 2004

286 S. Merrington and S. Stanley, 'What Works': Revisiting the Evidence in England and Wales, Probation Journal, 5:1, pp. 7-20,2004

287 'Jail thinking courses show you can't teach an old lag new tricks.' The Times, 7 August 2003.
http://www.communitycare.co.uk/2003/08/04/monday-4-august-2003/
See also:
'Prisoners fail to curb the inner man.' The Times, 18 November 2003

288 'Release me from this paperwork.' The Times, 5 August 2003

289 Home Office Research Findings no.161 (2003). An Evaluation of Cognitive Behavioural Treatment for Prisoners
http://library.college.police.uk/docs/hofindings/r161.pdf

290 Another One Bites the Dust: Recent Initiatives in Correctional Reform

in New Zealand. Newbold, G., Professor Canterbury University, The
Australian and New Zealand Journal of Criminology, vol. 41, no.3, 2008,
pp.384-401

http://search.informit.com.au/documentSummary;dn=434272382
137898;res=IELNZC

291 'Community Rehabilitation Companies not having any impact, say
inspectors': HM Inspectorate of Prisons, Media Release, July 2017
http://www.justiceinspectorates.gov.uk/hmiprisons/media/press-
releases/2017/06/support-for-prisoners-leaving-jail-community-
rehabilitation-companies-not-having-any-impact-say-insp

292 '£3.7 billion flop: Damning verdict on Cameron-era bid to cut crime.' Daily
Mail, 21 June 2017

293 National Offender Management Service Annual Report and Accounts,
2013-14
https://www.gov.uk/government/uploads/system/uploads/attachment_data/
file/322699/NOMS_AR_2014_web.pdf

294 Avon and Somerset Probation Trust Report and Accounts, 1 April to 31
October 2014
https://www.gov.uk/government/uploads/system/uploads/attachment_data/
file/407040/HC987_Avon_and_Somerset_Probation_Trust_Report_and_
Accounts_2014__web_.pdf

295 Mail Online, 17 January 2012, 'Thug who punched 92-year-old widower in
row over dog escapes jail because it would disrupt his anger management
course.'
http://www.dailymail.co.uk/news/article-2087946/Thug-punched-frail-92-year-
old-widower-row-dog-escapes-jail-disrupt-anger-management-course.html

296 'Judge: fingerprints aren't robust proof.' The Daily Telegraph, 19 November
2010

297 'Monster who strangled girl gets payout... because jail harmed his human
rights.' Daily Mail, 3 March 2014
http://www.dailymail.co.uk/news/article-2571658/Monster-strangled-
girl-gets-payout-jail-harmed-HIS-human-rights-Rapist-says-wasnt-given-
rehabilitation.html

298 A Channel 4 investigation, 'Interviews with Lifers in Gartree Prison', 2013

299 *Admirable Evasions* Theodore Dalrymple, Encounter Books, New York, 2015

300 'Restorative Justice could actually restore justice.' The *Daily Telegraph*, 31 October 2009

http://www.telegraph.co.uk/comment/personal.-view/6475013/Restorative-justice-could-actually-restore-justice.html

301 Ministry of Justice: Does Restorative Justice affect Reconviction? The 4th report from the evaluation of three schemes

http://restorativejustice.pbworks.com/f/MinistryOfJusticeJune08ReportOn RjAndRe-offending.pdf

302 Restorative Justice an Overview: A Report by the Home Office Research Development and Statistics Directorate 1999

http://fbga.redguitars.co.uk/restorativeJusticeAnOverview.pdf

303 Home Office Crime Reduction Series, Paper 9. Exploratory Evaluation of Restorative Justice Schemes 2001 https://www.restorativejustice.org.uk/sites/default/files/resources/files/An%20Exploratory%20Evaluation%20of%20Restorative%20Justice%20Schemes.pdf

304 'Hundreds of repeat knife offenders still avoiding jail.' The *Daily Telegraph*, 9 September 2016

305 'Silent police cars are useless.' The *Daily Telegraph*, 2 September 2015.

http://www.telegraph.co.uk/news/uknews/law-and-order/11837154/Police-cars-without-sirens-are- risking-lives-say-officers.html

306 'Criminals freed by worrying rate of court mistakes.' The *Daily Telegraph*, 24 October 2009

307 'Thousands of electronic tags tampered with.' Result of Freedom of Information request reported on in.' *Daily Mail*, 4 August 2012

308 'Half of tagged offenders breach their curfews, inspectors claim.' The *Daily Telegraph*, 14 June 2012

http://www.telegraph.co.uk/news/uknews/law-and-order/9330200/Half-of-offenders-with-electronic-tags-breach-curfews-inspectors-claim.html

309 'Government overcharged by companies monitoring tagged offenders.' The *Daily Telegraph*, 11 July 2013

http://www.telegraph.co.uk/news/uknews/crime/10173615/G4S-and-Serco-Taxpayers-overcharged-by-tens-of-millions-over-electronic-tagging.html

310 'Hundreds of sex offenders are on the run in the UK.' *Daily Express*, 20 March 2016

http://www.express.co.uk/news/uk/654007/Hundreds-sex-offenders-run-UK-Home-Office-Data-Protection

311 '700 sex crime culprits have been taken off offender list.' *Daily Mail*, 22 March 2016

http://www.dailymail.co.uk/news/article-3503557/Sex-crime-culprits-taken-offender-list-hundreds-past-four-years-protect-human-rights.html

312 'Absconding: Why do prisoners take the risk?' *BBC News*, 19 May 2014.

http://www.bbc.co.uk/news/uk-england-27292555

See Also:

National Audit Office, Ministry of Justice 2013/14, The Performance of the Ministry of Justice

https://www.nao.org.uk/report/departmental-overview-performance-ministry-justice-2013-14/

313 '18 On-the-run Criminals who can't be named... because it infringes their privacy.' *Daily Mail*, 22 May 2014

http://www.dailymail.co.uk/news/article-2635646/18-run-Criminals-named-infringes-personal.-privacy.html

314 'Reward for help in catching killer.' *Bristol Evening Post*, 2 September 2013

315 'Foreign prisoners squad is disbanded.' The *Daily Telegraph*, 24 September 2006.

http://www.telegraph.co.uk/news/uknews/1529662/Foreign-prisoners-squad-is-disbanded.html

316 Criminal Justice Statistics Quarterly Update June 2014 England and Wales, Ministry of Justice Bulletin

https://www.gov.uk/government/uploads/system/uploads/attachment_data/file/376898/Criminal-justice-statistics-update_to-june-2014.pdft

317 'Powers to stop UK jihadists from returning to Britain (introduced in 2015), have never been used.' The *Daily Telegraph*, 14 January 2017

318 'Now justice is a joke says veteran bobby.' *Daily Express*, 11 February 2011

http://www.express.co.uk/news/uk/228396/Now-justice-is-a-joke-says-veteran-bobby

319 'Dear Mrs Lawrence, would you like to know how your girl's killer is getting on?' The *Sun* Newspaper, 28 May 1996

# Chapter 4

320 'Monster let out for walks.' *Bristol Evening Post*, 29 March 2010
http://www.bristolpost.co.uk/Bristol-family-s-fury-killer-pregnant-Bristol-mother-let-walks/story-11242954-detail/story.html

321 '30 years for the pair who starved and killed four-year-old son.' The *Daily Telegraph*, 3 August 2013
http://www.telegraph.co.uk/news/10219872/Daniel-Pelka-Mother-and-stepfather-get-30-years-for-campaign-of-unimaginable-cruelty.html

322 *Sky News*, 5 March 2009: 'Actor's killer smirks as he is jailed.'
http://news.sky.com/story/675396/actors-killer-smirks-as-hes-jailed-for-life

323 'Taxi yob faces life over death of a gentle giant.' *Daily Express*, 20 June 2011

324 'Fury as 'happy-slap' killers will walk free in 18 months.' *Daily Express*, 27 July 2010

325 'Arrests follow Bristol blast.' *The Herald*, Scotland, 25 February 1989.
http://www.Heraldscotland.com/news/11996790.Arrests_follow_Bristol_blast/

326 'Frenchman raped at gunpoint.' *New Zealand Herald*, 10 September 2009

327 The story of Stephen Griffiths is taken with the author's permission from the essay, *Murder Most Academic*, by Theodore Dalrymple, published in The City Journal, New York, 2010
http://www.city-Journalorg/2011/21_2_otbie-homicide-studies.html

328 *Deserter: The Last Untold Story of the Second World War*, Charles Grass, 2013, Harperpress

329 'The Meaning of Violence.' BBC 2, Presented by Michael Portillo, May 2012

330 Research by Herbert Jager referred to in: *International Handbook of Violence Research*, edited by Wilhelm Heitmeyer & John Hagen, (2005)
https://books.google.co.uk books?id=A4mqsikVDcC&printsec=frontcover &source= gbs_book_other_versions#v=onepage&q&f=fal.se
See also:
Perpetrators of the Holocaust. A Histiography. Loughborough University.
https://dspace.lboro.ac.uk/dspace-jspui/bitstream/2134/13336/3/
Szejnmann%20-%20Perpetrators%20of%20the%20Holocaust%20-%20

Final%20and%20Revised%20Text%20-%206-3-08.pdf

331 Research by Ulrich Herbert referred to in: International Handbook of Violence Research, edited by Wilhelm Heitmeyer & John Hagen, (2005) https://books.google.co.uk/books?id=A4mqsik_VDcC&printsec=frontcover&source=gbs_book_other_versions#v=onepage&q&f=fal.se

332 *Ordinary Men: Police Reserve Battalion 101 and the Final Solution in Poland*, by Christopher Browning (1992)

333 *BBC Radio 4*, Today Programme, May 2014

334 *Serial killers: An Interview with Arthur Shawcross*, BBC TV programme, 2012.

See also:

*Talking with serial killers*, Christopher Berry-Dee, 2003, John Blake Publishers.

335 *Serial killers: An Interview with Arthur Shawcross,* BBC TV programme, 2012.

See also:

*Talking with serial killers*, Christopher Berry-Dee, 2003, John Blake Publishers

336 *Reducing Crime: A Review*, John Birt, 20 December 2002

337 British Medical Journal, 2006, September 2003: 333(7569): 652. http://www.ncbi.nlm.nih.gov/pmc/articles/PMC1570809 /

338 *BBC Radio News* item, 30 July 2014, 'Increase in violent attacks against prison officers by inmates.'

and:

*BBC Radio News* item, 30 July 2015, "significant rise in homicides by prison inmates and in assaults against prison staff"

339 'Man guilty of Donald Lock road rage killing.' *BBC News*, 16 May 2016 http://www.bbc.co.uk/news/uk-england-36305405

see also:

'Great-grandfather murdered in road rage stabbing.' The *Daily Telegraph*, 18 July 2015 http://www.telegraph.co.uk/news/uknews/crime/11745733/Manhunt-as-motorist-stabbed-to-death-after-car-crash.html

340 'Son hired hitman to kill parents for fussing.' *Daily Express*, 30 July 2009.
http://www.express.co.uk/news/uk/117193/Son-hired-hitman-to-kill-his-parents-for-fussing

341 'How love struck boy was lured to his death.' *BBC News*, 4 September 2009
http://news.bbc.co.uk/1/hi/uk/8048635.stm

342 'Beaten for £5 and left in the snow.' *Daily Express*, 6 February 2009

343 'Former soldier beaten to death by gang for £5.' The *Daily Telegraph*, 24 April 2008
http://www.telegraph.co.uk/news/uknews/1900412/Veteran-beaten-to-death-by-gang-for-5.html

344 'Gentle soul who met a cruel death on his way to church.' The *Daily Telegraph*, 29 December 2012

345 'Mob kills boy of 16.' *Daily Express*, 12 February 2008

346 'How can children be so evil?' *Daily Mail*, 7 April, 2009:
http://www.dailymail.co.uk/news/article-1167708/Brothers-charged-attempted-murder-young-playmates-slashed-head-toe-Stanley-knife.html
see also:
'Tortured, punched, burned and stamped on.' *Daily Mail*, 4 September 2009:
http://www.dailymail.co.uk/news/article-1211070/Aged-10-11-brothers-known-sadistic-thugs-So-free-torture-innocent-boys.html

347 'Mohammed Arshad trial: Andrew John Bayliss jailed for 30 years.' *Birmingham Mail*, 7 April 2011
http://www.birminghammail.co.uk/news/local.-news/mohammed-arshad-trial-andrew-john-152020

348 'Murder hunt after war veteran dies from doorstep mugging.' The *Guardian*, 19 August 2010
https://www.theguardian.com/uk/2010/aug/19/murder-hunt-war-veteran-geoffrey-bacon
and:
'Second World War veteran killed for £40 and bus pass.' The *Daily Telegraph*, 19 August, 2010

349 'Gang beat a dad to death in house raid.' *Daily Express*, 18 January, 2008

350 'Pensioner's torturers are jailed for life.' The *Daily Telegraph*, 21 May 2009

And:

'Pair jailed for life after torture and murder of OAP.' *Bournemouth Daily Echo* 20 May 2009 http://www.bournemouthecho.co.uk/news/4383000. Pair_jailed_for_life_after_torture_and_murder_of_OAP

351 'Head battered by ex-pupil who had a 2-year grudge.' *Daily Express*, 22 April, 2010
http://www.express.co.uk/posts/view/170653/Headteacher-battered-by-ex-pupil-who-had-20-year-grudge

352 'Beaten to death by yobs over a Halloween hat.' *Daily Express*, 3 November, 2009
http://www.express.co.uk/news/uk/137782/Beaten-to-death-by-yobs-over-a-Halloween-hat

353 'Gang kicked man to death for a cigarette.' *Daily Express*, 8 December 2009
http://www.express.co.uk/news/uk/144728/Gang-kicked-man-to-death-for-a-cigarette

354 'Thug stabbed teenager who asked friend to take feet off bus seat.' *The Daily Telegraph*, 16 June 2012.
http://www.telegraph.co.uk/news/uknews/law-and-order/9333864/Thug-stabbed-teenager-who-asked-friend-to-take-feet-off-bus-seat.html

355 'Thugs killed graduate, 23, in row over sweet paper.' *Daily Express*, 5 March, 2008
http://www.express.co.uk/news/uk/36974/Thugs-killed-graduate-23-in-row-over-sweet-wrapper

356 'Kill her and I'll buy you breakfast: Boy, 16, accused of murdering his 15-year-old ex for a DARE.' *Daily Mail* 23 June 201.
http://www.dailymail.co.uk/news/article-2006944/Killed-dare-Schoolboy-murdered-ex-girlfriend-free-breakfast.html

357 'Youth jailed for murdering student in senseless knife attack.' *The Guardian*, 23 June 2006
https://www.theguardian.com/uk/2006/jun/23/ukcrime

358 'Who fired up the thug who lit these flames?' *The Times*, 14 April 2012
http://www.thetimes.co.uk/tto/opinion/columnists/gilescoren/article3383788.ece

359 'Over half of those held in riots have been rearrested.' *Daily Mail*, 3 August 2012

http://www.dailymail.co.uk/news/article-2183498/London-riots-Almost-half-held-riots-arrested-crimes-including-rape-threats-kill-robbery.html

360 'Youngest looter in London riots back in court a week later.' The *Daily Telegraph*, 17 September 2011

361 'Its not about Criminality and cuts… it's about culture.' article by David Starkey, The *Daily Telegraph*, 20 August 2011
http://www.telegraph.co.uk/news/uknews/law-and-order/8711621/UK-riots-Its-not-about-Criminality-and-cuts-its-about-culture… -and-this-is-only-the-beginning.html

362 'TVs, computers, clothes and shoes, images of the spoils posted on line.' The *Daily Telegraph*, 9 August 2011
http://www.telegraph.co.uk/news/uknews/crime/8690268/London-riots-TVs-computers-clothes-and-shoes-images-of-the-spoils-online.html

363 'Stab victim raped and burnt girl.' *Daily Express*, 15 May 2008
http://www.pressreader.com/uk/daily-express/20080515/281702610451356

364 'Chilling truth about video games your children got for Christmas.' *Daily Mail*, 27 December 2013
http://www.dailymail.co.uk/sciencetech/article-2529677/Chilling-truth-video-games-children-got-Christmas.html

365 'Massacre prompts call for film talks.' The *Daily Telegraph*, 28 July, 2012

366 'April's mother must not blame herself – online porn is the evil.' The *Daily Telegraph*, 1 June 2013
http://www.telegraph.co.uk/news/uknews/crime/10091643/April-Jones-mother-must-not-blame-herself-online-porn-is-the-evil-here.html

367 'Violence on video brings pressure for regulation.' The *Times*, 18 August 1997

368 'Chilling truth about video games your children got for Christmas.' *Daily Mail*, 27 December 2013
http://www.dailymail.co.uk/sciencetech/article-2529677/Chilling-truth-video-games-children-got-Christmas.html

369 'Sex and violence video ban for young offenders.' The *Daily Telegraph*, 18 August, 1997

370 'Olympic song 'too violent' for school play.' The *Daily Telegraph*, 2 June 2012

371 'Murder call TV firm fined.' The *Daily Telegraph*, 6 July 2013
http://www.telegraph.co.uk/news/uknews/terrorism-in-the-uk/10162099/
Muslim-television-channel-fined-after-preacher-of-hate-incited-murder-live-
on-air.html

## Chapter 5

372 Prison Reform Trust. Prison, the Facts
http://www.prisonreformtrust.org.uk/Portal.s/0/Documents/Bromley%20
Briefings/summer%202016%20briefing.pdf
373 'Time served for murder.' *Mail Online*, 3 January 2012
374 This data has been compiled from Home Office bulletins and 'Homicide
Firearm Offences and Intimate Violence; Crime in England and Wales
Supplementary Volumes', for years 1900–2011 as well as newspaper reports
for the same period.
375 2012-2014 data: Office for National Statistics, Crime Statistics, Focus on
Violent Crime and Sex Offences 2013/14
http://webarchive.nationalarchives.gov.uk/20160105160709/http://www.
ons.gov.uk/ons/rel/crime-stats/crime-statistics/focus-on-violent-crime-and-
sexual.-offences--2013-14/index.html%20
Then:
Chapter 2: Violent crime and Sexual. Offences – Homicide
Then: previous homicide convictions
376 'Scores of life-term prisoners freed to kill again.' The *Daily Telegraph*, 4 July
2015
https://www.google.co.uk/?gws_rd=ssl#q=Scores+of+life-term+prisoners+free
d+to+kill+again
377 Office for National Statistics, Crime Statistics, Focus on Violent Crime and
Sex Offences 2013/14
http://webarchive.nationalarchives.gov.uk/20160105160709/http://www.
ons.gov.uk/ons/rel/crime-stats/crime-statistics/focus-on-violent-crime-and-
sexual.-offences--2013-14/index.html%20
378 Second killing analysis of 103 killers freed to kill again, sourced from Home
Office bulletins (e.g. Homicide Firearm Offences and Intimate Violence

Reports; Crime in England and Wales Supplementary Volumes) for various years as well as newspaper reports, for the period 1900–2011

379 'The real me is a loving person – how Karolina killer Hayes made his case for release after three child rapes.' *Bristol Evening Post*, 12 April 2006

380 'Sex beasts given hope of walking the streets unchecked.' *Daily Express*, 22 April 2010
http://www.express.co.uk/news/uk/170666/Sex-beasts-given-hope-of-walking-street-unchecked

381 This data has been compiled from Home Office bulletins (e.g. Homicide Firearm Offences and Intimate Violence Reports; Crime in England and Wales Supplementary Volumes) for various years as well as newspaper reports for the period 1900–2012.

382 Based on an analysis of 91 killers released to kill again, sourced from home office bulletins (e.g. Homicide Firearm Offences and Intimate Violence Reports; Crime in England and Wales Supplementary Volumes) for various years as well as newspaper reports for the period 1900–2012.

383 Taken from: True Crime Journal, January 2008

384 'Sentences for dangerous killers.' The *Daily Telegraph*, 10 July 2013

385 'Murderer of Jacqueline Ross sentenced to life imprisonment with a minimum tariff of 22 years.' *Macclesfield Express*, 30 November 2005
http://www.macclesfield-express.co.uk/news/local.-news/22-years-murdering-loved-wife-2539322
and:
*Manchester Evening News*, 5 September 2007 'Dog Walker Murder: Was sex the motive?'
http://www.manchestereveningnews.co.uk/news/local.-news/dog-walker-murder-was-sex-the-motive-1090090

386 The *Bucks Herald*, 24 March 2015, Mrs Buck criticises the release system
http://www.bucksHerald.co.uk/news/more-news/my-husband-could-still-be-al.ive-today-widow-of-man-murdered-by-convict-on-day-release-slams-prison-protocols-1-6651552
See also: 'Failures that let murderer out on day release to kill yet again.' *Daily Mail*, 24 March 2015.
And: *Mail Online,* 21 October 2013, 'European Court Ruling prevents

judge form giving Whole Life Term to McLoughlin.'
http://www.dailymail.co.uk/news/article-2470058/Triple-killer-Ian-
McLoughlin-murdered-Good-Samaritan-jailed-40-years.html
And: Court of Appeal. upholds the principle of Whole-Life prison terms.
*BBC News Online*, 18 February, 2014
http://www.bbc.co.uk/news/uk-26236225

387 'Betrayal of a hero.' *Daily Mail* 24 March 2015

388 '£150 m legal bill for troops just 'doing duty'.' The *Sunday Telegraph* 18
October 2015
http://www.telegraph.co.uk/news/uknews/defence/11938476/150m-legal-
bill-for-troops-just-doing-their-duty.html
see also: 'Clearing the Fog of Law.' pamphlet by *Policy Exchange*
https://policyexchange.org.uk/wp-content/uploads/2016/09/clearing-the-
fog-of-law.pdf

389 'Defeat of Iraq War Vultures.' *Mail Online*, 15 August 2016
http://www.dailymail.co.uk/news/article-3740507/Legal-firm-spent-
taxpayer-millions-hounding-troops-closes-down.html

390 'Nearly 60 Iraq killings claims against UK soldiers dropped.' *BBC News 24*,
January 2016
http://www.bbc.co.uk/news/uk-35395892

391 'Freed robber obsessed with the rich guilty of stabbing financier to death.'
The *Guardian*, 16 December 2005
https://www.theguardian.com/uk/2005/dec/16/ukcrime.hughmuir

392 HM Inspectorate of Probation Serious Further Offence review: Damian
Hanson and Elliot White, 2006
http://www.justiceinspectorates.gov.uk/probation/wp-content/uploads/
sites/5/2014/03/hansonandwhitereview-rps.pdf

393 *Confessions of a Country Magistrate.* by Edward Grierson. Published by Victor
Gollancz, 1972

394 'Teenage paedophile jailed for raping girl, 11.' The *Daily Telegraph*, 18 April,
2013
http://www.telegraph.co.uk/news/uknews/crime/10003638/Teenage-
paedophile-convicted-of-raping-11-year-old-while-on-supervision-order.html

395 'At Liberty to Kill and Rape Again.' *Daily Mail*, 2 July 1997

396 'Teenage hitman, 15, caught on CCTV gunning down innocent mother, is jailed for life.' *Mail Online*, 24 May 2011
http://www.dailymail.co.uk/news/article-1390069/Schoolboy-hitman-Santre-Sanchez-Gayle-15-convicted-murder.html

397 An analysis of data found in Home Office Bulletin, 17/05, Offender Management Caseload Statistics 2004, published 2005

398 'Raped, Tortured, then told: You are going to die slowly.' The *Daily Telegraph*, 14 January 2006
http://www.telegraph.co.uk/news/uknews/1507784/Raped-tortured-then-told-You-are-going-to-die-slowly.html

399 'Supervised Criminals continue crime wave.' The *Daily Telegraph*, 22 October 2006
http://www.telegraph.co.uk/news/uknews/1532053/Supervised-Criminals-continue-crime-wave.html

400 'One in eight accused of murder is a criminal on probation.' The *Independent*, 2 July 1997

401 'Killing and raping while on probation.' *Daily Mail*, 2 July 1997

402 'Killers strike on probation.' The *Times*, 27 January 2000.
See also:
'Killing and raping while on probation.' *Daily Express*, 2 July 1997

403 Home Office Probation Statistics England and Wales 2002
http://webarchive.nationalarchives.gov.uk/20110220105210/rds.homeoffice.gov.uk/rds/pdfs2/probation2002.pdf

404 HO Bulletin 15/04 Offender Management Caseload Statistics 2003, published December 2004
http://webarchive.nationalarchives.gov.uk/20110220105210/rds.homeoffice.gov.uk/rds/pdfs04/hosb1504.pdf

405 Ministry of Justice, 2012 Compendium of reoffending statistics and analysis
https://www.gov.uk/government/uploads/system/uploads/attachment_data/file/278126/2012-compendium-reoffending-stats-analysis.pdf

406 Ministry of Justice Proven Reoffending Statistics, Quarterly Bulletin, January to December 2012/13
https://www.gov.uk/government/uploads/system/uploads/attachment_data/file/368403/proven-reoffending-jan12-dec12.pdf

407 'Life Sentence for jeweller killer.' *BBC Online News Channel*, 5 May 2005:
See also:
'Pair jailed for role in fatal robbery.' *The Guardian*, 22 March 2005
https://www.theguardian.com/uk/2005/mar/22/ukcrime.ukguns1
and: HM Inspectorate of Probation Enquiry into the supervision of Peter
Williams by Nottingham City Youth Offending Team, 2005
http://www.justiceinspectorates.gov.uk/probation/wp-content/uploads/
sites/5/2014/03/peterwilliamsenquiry-rps.pdf

408 'Probation Service faces new accusation of failing to supervise harmful
offenders.' *The Times*, 29 March 2004.
See also: 'Harmful offenders lack supervision.' *The Times*, 29 March 2004
(page 10)

409 'Probation system failed to stop constable's killer.' *The Times*, 26 March
2004

410 'Probation system failed to stop constable's killer.' *The Times*, 26 March 2004:
see also: 'Probation boss takes the blame for errors that led to killing of PC.'
*The Daily Telegraph*, 26 March 2004

411 'Probation service failing to learn lessons over murder of French students,
inquiry finds.' *The Guardian*, 2 November 2009
https://www.theguardian.com/society/2009/nov/02/probation-service-
monitoring-inquiry-sonnex

412 Home Office Probation Circular 36/97: Serious Incident Reports: Analysis

413 'Copycat killing by murderer 25 years on.' *Mail Online*, 21 April 2012
See also:
'49 monsters given hope of freedom by the European Court of Human
Rights.' *Mail Online*, 10 July 2013
http://www.dailymail.co.uk/news/article-2359106/49-monsters-given-hope-
freedom-Theyre-UKs-notorious-killers-seek-parole.html

414 Section of an internal report prepared by the Avon and Somerset Probation
Service, 2004

415 Home Office, Probation Statistics England and Wales 2002, published
January 2004
http://webarchive.nationalarchives.gov.uk/20110220105210/rds.homeoffice.
gov.uk/rds/pdfs2/probation2002.pdf

416 HO Bulletin 15/04 'Offender Management Caseload Statistics 2003, published December 2004
http://webarchive.nationalarchives.gov.uk/20110220105210/rds.homeoffice.gov.uk/rds/pdfs04/hosb1504.pdf

417 Ministry of Justice, 2012 Compendium of reoffending statistics and analysis
https://www.gov.uk/government/uploads/system/uploads/attachment_data/file/278126/2012-compendium-reoffending-stats-analysis.pdf

418 Ministry of Justice, Proven reoffending Statistics, Quarterly Bulletin, January to December 2012, England and Wales
https://www.gov.uk/government/uploads/system/uploads/attachment_data/file/368403/proven-reoffending-jan12-dec12.pdf

419 Annex B: Serious Further Offences, Reoffending Data 2013/14
https://www.gov.uk/government/uploads/system/uploads/attachment_data/file/472526/annex-b-serious-further-offences-reoffending-data-2013-14.pdf

420 Ministry of Justice, 2012 Compendium of reoffending statistics and analysis
https://www.gov.uk/government/uploads/system/uploads/attachment_data/file/278126/2012-compendium-reoffending-stats-analysis.pdf

421 Home Office Probation Circular 22/2008: http://webarchive.nationalarchives.gov.uk/20101216070244/http://www.probation.homeoffice.gov.uk/files/pdf/PC22%202008.pdf
and:
Ministry of Justice, Compendium of reoffending statistics and analysis 2012
https://www.gov.uk/government/uploads/system/uploads/attachment_data/file/278126/2012-compendium-reoffending-stats-analysis.pdf

422 'Prisoners freed under supervision carried out 61 violent crimes.' The *Guardian*, 24 October 2006
http://www.theguardian.com/uk/2006/oct/24/ukcrime.immigrationpolicy

423 'Sex attackers on register rise by 50% in five years.' *Daily Mail*, 12 October 2009

424 'Judges are told to spare the muggers.' *Daily Mail*, 10 April 2003

425 'Violent burglars could still be spared jail terms.' The *Daily Telegraph*, 12 March 2010

426 'Knife teens could be spared jail if they're from troubled home.' *Daily Mail*, 6 October 2016. (An example of how Sentencing Council direction undermines parliamentary law).

427 'My jail term for thug is pathetic, says judge.' The *Daily Telegraph*, 13 October 2012

http://www.dailymail.co.uk/news/article-2216674/Samual.-Evans-Judge-brands-sentencing-powers-pathetic-jails-thug-years.html

428 'I have never seen anything so wet in all my life.' *Mail Online*, 29 January 2011

http://www.dailymail.co.uk/news/article-1351459/Judge-slams-soft-sentencing-options-prevented-jailing-burglar.html

429 'How chief judge is so out of touch on crime.' *Daily Express*, 28 June 2006

430 'Judge's fury that he cannot lock up pervert for longer.' *Daily Mail*, 16 December 2014

431 'Scores of rapists and killers allowed home on bail after they are convicted.' *Daily Mail*, 19 March 2015

http://www.dailymail.co.uk/news/article-3001663/The-rapists-killers-allowed-home-bail-convicted-210-sent-home-2013-awaiting-sentencing.html

432 'I quit, says JP forced to let serial convicts go free on bail.' *Daily Mail*, 12 August, 2015

433 'One killing each week by a thug on bail.' *Daily Mail*, 3 February 2015

434 Statement by the Sentencing Advisory Panel concerning the large numbers of 'Bail Act offences' committed each year.

http://www.criminalsolicitor.net/forum/forum_posts.asp?TID=2386

See also:

'One fifth of murder suspects committed crime while on bail.' The *Daily Telegraph*, 23 March 2008

http://www.telegraph.co.uk/news/uknews/1582527/One-fifth-of-murder-suspects-committed-crime-while-on-bail.html

435 'One killing each week by a thug out on bail.' *Daily Mail*, 3 February 2015

http://www.dailymail.co.uk/news/article-2937167/One-killing-week-thug-bail-Offenders-committed-two-rapes-week-sexual.-assault-child-day-await-trialhtml

436 'Killers on Bail.' *Mail Online*, 24 April 2008

437 'One killing each week by a thug out on bail.' *Daily Mail*, 3 February 2015

http://www.dailymail.co.uk/news/article-2937167/One-killing-week-thug-bail-Offenders-committed-two-rapes-week-sexual.-assault-child-day-await-trialhtml

438 'Murdered girl's father lashes inquiry refusal.' *Western Daily Press*, 20 June 1992

439 'Eight bailed prisoners went on to rape or kill last year.' The *Daily Telegraph*, 18 July 2009

440 'Parents seek justice for murdered nurse.' The *Daily Telegraph*, 6 November 2010

441 'Shopkeeper is facing murder charge after turning knife on thug.' *Daily Express*, 21 February 2008
http://www.express.co.uk/news/uk/35607/Shopkeeper-is-facing-murder-charge-after-turning-knife-on-Thug

442 'One fifth of murder suspects committed crime while on bail.' The *Guardian*, 24 March 2008

443 'Tough on crime?' *Daily Mail*, 14 April 2006

## Chapter 6

444 Christoph, J. B., (1962), *Capital Punishment and British Politics, The British Movement to Abolish the Death Penalty* (Allen & Unwin)

445 Christoph, J. B., (1962), *Capital Punishment and British Politics, The British Movement to Abolish the Death Penalty* (Allen & Unwin)

446 Christoph, J. B., (1962), *Capital Punishment and British Politics, The British Movement to Abolish the Death Penalty* (Allen & Unwin)

447 Christoph, J. B., (1962), *Capital Punishment and British Politics, The British Movement to Abolish the Death Penalty* (Allen & Unwin)

448 Murder (Abolition of Death Penalty) Bill, Hansard, House of Commons debate, 21 December 1964 vol. 704 cc870-1010
http://hansard.millbanksystems.com/commons/1964/dec/21/murder-abolition-of-death-Penalty-bill

449 Christoph, J. B., (1962), *Capital Punishment and British Politics, The British Movement to Abolish the Death Penalty* (Allen & Unwin)

450 Christoph, J. B., (1962), *Capital Punishment and British Politics, The British Movement to Abolish the Death Penalty* (Allen & Unwin)

451 Christoph, J. B., (1962), *Capital Punishment and British Politics, The British Movement to Abolish the Death Penalty* (Allen & Unwin)

452 Death Penalty Poll Results: UK Polling Report You Gov on
http://ukpollingreport.co.uk/blog/archives/3802

453 'Support for the death Penalty drops below 50% for the first time.' *BBC
News*, 26 March 2015
http://www.bbc.co.uk/news/uk-32061822

454 Society and Homicide in 13th Century England, James Given, 1977,
Stanford University Press (originally found in Manuel Eisner, The Long
Term Historical Trends in Violent Crime, Crime and Justice, vol. 30, (2003)
pp.83-142.
Now available as:
Manuel Eisner, Long-Term Historical Trends in Violent Crime
http://www.vrc.crim.cam.ac.uk/vrcresearch/paperdownload/manuel-eisner-
historical-trends-in-violence.pdf

455 Historical Trends in Violent Crime: A Critical. Review of the Evidence, T.R.
Gurr, 1981
(found in Manuel Eisner, The Long Term Historical Trends in Violent
Crime, Crime and Justice, vol. 30, (2003) pp.83-142

456 Homicide, Firearm Offences and Intimate Violence, Supplementary Volume
2 to Crime in England and Wales 2010/2011 (table 1.01)
https://www.gov.uk/government/uploads/system/uploads/attachment_data/
file/116483/hosb0212.pdf

457 International handbook of Violence Research, Vol. 1, edited by Wilhelm
Heitmeyer and John Hagen
https://books.google.co.uk/books?id=A4mqsik_
VDcC&printsec=frontcover&source=gbs_book_other_
versions#v=onepage&q&f=fal.se

458 The Long Term Historical Trends in Violent Crime, Manual. Eisner, found
in Manuel Eisner, The Long Term Historical Trends in Violent Crime,
Crime and Justice, vol. 30, (2003) pp.83-142.
Now available as:
Manuel Eisner, Long-Term Historical Trends in Violent Crime
http://www.vrc.crim.cam.ac.uk/vrcresearch/paperdownload/manuel-eisner-
historical-trends-in-violence.pdf

459 *Crime in Early Modern England 1550-1750*. J.A. Sharpe, Longman 1986

460 Emsley, C., (1991), *Crime and Society in England 1750-1900*, Longman

461 *The Floating Brothel*, by Sian Rees, (2001), Headline.

462 Sunstein C.,R., Llewellyn K.,N.,Vermeule B.,D., 'Is Capital Punishment Morally Required? The Relevance of Life-Life Trade-offs', University of Chigago, Public Law and legal Theory Working Paper no. 85, 2005. http://chicagounbound.uchicago.edu/cgi/viewcontent. cgi?article=1162&context=public_law_and_legal_theory

463 The Death Penalty Deters Crime and Saves Lives. Address given to the Subcommittee on the Constitution, Civil Rights, and Property Rights of the Committee on the Judiciary of the United States, 2007. Given by Dr. David B. Mulhausen, Research Fellow in Empirical. Policy Analysis, Centre for Data Analysis, The Heritage Foundation http://www.heritage.org/research/testimony/the-death-Penalty-deters-crime-and-saves-lives

464 Sunstein C. R., Llewellyn K. N.,Vermeule B. D., 'Is Capital Punishment Morally Required? The Relevence of Life-Life Tradeoffs', University of Chigago Public Law and legal Theory Working Paper no. 85, 2005. http://chicagounbound.uchicago.edu/cgi/viewcontent. cgi?article=1162&context=public_law_and_legal_theory

465 The Death Penalty Deters Crime and Saves Lives. Evidence submitted to the Subcommittee on the Constitution, Civil Rights, and Property Rights of the Committee on the Judiciary of the United States, 2007, by Dr David B. Mulhausen, Research Fellow in Empirical. Policy Analysis, Centre for Data Analysis, The Heritage Foundation http://www.heritage.org/research/testimony/the-death-Penalty-deters-crime-and-saves-lives

466 The Death Penalty Deters Crime and Saves Lives. Evidence submitted to the Subcommittee on the Constitution, Civil Rights, and Property Rights of the Committee on the Judiciary of the United States, 2007, by Dr David B. Mulhausen, Research Fellow in Empirical. Policy Analysis, Centre for Data Analysis, The Heritage Foundation http://www.heritage.org/research/testimony/the-death-Penalty-deters-crime-and-saves-lives

467 Crime in the United States, U.S. Department of Justice, federal. Bureau of

Investigation, Criminal Justice Information Service Division
https://ucr.fbi.gov/crime-in-the-u.s/2014/crime-in-the-u.s.-2014/tables/
table-1

468 Uniform Crime Reporting Statistics, U.S. Department of Justice, Federal.
Bureau of Investigation, Crime in Texas
https://www.ucrdatatool.gov/Search/Crime/State/RunCrimeStatebyState.
cfm

469 United States and Texas Populations 1850-2015. Data from the Texas
Library and Archives
https://www.tsl.texas.gov/ref/abouttx/census.html

470 Crime in the United States, U.S. Department of Justice, federal. Bureau of
Investigation, Criminal Justice Information Service Division
https://ucr.fbi.gov/crime-in-the-u.s/2014/crime-in-the-u.s.-2014/tables/
table-1

471 Its Incredible How Much Safer America Has Become Since the 1980's. FBI
Crime Report shows America is still getting safer
http://uk.businessinsider.com/fbi-crime-report-shows-america-is-still-
getting-safer-2015-1?r=US&IR=T

472 'London worse for crime than New York.' The *Daily Telegraph*, 21 October
2017

473 Death Penalty Information Centre
http://www.deathPenaltyinfo.org/executed-possibly-innocent

474 U.S. Department of Justice, Office of Justice Programmes, Bureau of Justice
Statistics. Capital Punishment 2013
http://www.bjs.gov/content/pub/pdf/cp13st.pdf

475 Data.gov A Summary of Recorded Crime Data 1898-2001
https://Data.gov.uk/dataset/recorded-crime-data-1898-2001-02/resource/
b5b1c3fe-338e-472e-b844-75108c57436c

476 Home Office Statistical Bulletin Crime in England and Wales 2010/11
HOSB 10/11
https://www.gov.uk/government/uploads/system/uploads/attachment_data/
file/116417/hosb1011.pdf

477 Office for National Statistics, Crime in England and Wales 2014
http://www.ons.gov.uk/ons/dcp171778_371127.pdf

478  Home Office Statistics, Crime in England and Wales, 2012.
     http://webarchive.nationalarchives.gov.uk/20160105160709/http://
     www.ons.gov.uk/ons/rel/crime-stats/crime-statistics/period-ending-
     december-2012/stb-crime-in-england-and-Wales--year-ending-
     december-2012.html (Appendix Table A4).

479  'Murder increase sparks warning from police chief.' The *Times*, 20 January,
     2017

480  Christoph, J. B., (1962), Capital Punishment and British Politics, The
     British Movement to Abolish the Death Penalty (Allen & Unwin)

481  Romilly, S., (1886) *The Punishment of Death*, John Murray

482  Home office, Offences initially recorded as homicides, England and Wales,
     1961-2011
     http://www.homeoffice.gov.uk/publications/science-research-statistics/
     research-statistics/crime-research/hosb0212/hosb0212?view=Binary

483  West, D., Murder Followed by Suicide: an inquiry carried out for the
     Institute of Criminology, Cambridge, Heinemann (1965)

484  The National Confidential. Inquiry into homicide followed by suicide by
     people with mental illness 2016
     http://research.bmh.manchester.ac.uk/cmhs/research/
     centreforsuicideprevention/nci/reports/2016-report.pdf

485  Homicides, Firearm Offences and Intimate Violence 2010/11:
     Supplementary Volume 2 to Crime in England and Wales 2010/11, table 1e,
     and table 1.01
     https://www.gov.uk/government/uploads/system/uploads/attachment_data/
     file/116483/hosb0212.pdf

486  The Death Penalty Deters Crime and Saves Lives. Address given to the
     Subcommittee on the Constitution, Civil Rights, and Property Rights of
     the Committee on the Judiciary of the United States, 2007. By Dr David B.
     Mulhausen, Research Fellow in Empirical. Policy Analysis, Centre for Data
     Analysis, The Heritage Foundation
     http://www.heritage.org/research/testimony/the-death-Penalty-deters-crime-
     and-saves-lives

487  'Life for murderer who killed 10 years ago.' The *Independent*, 5 November,
     2002

488 This data has been compiled from Home Office bulletins (e.g. Homicide Firearm Offences and Intimate Violence Reports; Crime in England and Wales Supplementary Volumes) for various years as well as newspaper reports for the period 1900–2012.

489 Data on numbers of police killed by Criminals found www.policememorial.org.uk/ Forces/ForcesList.htm (The historical data was extracted in 2014 from this site but during a more recent search it could not be found.)

490 Homicide in England and Wales 1967–71, Home Office Study 31, by Evelyn Gibson http://library.npia.police.uk/docs/hors/hors31.pdf.

491 This analysis is based on figures from:
Data.gov A Summary of Recorded Crime Data 1898–2001, https://Data.gov.uk/dataset/recorded-crime-data-1898-2001-02/resource/ b5b1c3fe-338e-472e-b844-75108c57436c
and:
Home Office Statistical Bulletin, Homicides, Firearm Offences and Intimate Violence 20/10/11, Supplementary Volume 2 to Crime in England &Wales https://www.gov.uk/government/uploads/system/uploads/attachment_data/ file/116483/hosb0212.pdf
and:
HO Statistics 02/05, Total., Convictions for Homicide 1965-1996 http://webarchive.nationalarchives.gov.uk/20110220105210/rds.homeoffice. gov.uk/rds/pdfs05/hosb0205.pdf

492 Office for National Statistics, Crime in England and Wales 2015: http://www.ons.gov.uk/peoplepopulationandcommunity/crimeandjustice/ bulletins/crimeinenglandandWales/yearendingdecember2015
and:
'Homicide in England and Wales up 14%.' The *Guardian*, 21 January 2016 https://www.theguardian.com/uk-news/2016/jan/21/england-Wales- homicides-rise-knife-gun-crime

493 'Murder increase sparks warning from police chief.' The *Times*, 20 January, 2017

494 Dobson, R., (2002), *Medical Advances mask epidemic of violence by cutting homicide rates.* British Medical Journal, 325: 615, September 21st

https://www.ncbi.nlm.nih.gov/pmc/articles/PMC1124155/

495 Data.gov A Summary of Recorded Crime Data 1898-2001
https://Data.gov.uk/dataset/recorded-crime-data-1898-2001-02/resource/
b5b1c3fe-338e-472e-b844-75108c57436c

496 Home Office Statistical Bulletin Crime in England and Wales 2010/11
HOSB 10/11
https://www.gov.uk/government/uploads/system/uploads/attachment_data/
file/116417/hosb1011.pdf

497 National Statistics Crime in England and Wales, year ending June 2012,
Appendix tables A4
http://webarchive.nationalarchives.gov.uk/20160105160709/
http://www.ons.gov.uk/ons/publications/re-reference-tables.
html?edition=tcm%3A77-274949

498 National Statistics, Crimes detected in England and Wales 2012/13, Data
Tables: Crimes detected in England and Wales 2012/13

499 Data.gov A Summary of Recorded Crime Data 1898-2001
https://Data.gov.uk/dataset/recorded-crime-data-1898-2001-02/resource/
b5b1c3fe-338e-472e-b844-75108c57436c

500 Home Office Statistical Bulletin, Crime in England and Wales 2010/11,
HOSB 10/11
https://www.gov.uk/government/uploads/system/uploads/attachment_data/
file/116417/hosb1011.pdf

501 National Statistics Crime in England and Wales, year ending June 2012,
Appendix tables A4
http://webarchive.nationalarchives.gov.uk/20160105160709/
http://www.ons.gov.uk/ons/publications/re-reference-tables.
html?edition=tcm%3A77-274949

502 National Statistics, Crimes detected in England and Wales 2012/13, Data
Tables: Crimes detected in England and Wales 2012/13
https://www.gov.uk/government/statistics/crimes-detected-in-england-and-
Wales-2012-to-2013

503 The calculation assumes a gradual change in the numbers of lives saved from
the early 1970s, not reaching the improvement factor of 5 until the mid to
late 1980s

504 Data.gov A Summary of Recorded Crime Data 1898-2001
https://www.gov.uk/government/statistics/historical-crime-data

505 Home Office Statistical Bulletin Crime in England and Wales 2010/11
HOSB 10/11
https://www.gov.uk/government/uploads/system/uploads/attachment_data/
file/116417/hosb1011.pdf

506 Home Office Statistics, Crime in England and Wales, 2012.
http://webarchive.nationalarchives.gov.uk/20160105160709/http://
www.ons.gov.uk/ons/rel/crime-stats/crime-statistics/period-ending-
december-2012/stb-crime-in-england-and-Wales--year-ending-
december-2012.html

507 Office for National Statistics, Crime in England and Wales 2014
http://www.ons.gov.uk/ons/dcp171778_371127.pdf

508 Office for National Statistics, Crime in England and Wales 2015: http://
www.ons.gov.uk/peoplepopulationandcommunity/crimeandjustice/
bulletins/crimeinenglandandWales/yearendingdecember2015
and:
'Homicide in England and Wales up 14%', The *Guardian*, 21 January 2016
https://www.theguardian.com/uk-news/2016/jan/21/england-Wales-
homicides-rise-knife-gun-crime

509 '275,000 persons go missing every year.' The *Independent*, 10th October 2009
http://www.independent.co.uk/news/uk/home-news/the-missing-each-year-
275000-britons-disappear-1801010.html

510 UK Missing Persons Bureau 2013 Report
http://www.missingpersons.police.uk/en/resources/missing-persons-data-
analysis-2012-13

511 Home Office, Missing Children and Adults
https://www.gov.uk/government/uploads/system/uploads/attachment_data/
file/117793/missing-persons-strategy.pdf

512 The UK Missing Persons Bureau 2011/2012
http://www.missingpersons.police.uk/en/resources/missing-persons-data-
and-analysis-2010-2011

513 'Becky Goddard murder: Christopher Halliwell given a whole life sentence.'
*BBC News*, 23 September 2016

http://www.bbc.co.uk/news/uk-england-37450337

514 'As the death toll rises, is 'The Pusher' on the prowl?' The *Daily Telegraph*, 17 January 2015

515 A Study into Decision Making at the Scene of Unexpected Death: A Report for the Forensic Science Regulator concerning the 2012 Audit of Forensic Pathologist's Reports. Published by the Forensic Pathology Unit of the Home Office, January 2015
https://www.gov.uk/government/uploads/system/uploads/attachment_data/file/484298/Report_into_the_2012_FSR_FP_Audit_Publication_copy_pdf.pdf

516 A Study into Decision Making at the Scene of Unexpected Death: A Report for the Forensic Science Regulator concerning the 2012 Audit of Forensic Pathologist's Reports. Published by the Forensic Pathology Unit of the Home Office, January 2015
https://www.gov.uk/government/uploads/system/uploads/attachment_data/file/484298/Report_into_the_2012_FSR_FP_Audit_Publication_copy_pdf.pdf

517 'Random attacks by thugs every 30 seconds.' *Daily Mail*, 2 November 2009
http://www.dailymail.co.uk/news/article-1224565/Random-attack-thugs-30-seconds-stranger-assaults-soar-binge-Britain.html

518 Homicide in England and Wales 1967-71, Home Office Study 31, by Evelyn Gibson
http://library.npia.police.uk/docs/hors/hors31.pdf

519 Data.gov A Summary of Recorded Crime Data 1898-2001
https://www.gov.uk/government/statistics/historical-crime-data

520 Office for National Statistics, Crime Statistics, Focus on Violent Crime and Sex Offences 2013/14, Chapter 2 Violent Crime and Sexual. Offences – Homicide
http://www.ons.gov.uk/ons/rel/crime-stats/crime-statistics/focus-on-violent-crime-and-sexual.-offences--2013-14/index.html

521 Home Office Statistical Bulletin Crime in England and Wales 2010/11 HOSB 10/11
https://www.gov.uk/government/uploads/system/uploads/attachment_data/file/116417/hosb1011.pdf

522 Home Office Statistics, Crime in England and Wales, 2012

http://webarchive.nationalarchives.gov.uk/20160105160709/http://
www.ons.gov.uk/ons/rel/crime-stats/crime-statistics/period-ending-
december-2012/stb-crime-in-england-and-Wales--year-ending-
december-2012.html

523 Office for National Statistics, Crime in England and Wales 2014
http://www.ons.gov.uk/ons/dcp171778_371127.pdf

524 Crime in England and Wales 2003/2004: Supplementary Volume 1:
Homicide and Gun Crime 02/05
http://webarchive.nationalarchives.gov.uk/20110220105210/rds.homeoffice.
gov.uk/rds/pdfs05/hosb0205.pdf

525 Homicides, Firearm Offences and Intimate Violence 2010/11:
Supplementary Volume 2 to Crime in England and Wales 2010/12
https://www.gov.uk/government/uploads/system/uploads/attachment_data/
file/116483/hosb0212.pdf

526 'Girl, 14 years old, orders the fatal stabbing of a teenage boy.' The *Daily
Telegraph*, 6 April, 2013

527 'Men jailed for Ben Gardner Halloween hat murder.' *BBC News*, 15 October
2010: and: 'Heartbreak over Halloween killing.' *BBC News*, 3 November
2009
http://www.bbc.co.uk/news/uk-england-london-11551380

528 Homicide England and Wales, Home Office research Study no 31, table 2,
'homicide method'

529 Data.gov A Summary of Recorded Crime Data 1898-2001
https://www.gov.uk/government/statistics/historical-crime-data

530 Office for National Statistics, Crime Statistics, Focus on Violent Crime and
Sex Offences 2013/14, Chapter 2 Violent Crime and Sexual. Offences –
Homicide
http://www.ons.gov.uk/ons/rel/crime-stats/crime-statistics/focus-on-violent-
crime-and-sexual-offences--2013-14/index.html

531 Office for National Statistics, Crime in England and Wales 2014
http://www.ons.gov.uk/ons/dcp171778_371127.pdf

532 HUNT, I. M., Asmin, B., et al., 2010, Homicide convictions in different
age groups: a national survey. Journal of Forensic Psychiatry & Psychology,
2010

http://www.tandfonline.com/doi/abs/10.1080/14789940903513195

533 Focus on Violent Crime and Sexual Offences: year Ending March 2015
http://www.ons.gov.uk/peoplepopulationandcommunity/
crimeandjustice/compendium/focusonviolentcrimeandsexualoffences/
yearendingmarch2015

534 Statistical Bulletin: Crime in England and Wales, March 2014. Police
recorded crime: Home Office
http://webarchive.nationalarchives.gov.uk/20160105160709/http://www.
ons.gov.uk/ons/dcp171778_371127.pdf

535 Office for National Statistics: Statistical Bulletin: Crime in England and
Wales year ending December 2015
http://www.ons.gov.uk/peoplepopulationandcommunity/crimeandjustice/
bulletins/crimeinenglandandwales/yearendingdecember2015

536 Data.gov A Summary of Recorded Crime Data 1898-2001
https://www.gov.uk/government/statistics/historical-crime-data

537 Home Office Statistical Bulletin, Crime in England and Wales 2010/2011
https://www.gov.uk/government/uploads/system/uploads/attachment_data/
file/116417/hosb1011.pdf

538 National Statistics Crime in England and Wales, year ending June 2012,
Appendix tables A4
http://webarchive.nationalarchives.gov.uk/20160105160709/
http://www.ons.gov.uk/ons/publications/re-reference-tables.
html?edition=tcm%3A77-274949

539 National Statistics, Crimes detected in England and Wales 2012/13, Data
Tables: Crimes detected in England and Wales 2012/13
https://www.gov.uk/government/statistics/crimes-detected-in-england-and-
wales-2012-to-2013

540 Statistica: The Statistics Portal
http://www.statista.com/statistics/303493/threats-to-kill-in-england-and-
wales-uk-y-on-y/

541 Statistical Bulletin: Crime in England and Wales, March 2014. Police
recorded crime: Home Office
http://webarchive.nationalarchives.gov.uk/20160105160709/http://www.
ons.gov.uk/ons/dcp171778_371127.pdf

542 Data supplied by Gawain Towler, Press Officer, EFD Group in the European Parliament, UK Independence Party. Results of a Freedom of Information Act Request no. 2012030001415. Numbers of non-UK subjects charged with murder and rape.

543 'Immigrant gang land.' *Daily Express*, 18 April 2008.
See also: 'Judges must start laying down the law.' *Daily Express*, 18 April 2008.

544 'Polish criminal left free to kill pensioner after lying over identity.' The *Daily Telegraph*, 22 July 2011

545 'Wanted thug let into Britain to strike again.' *Daily Express*, 14 March 2008

546 Robert Rowthorn (2014) The Economic Consequences of large-scale immigration. Civitas
http://www.civitas.org.uk/pdf/LargescaleImmigration.pdf

547 Homicide Statistics, House of Commons Research Paper 99/56, published 27 May 1999
http://researchbriefings.files.parliament.uk/documents/RP99-56/RP99-56.pdf

548 Homicides, Firearm Offences and Intimate Violence 2010/11: Supplementary Volume 2 to Crime in England and Wales 2010/11
https://www.gov.uk/government/uploads/system/uploads/attachment_data/file/116483/hosb0212.pdf

549 Metropolitan Police Crime Figures for London 2015.
http://www.met.police.uk/crimefigures/
(This reports 117 homicides for London for 2015. The national population for the capital that year was 8.6 million, which calculates to 1.4 homicides per 100,000 population of the Capital)

550 Office for National Statistics Crime in England and Wales 2015
http://www.ons.gov.uk/peoplepopulationandcommunity/crimeandjustice/bulletins/crimeinenglandandwales/yearendingdecember2015

551 Office for National Statistics: Population Estimates for England and Wales 2015
http://www.ons.gov.uk/peoplepopulationandcommunity/populationandmigration/populationestimates

552 'London worse for crime than New York.' The *Daily Telegraph*, 21 October 2017

553  Metropolitan Police Homicide Statistics found on:
     http://maps.met.police.uk/tables.htm

554  Citizens Report: Teenage Murders in London 2005-2015
     http://www.citizensreportuk.org/reports/teenage-murder-london.html

555  Operation Trident figures reported by the *BBC Radio News*, 19 October
     2004

556  'London Gun crime rises as shootings nearly double.' The *Guardian*, 3
     November 2009.
     https://www.theguardian.com/uk/2009/nov/03/london-gun-crime-
     shootings-rise

557  'Violent inner-city crime, the figures, and a question of race.' Data obtained
     from a Freedom of Information Act request and reported on in The *Sunday
     Telegraph*, 26 June 2010
     http://www.telegraph.co.uk/news/uknews/crime/7856787/Violent-inner-
     city-crime-the-figures-and-a-question-of-race.html

558  'Teenager stabbed to death schoolboy as part of a 20-strong gang at Tube
     station.' *Daily Mirror*, 24 April 2013
     http://www.mirror.co.uk/news/uk-news/sofyen-belamouadden-killing-
     teenager-junior-1852064

559  London Murders (all), 2006-2012, Citizens Report, London Murders
     http://www.citizensreportuk.org/reports/london-murders.html

560  Homicide in London, 2008-2009, from Metropolitan Police web site,
     http://maps.met.police:uk/tables.htm

561  'Killer, 15 laughs as he is jailed for 'primeval murder'.' *Daily Mail*, 16
     September 2014
     http://www.dailymail.co.uk/news/article-2756418/Schoolboy-aged-just-14-
     stabbed-market-trader-death-asked-hand-stolen-watch-LAUGHS-jailed-life.
     html

## Chapter 7

562  Statistics released by the Attorney General's Office on referrals to the Court
     of Appeal of cases thought to be unduly lenient. Found on:
     www.attorneygeneral.co.uk

563 'Appeals win 200 longer jail sentences.' The *Daily Telegraph*, 12 June 2006.

564 'Killer's longer term.' The *Daily Telegraph*, 12 March 2010 and 'Suffolk bolt gun killer's minimum sentence increased.' *BBC News*, 12 March 2010
https://innertemplelibrary.wordpress.com/2010/03/12/suffolk-bolt-gun-killers-minimum-sentence-increased-bbc-news/

565 Statement by Sir Igor Judge: Unduly Lenient Sentence Statistics, 22 June 2007
http://www.judiciary.gov.uk/publications_media/general/unduly_lenient_sentence_220607.htm

566 'Judges too lenient, 4 in 10 believe.' The *Daily Telegraph*, 25 May 2013

567 'Public lose faith in ability of politicians to deal with crime.' The *Sunday Telegraph*, 2 July 2006
http://www.telegraph.co.uk/news/uknews/1522852/Public-loses-faith-in-ability-of-politicians-to-deal-with-crime.html

568 'Time served for murder.' *Mail Online*, 3 January 2012

569 The Penalty for Murder. Louis Blom-Cooper Q.C., 1972

570 Prison Population Statistics, House of Commons Library Paper, No. SN/SG/4334, 29 July 2013
http://researchbriefings.files.parliament.uk/documents/SN04334/SN04334.pdf

571 'Freed attacker killed woman.' The *Daily Telegraph*, 23 February 2010:
http://news.bbc.co.uk/1/hi/england/hampshire/8528364.stm

572 Statement by Jack Straw in House of Commons in December 2007, concerning the killing of Amanda Murphy by Andrew Mournian

573 'Killing a man? It's no big deal.' *Daily Mail*, 27 February 2014:
http://www.dailymail.co.uk/news/article-2568819/Killing-man-Its-no-big-deal-As-Attorney-General-deluged-calls-increase-sentence-sneer-mother-thug-punched-Aspergers-sufferer.html
and:
'Savage past of one-punch killer.' *Mail Online*, 28 February 2014:
http://www.dailymail.co.uk/news/article-2570570/Savage-past-one-punch-killer-calls-Capone-gang-robbed-teenager-bus.html
and :
'Lewis Gill, the man who killed Andrew Young with a single punch.' The

*Huffington Post*, 20 March 2014

http://www.huffingtonpost.co.uk/2014/03/20/lewis-gill-has-sentence-reviewed-killing-andrew-young_n_5000058.html

574 The National Confidential Inquiry into homicide followed by suicide by people with mental illness, 2016

http://research.bmh.manchester.ac.uk/cmhs/research/centreforsuicideprevention/nci/reports/2016-report.pdf

575 'One person a week dies at the hands of psychiatric patients.' The *Sunday Telegraph*, 24 September 2006

http://www.telegraph.co.uk/news/uknews/1529664/Report-reveals-doctors-failed-to-act-in-cases-with-a-history-of-violence.html

576 'Killer who murdered passerby was released without going before mental health tribunal.' The *Daily Telegraph*, 8 February 2013

http://www.telegraph.co.uk/news/uknews/crime/9856695/Killer-who-murdered-passerby-was-released-without-going-before-mental-health-tribunal.html

577 'Mentally ill patients kill 96 in London over 8 years, says trusts.' *BBC News*, 8 October 2013

http://www.bbc.co.uk/news/uk-england-london-24437484

578 'Killer who murdered passerby was released without going before mental health tribunal.' The *Daily Telegraph*, 8 February 2013

http://www.telegraph.co.uk/news/uknews/crime/9856695/Killer-who-murdered-passerby-was-released-without-going-before-mental-health-tribunal.html

579 'One person a week dies at the hands of psychiatric patients.' The *Sunday Telegraph*, 24 September 2006

http://www.telegraph.co.uk/news/uknews/1529664/Report-reveals-doctors-failed-to-act-in-cases-with-a-history-of-violence.html

580 'Doctors thought schizophrenic killer was faking illness.' The *Daily Telegraph*, 1st March 2013

http://www.telegraph.co.uk/news/uknews/crime/9902815/Schizophrenic-killer-turned-away-from-hospital-twice.html

581 'Mentally ill school bus killer hadn't been treated for 12 years.' *Daily Mail*, 16 September 2014

http://www.dailymail.co.uk/news/article-2756416/Damning-report-reveals-12-years-social-services-failures-allowed-schizophrenic-man-stab-schoolgirl-death-bus.html

582 'Court let youth, 17, go free to rape.' *Daily Express*, 4 June 2008

583 'Widow demands enquiry into stranger killing of 'remarkable husband'.' *Dorset Echo*, 10 October 2016,

http://www.dorsetecho.co.uk/news/national/14792567.Grieving_widow_demands_inquiry_into_stranger_stabbing_of__remarkable__husband/

and:

'Widow's fury at officials who left crazed cannabis addict free to kill: New father was knifed to death SIX days after assault case was dropped.' *Daily Mail*,

http://www.dailymail.co.uk/news/article-3830357/Widow-Islington-stab-victim-Dr-Jeroen-Ensink-speak-sentencing-Femi-Nandap.html

584 'A 'Postcode lottery' for sentences.' The *Sun*, 1 January 2013. Data based on a Freedom of Information Act request by Philip Davies MP.

585 'Three men jailed for gratuitous attack.' *Daily Mail*, 28 March 2012

http://www.dailymail.co.uk/news/article-2121651/Three-jailed-gratuitous-attack-man-died-broke-bone-face.html

586 *Obsessive Poisoner, The Strange Story of Graham Young*, by his sister Winifred Young, 1973, Robert Hale, London

587 'The killing of Gunner Lee Rigby.' *Daily Mail*, 27 February 2014 (This paper version refers to the judge's comments that 'Adebelajo was beyond rehabilitation'.)

also:

'The final insult: Court terror for Lee Rigby's family as his Muslim killers are dragged from dock shouting 'Allahu akbar' while fighting prison guards – before judge tells them life will NOT mean life.' *Mail Online*, 26 February 2014

http://www.dailymail.co.uk/news/article-2568317/Justice-Lee-Rigby-Soldiers-family-arrive-court-wearing-matching-t-shirts-act-solidarity-ahead-sentencing-two-Muslim-converts-murdered-him.html

588 1997 Criminal Sentences Act. This introduced Mandatory Life Sentences for a second conviction of a listed dangerous violent or sex crime.

http://www.legislation.gov.uk/ukpga/1997/43/pdfs/ukpga_19970043_en.pdf

589  'Killer grinned as he took Sarah Payne', The *Daily Telegraph*, 15 November 2001

http://www.telegraph.co.uk/news/uknews/1362446/Killer-grinned-as-he-took-Sarah-Payne.html

590  Section 225 of the Criminal Justice Act 2003 introduced 'Indeterminate Imprisonment for Public Protection' (IPPs):

http://www.legislation.gov.uk/ukpga/2003/44/contents

also see:

for information on IPPs, Discretionary Life, Mandatory Life, Automatic Life sentences: online

http://www.justice.gov.uj/offenders/types-of-offender/life

591  Gov.UK. Offender Management Statistics: Prison Population Tables 2002-2012

http://www.gov.uk/government/publications/offender-managment-statistics-quarterly-2

592  'A Low Risk, said Probation.' *Evening Standard*, 15 March 2006

593  A New Parole System for England and Wales. A Justice Report (see page 66, para A.2)

http://www.nuffieldfoundation.org/sites/default/files/A%20New%20Parole%20System%20for%20England%20and%20Wales.pdf

594  Criminal Justice and Immigration Act 2008

http://www.legislation.gov.uk/ukpga/2008/4/pdfs/ukpga_20080004_en.pdf

595  Explanatory Notes to Criminal Justice and Immigration Act 2008, Chapter 4 (see para: 14)

http://www.banksr.co.uk/images/Statutes/2008-2010/2008/Counter-Terrorism_Act_2008_Explanatory_Note.pdf

596  Ministry of Justice, Offender Management Caseload Statistics Bulletin, England and Wales, 2014

https://www.gov.uk/government/uploads/system/uploads/attachment_data/file/424872/offender-management-statistics-bulletin-oct-dec-2014.pdf

597  Tom Ellis and Peter Marshall. Does Parole Work? A Post Release Comparison of Reconviction Rates for Paroled and non-Paroled Prisoners. Home Office Research Bulletin 39, 1998

http://journals.sagepub.com/doi/pdf/10.1177/000486580003300304

598 Does Parole Work? Empirical Evidence from England and Wales. Professor Shute, Birmingham University.
https://kb.osu.edu/dspace/bitstream/handle/1811/72860/OSJCL_V2N1_315.pdf

599 'Reoffending rate of killers and rapists is higher than we think, says Parole Board.' *Mail Online*, 7 January 2011
http://www.dailymail.co.uk/news/article-1345078/Number-prisoners-offend-released-licence-far-higher-know-admits-parole-board-boss.html

600 Thematic report by HM Inspectorate of Prisons: Unintended consequences: Finding a way forward for prisoners serving sentences of imprisonment for public protection. November 2016
https://www.justiceinspectorates.gov.uk/hmiprisons/wp-content/uploads/sites/4/2016/11/Unintended-consequences-Web-2016.pdf

601 Parole Board Report for England and Wales, 2013/14

602 Parole Board Report for England and Wales, 2014/15
https://www.gov.uk/government/uploads/system/uploads/attachment_data/file/446277/Parole_Board_for_England_and_Wales_Annual_Report_2014.15.pdf

603 'Justice Secretary rejects call to move Kenneth Noye to an open prison.' The *Guardian*, 23 October 2015

604 'Judge's outrage over rapist who was given a day release...only to strike again.' *Daily Mail*, 4 June 2015
http://www.dailymail.co.uk/news/article-3110062/Judge-s-outrage-rapist-given-day-release-attack-27-year-old-woman-home-friend-forced-watch.html

605 'Mark Shirley sentenced to life for third rape.' The *Independent*, 27 September 2012
http://www.independent.co.uk/news/uk/crime/rapist-murderer-mark-shirley-set-to-die-in-jail-as-judge-hands-him-16-life-sentences-8182345.html

606 The top ten longest prison sentences in the world, found on:
http://Akorra.com

607 The previous conviction history of Damien Hanson is reported on in HM Inspectorate of Probation Serious Further Offence review: Damian Hanson

and Elliot White, 2006

http://www.justiceinspectorates.gov.uk/probation/wp-content/uploads/
sites/5/2014/03/hansonandwhitereview-rps.pdf

608 United States Crime Rates 1960-2015. Compiled from Federal Bureau of
Investigation Uniform Crime Reports
http://www.disastercenter.com/crime/uscrime.htm

609 U.S. Department of Justice, FBI Uniform Crime Reporting Statistics site
http://www.ucrdatatool.gov/index.cfm.

610 Correctional Populations in the United States 2014, U.S. Department of
Justice, Office of Justice Programs, Bureau of Justice Statistics
https://www.bjs.gov/content/pub/pdf/cpus14.pdf

611 Submission to the Sentencing and Parole Reform Bill Law and Order
Committee, Parliament Buildings, Wellington, New Zealand (by Professor J
Walsh)
https://www.parliament.nz/en/pb/sc/submissions-and-advice/document/
49SCLO_EVI_00DBHOH_BILL9040_1_A18696/professor-jennifer-walsh
then choose 'full text', which goes to:
https://www.parliament.nz/resource/en-NZ/49SCLO_EVI_00DBHOH_
BILL9040_1_A18696/cb4ebc89e99e1c99c0a99d5c0baecf004091d830

612 *BBC Radio World News*, 26th May, 2010

613 United States Crime Rates 1960-2015. Compiled from Federal Bureau of
Investigation Uniform Crime Reports
http://www.disastercenter.com/crime/uscrime.htm

614 Maurin, E., & Ouss, A., (2009), Sentence Reductions and Recidivism:
Lessons from the Bastille Day Quasi Experiment. Bonn, Germany: Institute
for the Study of Labour (IZA).
http://www.coll.mpg.de/economix/2009/Maurin.pdf

615 Tough for Whom? Assessing the Impact of Discretion on California's Three
Strikes Law. Jennifer Walsh, PhD
http://www.academia.edu/6381354/Tough_for_Whom_Assessing_the_
Impact_of_Discretion_on_California_s_Three_Strikes_Law

616 Submission to the Sentencing and Parole Reform Bill Law and Order
Committee, Parliament Buildings, Wellington, New Zealand (by Professor
Jennifer Walsh, 2009)

https://www.parliament.nz/en/pb/sc/submissions-and-advice/
document/49SCLO_EVI_00DBHOH_BILL9040_1_A18696/professor-
jennifer-walsh

then choose 'full text', which goes to:

https://www.parliament.nz/resource/en-NZ/49SCLO_EVI_00DBHOH_
BILL9040_1_A18696/cb4ebc89e99e1c99c0a99d5c0baecf004091d830

617 *Confessions of a Country Magistrate*, by Edward Grierson. Published by Victor
Gollancz, 1972

618 Three Strikes five years on: Press Release, Sensible Sentencing Trust, 2015
http://www.scoop.co.nz/stories/PO1506/S00005/three-strikes-five-years-on.
htm

619 Sensible Sentencing Trust: Three Strikes:
http://sst.org.nz/our-aims/sst-three-strikes-policy/

620 'Anger as Europe backs killers,' The *Daily Telegraph*, 10 July 2013:
http://www.pressreader.com/uk/the-daily-telegra
ph/20130710/281487863943855
and:
*BBC News*, 24 January 2014

621 'Harry Roberts, police killer freed from jail.' *BBC News*, 12 November 2014
http://www.bbc.co.uk/news/uk-england-london-30016319

622 The top ten longest prison sentences in the world, found on
http://Akorra.com

623 Romilly, S., (1886) *The Punishment of Death*, John Murray

624 'Blunkett: Scrapping of indeterminate sentences.' *BBC News*, 13 March
2014
http://www.bbc.co.uk/news/uk-26561380

625 Criminal Justice and Courts Act 2015, (section 23A)
http://www.safeguardingdurhamadults.info/SiteCollectionDocuments/
Policies%20and%20Procedures/Miscellaneous%20linked%20files/
CJACA%20Explanation%20Section%201.pdf

626 Offender Management Statistics Bulletin, England and Wales, Quarterly,
January to March 2016
https://www.gov.uk/government/uploads/system/uploads/attachment_data/
file/541499/offender-management-statistics-quarterly-bulletinjan2mar-2016.pdf

# Index

www.ingramcontent.com/pod-product-compliance
Lightning Source LLC
Chambersburg PA
CBHW072114270326
41931CB00010B/1550